Postcards
to the Future

Postcards to the Future

Mercurial Musings

1995-2021

Anne Whitaker

12WTH PUBLICATIONS

BOOKS BY ANNE WHITAKER
2009 *Jupiter Meets Uranus: From Erotic Bathing to Star Gazing.*
Original research study of the 1997 Jupiter Uranus conjunction
(USA, American Federation of Astrologers)

e-publications:

2013 *Rumbold Raven's Magic Menagerie*
(Children's poetry book, illustrated by Albert Ennemoser)

2014 *Jupiter Meets Uranus and Tales from the Wild Ride*
(Republished study of 1997 research, including new research on the 2010/11 Jupiter-Uranus conjunction)

2015 W*isps from the Dazzling Darkness: An Open-minded 'Take' on Paranormal Experience*

2015 *The Moon's Nodes in Action*
(An original research study)

All e-books designed and produced by co-occurrence.com and published by Writing from the Twelfth House, Glasgow, Scotland, UK.

First published by
Writing from the Twelfth House Publications
Glasgow, Scotland, 2021

Copyright © Anne Whitaker 2021

All rights reserved.
The moral rights of the author have been asserted

ISBN 9798453241064

Designed and typeset in Sabon by Rosamund Saunders

This book is dedicated with gratitude to the memory of

Ian Halliburton,

my husband, supporter and soulmate from 1982 until his death on 13.1.2020

Contents

Foreword by Frank C. Clifford	12
Anne Whitaker's natal chart	14
PREFACE: six things I love about astrology	15
ANGLES & DEGREES: power points of the zodiac	19
Fate, Uranus – and the astrologers' degree	20
Pisces' anaretic degree: the final degree of the zodiac	23
What happens when Pluto, Neptune and Uranus cross the IC?	26
CUSPS, HOUSES, TWINS: top topics of beginners' questions	33
Rian's question: born on the cusp: which sign am I?	34
How does astrology explain twins?	38
Astrological houses: placidus, equal – or what?	41
CYCLES: 'History fancies itself linear – but yields to a cyclical temptation'	47
The attraction of new horizons … the Jupiter cycle	48
The Saturn cycles – forging the 'diamond soul'	54
Cycles end, new ones begin. On being 'liminal'	63
Cycles: a Saturn-Pluto trio: 1: a vandalised ephemeris – Saturn-Pluto strikes?	66
Cycles: a Saturn-Pluto trio: 2: 'in my end is my beginning': paradox and the Saturn-Pluto cycle	69
Cycles: a Saturn-Pluto trio: 3: wall – what wall?	80

ETHICS & PRACTICE: where we must take care   83
 An astrologer's job description   84
 Answering a challenge: 'is it true that real astrologers do not
  charge for their services?'   86
 The ethics of astrological practice: a question
  needing an answer   89
 On becoming a responsible astrologer: how do you get there?   92

FATE: 'The power of fate is a wonder, dark, terrible wonder'   99
 A tale of Saturn, Capricorn, nodes and family history   101
 Encountering fate – in the middle of nowhere   104
 Review of *The Astrological World of Jung's Liber Novus –
  Daimons, Gods and the Planetary Journey* by Liz Greene   109
 Prediction and a personal story   120

HEALING & WOUNDING: all arts have their shadow   127
 The art of astrology: wounding, healing – or both?   128
 Reflecting on Chiron as his Aries trip begins   143

ASTROLOGY MEETS SCIENCE: differing lenses, same source   149
 'Astrology is a load of rubbish!' please, not that tedious
  old trope again   150
 Broken vows, genetics and astrology   153
 Scorpio's season, hallowe'en, dark matter   156
 Pluto, the nodes – and a black hole revealed   161
 Red chair moment: a Saturn return tale   164

INTERVIEWS: featuring the bacon sandwich motivational
 technique, plus other arcane delights   167
 20 Questions and a selfie: a day in the life of 12th-house
  astrologer Anne Whitaker   168
 My favourite interview Q & As   173

AFA interview: Jupiter, Uranus and the Purple People
   from Planet Zog ... 175
Anne and Victor's astro-spar ... 183

LUNAR STUFF: 'do not swear by the moon,
   for she changes constantly' ... 193
  The power of eclipses – and a personal tale ... 194
  Solar eclipse in Cancer: the old order changes ... 198
  Stopping smoking/solar eclipses ... 201
  Do you do Moondark? Maybe you should ... 204
  Sea tragedy at Moondark: the Iolaire disaster of 1919 ... 208

MY MARY SHELLEY OBSESSION: it has never gone away ... 213
  Mary, Dolly and Andi – O brave new world? ... 215
  Dreaming Frankenstein: the creation of a modern myth ... 221
  Of silver blobs and famous feminists ... 232

PLANETARY INGRESSES, TRANSITS, PROGRESSIONS:
   surveying possible futures ... 239
  Ingresses: Jupiter into Libra: putting flesh on symbolic bones ... 241
  Ingresses: Jupiter in Scorpio: Lord of the Starry Heavens
     enters 'The Great Below' ... 252
  Ingresses: Saturn enters Aquarius: prequel to
     a New World Order ... 265
  Ingresses: Pluto enters Aquarius in 2024: a major
     step in 'Boldly Going' ... 270
  Transits: 'Seems you can't outsmart Mother Nature' ... 273
  Transits: Saturn through Sagittarius: the Joyful Child
     grows up ... 276
  Transits: Uranus through Aries: fire and fury ... 283
  Progressions: Secondary Progressions: stepping into
     the mystery ... 292

Progressions: astrology's scary delights and a personal progressions story	302
Scotland: my own, my native land	305
Scotland's Horoscope	307
Teaching astrology: I never knew adult ed. could be such fun!	313
Returning to astrology: a lesson in 'never say never'	314
The pleasures of teaching	317
The big picture: don't focus on the chaos, look for the reason	321
The Aquarian Age: are we there yet?	322
The Fixed Cross: pointer to the new Air Age?	325
The air era beckons	329
Neptune and the 'gift' of uncertainty	332
The Twelfth House: where I live (behind the sofa …)	337
Whom doth the Grail serve? A personal quest in pursuit of vocation	338
Contemplating the 12th house: an optimist's take on self-undoing	353
PS: Windows to the future: Mary Shelley – with Greta Thunberg – has the last word	365
Waning and waxing crescents: windows to the future	367
Acknowledgements	381
About the author	382

Postcards to the Future

Foreword
by Frank C. Clifford

An in-depth knowledge of astrology requires an investigative and probing mind. To become proficient in the art, astrologers must learn more than the basics and how to apply them – they must test assumptions learned from books and teachers, put energy into researching the links between birth charts and biographies, and keep curious and observant – always keen to refine their craft.

Astrology must also be a deeply personal pursuit, for the way in which we approach and interpret a birth chart reflects our subjective view of the world. However open we astrologers may be to others' viewpoints and techniques, inevitably we relate to a birth chart from our own lens coloured by life experiences and interactions.

Postcards to the Future fulfils both criteria. It's a diverse compendium of astute, hard-won, professional observations that also contains many humorous and personal anecdotes. It's a sincere reflection of Anne Whitaker's pursuit of all things astrological, and her personal journey as a psychological astrologer and consultant.

Inside these pages, you'll find much food for thought on the transit cycles of Jupiter and Saturn. And the author isn't afraid to broach some contentious areas around the nature of astrology and the differences between its pop and psychological cousins. One of the richest sections is the chapter on ethics – a much-needed line of enquiry now that we're in the post-Saturn-Pluto era and beginning a 20-year Jupiter-Saturn period during which ethical issues in astrology will be at the forefront. There really is something here for everyone – from the curious beginner to the experienced practitioner.

The essays in *Postcards* are peppered with new perspectives on familiar topics – the sort of perceptive analyses only available to a writer after years of searching and researching the subject. And so we return to the aforementioned 'investigative and probing mind' that every astrologer could benefit from. In Anne Whitaker, we meet these through a Mercury-Pluto conjunction and Jupiter in Scorpio in the 3rd house – placements worthy of a writer, counsellor, teacher and mentor who has made astrology her creative passion for over 40 years.

Frank C. Clifford was honoured with The Charles Harvey Award for 'Exceptional Service to Astrology' from the Astrological Association in 2012, a writing award from ISAR in 2016, and a Regulus Award nomination in 2018. His books include the interpretation manual, *Getting to the Heart of Your Chart*, and a guide to forecasting, *The Solar Arc Handbook*. Frank teaches astrology and palmistry online and in person, and his courses are also available in Chinese, Japanese, and Turkish. To sign up for free videos, articles, news and live Q&As, please visit: londonschoolofastrology.com. His other website is: frankclifford.co.uk.

Anne Whitaker's natal chart (birth data withheld)

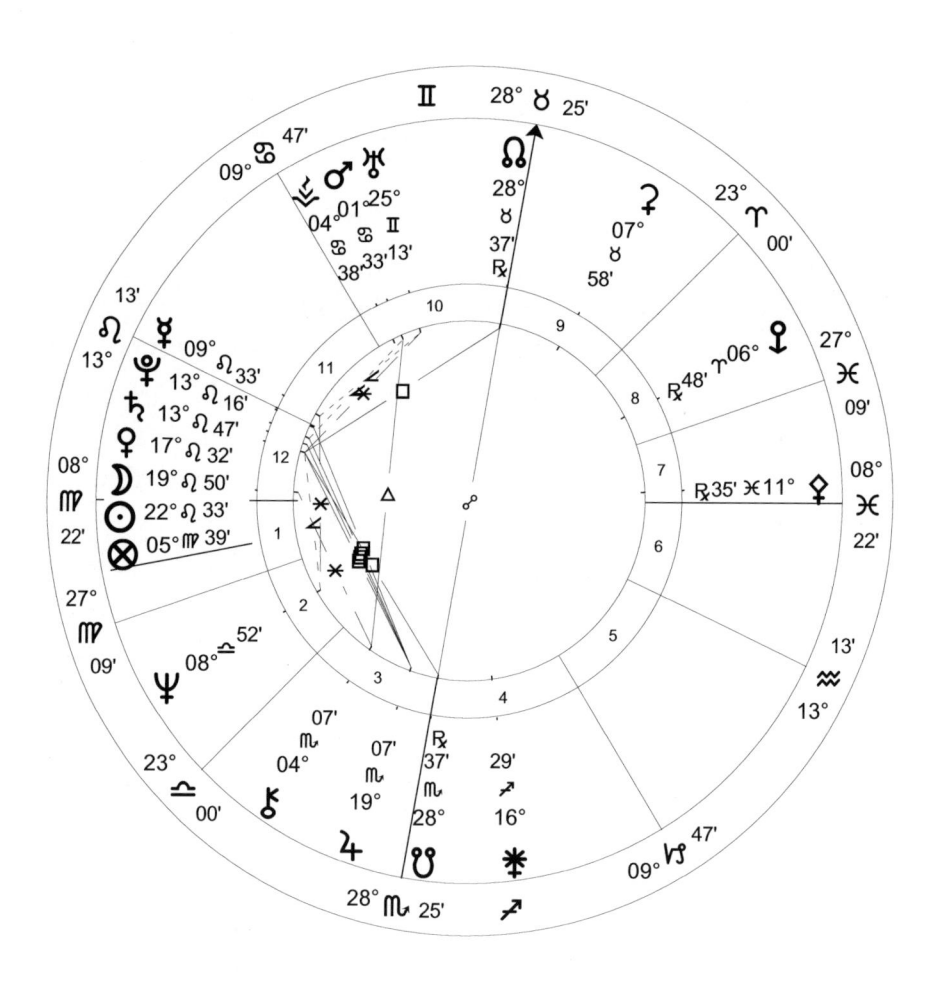

PREFACE:
Six things I love about astrology

(i)

'Six thousand years ago, when the human mind was still half asleep, Chaldean priests were standing on their watchtowers, scanning the stars.' – The Sleepwalkers by Arthur Koestler

I love knowing that the rational, mythical, symbolic and empirical art of astrology has been around for at least 6000 years. Our increasing contemporary awareness of the interconnectedness of all things was well known in antiquity. The ancient maxim 'As above, so below' still applies. Astrologers operate on the margins of our fragmenting, reductionist culture. But we represent an unbroken line to a time which in many ways was wiser than ours is now. Being a tiny thread in that weave gives me a deep sense of pride, connectedness and rootedness.

(ii)

I love being able to look out at the night sky, seeing the beauty of the lunar cycle and the visible planets in their ever-changing, ever-repeating patterns, knowing that being an astrologer offers one the privilege of perceiving not only astronomy but also symbolic meaning out there. I can still recall the exhilaration I felt on a freezing cold, clear night in January 1986 on a visit to the Outer Hebrides. My brother, a Merchant Navy captain, was able to point out Saturn to me – the first time I had ever seen that venerable planet with the naked eye. Saturn's meaning was also present that night: we were on our way back from the wake for an old uncle who had just died.

(iii)

I love the fact that I started out as a dismisser of our ancient art and ended up its devoted practitioner – having set out to confront my embarrassment at the inexplicable fascination I had developed for a subject which I considered to be beneath my intellectual consideration! This is the typical position of ignorance combined with arrogance from which many people dismiss astrology, not realising that there is a subject of great depth and power beyond the sun signs of astrology's public face. I embarked on a course of study with the Faculty of Astrological Studies in the early 1980s – to prove to myself through study rather than ignorant dismissal that there was nothing in astrology – and have kept up an unbroken interest since then for nearly forty years.

(iv)

I love how literal astrology can be. Saturn met Neptune in November 1989 and the Berlin Wall came down. There was a Jupiter-Uranus conjunction in Libra in July 1969 when a huge co-operative effort of unique scientific endeavour put the first human on the Moon. On the day Pluto first went into Sagittarius in January 1995, there was a massive earthquake in Japan and the city of Kobe went up in flames. At that same time, John Paul II, the best-travelled Pope ever, preached to an open-air audience of over a million people in Manila in the Philippines. To lower the tone somewhat, I was having lunch with a bank manager friend of mine on the day Saturn turned retrograde on my Scorpio IC on 7 March 1985. For no apparent reason (being sober at the time!) I passed out, just as another bank manager and friend of my friend was passing the restaurant window. They both ended up carting me home between them.

(v)

I love the impossibility of ever getting on top of, or to the end of, one's astrological studies. I have never applied myself to e.g. Chinese or Hindu astrology, not yet feeling I have enough of a grasp of the Western tradition into which I was born … and you can do hundreds or thousands of horoscope readings, teach hundreds of classes with thousands of students, and someone will still come up with a manifestation of e.g. Venus combined with Saturn or Mercury combined with Neptune which you have never before come across or thought of.

(vi)

I love astrology for the help it has given me (and countless other people who are willing to look within and try to be honest about themselves) in understanding the quirks and complexities, the gifts and pains of my personality and life pattern. My studies began as the next step in a lifelong quest to prove that our existence has some meaning, that we are not just butterflies randomly pinned to the board of fate, that we are each here because we have something unique to contribute to the Big Picture. Astrology has provided me with that proof. For that, and to that unbroken line of students and practitioners of our great art stretching right back to those ancient Chaldeans on their watchtowers, I will be forever grateful.

Thank you.

Written for World Astrology Day in
March 2014

ANGLES & DEGREES:
power points of the zodiac

I'm often asked about what clients or students can expect when the biggies, such as Uranus, Neptune and Pluto cross the Imum Coeli or I.C. Well, here is an account of one person's experiences, namely mine. Do not worry those of you in the throes of one of these heavy duty, life-changing transits. I have had all of them cross my I.C. and I'm still here (as far as I know).

The other two pieces in this section are from my Dell Horoscope *magazine column 'The Astro-view from Scotland' which I wrote for the last three years of that wonderful magazine which inspired generations of astrologers from 1935 to 2020. In them, I indulge my fascination for two of the most famous zodiacal degrees: the astrologers' degree, 24° Gemini 5', and the anaretic (final) degree 29° Pisces – the most potent one, in my view, coming as it does at the very end of the whole circle of the zodiac.*

Fate, Uranus – and the astrologers' degree

Anyone who has ever written a regular column will know that there are times when inspiration is – not to put too fine a point on it – notable by its absence. At other times, so many ideas are flying around that catching one by the tail to pin it down is, to say the least, *tricky*. And – you never know, as the last deadline is met, and you can now relax for a few weeks – which set of conditions is going to prevail the next time.

So, Reader, there I was, new deadline appearing over the horizon, and ... *nada*. Nix. No–thing. At all. Braincell dry as an old chewed-up bone. In this situation there are generally two options: blind panic – or blind faith. I have six fiery planets. This is often a curse, let me tell you, but in the matter of column deadlines, it is a blessing. So, armed with nothing but blind faith, I headed for the office.

To pass time sitting on the bus, I check my phone. A-ha! – there's a message on Messenger. A colleague is beginning a new project for the international company he works for, an unusual company where his boss is an astrology appreciator. He is making a podcast series on 'turning points': asking people to talk for five minutes on the one decision which changed their lives forever. He is inviting me to contribute.

'Ping!' went the braincell, hit by a mini bolt of inspiration. I had my topic. I'd ruminate on what it was that inspired me to take up, and continue, the long-term study and practice of astrology. That decision certainly changed MY life forever.

So – what was it?

Was it my youthful awe as I watched the Northern Lights enacting their glorious colourful dance, just above the skyline near our house? Perhaps it was lying cosy in bed, listening to the roaring gales of January tearing the world apart – wondering what the power was behind that raging wind. Was it the growing excitement, as I grew up, of being able to spot familiar constellations in the clear, unpolluted night skies of my native island?

Or: maybe the Fates had already decided, leaving me a clue to be decoded many years later via the placement of Uranus, the astrologers' planet, at 25° Gemini in the 10th house of my natal horoscope?

I have recently been revisiting the significance of the placement of Uranus' discovery degree, i.e. 24° Gemini 27'[1] in the horoscopes of those drawn to the practice of astrology. A dip into my horoscope collection, lifting out three male and three female birth charts, found that all six chosen prominent astrologers have this degree either conjunct, square or opposite natal planets, nodes or angles: Donna Cunningham, Michel Gauquelin, Liz Greene, Isabel Hickey, Johannes Kepler and Noel Tyl.

Furthermore, when I was 27 years old, progressed Sun crossed asteroid Urania, placed at 19° Virgo in my 1st house, square 10th-house Uranus. That year, as mentioned in an earlier column, I had a totally random encounter with a pair of astrologers who predicted my future astrological career.

So – did I choose that career, or did I come in with it already chosen? Was it Fate or Freewill? We will, of course, never be able to answer that question. *My* conclusion, hardly stunningly original, is that we dance to the tune of both. There are times when the power of Fate feels strongly present. Other times, the unglamorous wrestle with inertia, poor judgement, and other ills to haul our lives into a reasonably satisfying shape, feels very strongly to be determined mainly by our own conscious efforts.

In the latter case, a major ingredient in the shaping process is the power of inspiration, in my opinion. At 24 years of age, I was fortunate enough to have what I later realised was a mystical experience, something which has continued to inspire me. This may well have created a spiritual backdrop for the subsequent encounter with astrology as foreground; when I met those astrologers, I was going through a crisis involving wondering what, after all, my life was *for* ... not an uncommon state for one's late twenties.

---

[1]   All charts are accessible free from Astrodienst at astro.com.

Their accurate reading inspired me to investigate astrology further, initially via the UK's Faculty of Astrological Studies. On discovering that I, too, could produce accurate and affirming feedback from those strange marks on a piece of paper which seemed helpful to people trying to understand themselves better, I was hooked. For the rest of my life.

Astrology has continued to inspire because it continues to challenge me. It challenges me because we are working with living energies, patterns whose essential meanings we have established over millennia, but whose manifestations are endless and only partly predictable. Despite decades of experience, I still get that tight anxious feeling before every new client I see, being very aware of my responsibility at least to do no harm, at best to help the person before me see their life in a more constructive, bigger context.

I am, of course, always curious to find out what inspires people to engage with astrology – and to keep going once they get there. There is an occasional series running on my blog, in which astrologers tell their interesting, unusual tales of inspiration and – of course! – an inevitable amount of perspiration.

Dell Horoscope
January/February 2018

Pisces' anaretic degree: the final degree of the zodiac

The ruler of this issue's column is Neptune, dissolver of the old order, weaver of new dreams. Its source of inspiration is my astro-colleague Leah Whitehorse whose excellent article 'The 29th Degree: Tales from the Threshold' in *Dell*'s July/August 2019 issue sparked my imagination. She describes the final – or anaretic – degree of a sign as the ultimate 'no man's land', going on to describe in-between places as holding great mystery in fairy tales and folklore. Leah says: 'Dawn, dusk, midnight, the shore where sea meets land, crossroads … the 29th degree, too, is liminal. In my own studies, I have found that there's a sense of magic about these degrees, although this does not negate the potential difficulties.'

As I write this on the last day of May 2019, my progressed Moon is about to enter its anaretic degree, 29° Pisces, where it will remain for the whole month of June until entering Aries, the 8th house, and the beginning of a whole new twenty-seven-year cycle. I feel profoundly Neptunian in a liminal, poetic kind of way – but tough Neptune transits in recent years have taught me a deep, spiritual patience. T. S. Eliot expresses my anaretic, Piscean, Neptunian state most beautifully:

> *'I said to my soul, be still and wait without hope, for hope would be hope for the wrong thing; wait without love, for love would be love of the wrong thing; there is yet faith, but the faith and the love are all in the waiting. Wait without thought, for you are not ready for thought: So, the darkness shall be the light, and the stillness the dancing.'* [2]

From many years of work with clients and students, and observation of my own, family, and friends' horoscopes, I have noted an especially

---

[2] T. S. Eliot, *Four Quartets*, 'East Coker', Part iii.

potent quality to Pisces' 29th degree: whether natally via house position, planet, angle or Moon's nodes, or by transit and by progression. Why is this? Certainly, because it is anaretic – but most significantly because it is the very last degree of the whole zodiacal 360-degree circle prior to radical change. Aries beckons: with it, significant endings and early beginnings of a new life phase.

Neptune takes approximately 164 years to complete a whole transit cycle. Its most recent entry into Pisces being 2011-12, it fully enters Aries at the start of 2026. Curious to research what significant radical endings and rebirths might have occurred in history when Neptune was ending its most recent transit of Pisces, crossing the anaretic degree and fully entering Aries between 1860-62, I discovered the following. 1860: Abraham Lincoln is nominated US president. Lincoln's election for president was followed by South Carolina's succession from the Union. April 1862: (following Neptune's full entry into Aries on 14 February 1862) saw the beginning of the American Civil War. Furthermore, Lincoln issued the Emancipation Proclamation on 1 January 1863, abolishing slavery in the USA. [3]

There are equally striking examples if you research transiting Neptune's anaretic degree further back in history: a fine project, dear readers, to occupy you during the long winter months ahead!

Researching one's personal story can yield equally striking examples, as I discovered.

The Moon by progression takes 27.25 years to complete its cycle. The first time my progressed Moon crossed 29° Pisces during October 1964, I escaped a turbulent family life by going to university far too young; but it was the best thing for me, since my life began at last to open up beyond the confines of family. This was followed in November by the start of my first serious love affair.

Scroll forward another 27.25 years to February 1992, progressed

---

3   Obtained by googling 'Significant world events 1860-62'. Astrological data re: Neptune's ingresses from Michelsen's *Planetary Phenomena*.

Moon is at 29° Pisces once more. On the family front I found myself embattled with my mother and sister who were resisting calling me by the name I had adopted on leaving home all those years previously – I had decided it was time to take a stand on that issue. A few months after that very first honest conversation, my mother died.

I began attending seminars at the Centre for Psychological Astrology in London in late 1991. March 1992, with the progressed Moon at 0° Aries, found me sitting enthralled in my first Liz Greene seminar. The topic was 'Puer and Senex' – Jupiter and Saturn, the basic scaffolding upon which my whole horoscope hangs. As I listened, Liz was also describing the two archetypes around which my whole family life circled.

That day, almost twelve years after I began my astrological studies (Jupiter cycle, anyone?), I decided that only the diploma from the Centre would do. I graduated in 1998 (Saturn square, anyone?) – my fellow students having christened me 'the Flying Scot' since I had to pursue my studies by air from Glasgow to London. No webinars then.

In June 2019, progressed Moon is anaretic at 29° Pisces: my only brother, to whom I was very close through many family crises, is marrying again, acquiring a new wife and her family; and he no longer lives near me. I wish them every happiness – but it feels like a big life change for me.

On the career front, I also feel poised for some kind of change. But what is it to be? Well, I have a few ideas …

T.S. Eliot began this column, and I'd like to give him the final – most appropriate – say:

> *'For last year's words belong to last year's language and next year's words await another voice. And to make an end is to make a beginning.'* [4]

Dell Horoscope
November/December 2019

---

[4]   T. S. Eliot, 'Little Gidding' (Part 4 of *Four Quartets*).

What happens when Pluto, Neptune and Uranus cross the IC?

(My birth chart is on page 14)

Introduction

Liz Greene once wryly observed in one of her seminars that, if you wanted a relatively quiet and peaceful life, you should arrange to be born when the outer planets were as far away from the personal planets and angles as possible. 'I wish!' say many of you reading this, as indeed does the writer, who has all the outer planets bolted onto all the personal planets and has had anything *but* a quiet life.

(Encouraging note for the similarly challenged: I'm not young anymore, but I'm still here – more or less! – and pretty happy with what I have been able to make of my time on this earth to date.)

In similar vein, many people – depending on the horoscope yielded by their particular date, time, and place of birth – will never even experience one of the outer planets, Uranus, Neptune and Pluto, crossing their IC (for non-astrologers reading this, the IC symbolises the point of origin, roots and the core of a person's life).

However, I have had the lot – and am still here to tell the tale. Here it is.

A Plutonian Imagination

In my horoscope the IC is conjunct the South Node at 28° Scorpio. Pluto, its ruler, is placed in the 12th house conjunct Mercury, Saturn, Venus, Moon and Sun in Leo. As a child I would lie in bed watching the roses on the wallpaper turn into malevolent faces as daylight faded; I had to make bargains with them before they would let me sleep.

I read voraciously, and particularly recall the works of Victorian novelist H. Rider Haggard whose myth-steeped descriptions of his characters' adventures in Africa last century fascinated me. But da

Silva, the Dutch explorer whose frozen body was found centuries after his death in a cave high up Mt. Kilimanjaro, transferred himself from *King Solomon's Mines* to the wardrobe in my bedroom, on and off, for a couple of years. Getting to sleep was no mean feat with an imagination like mine.

My 'real' life – eating, sleeping, going to school – was incidental to my inner life which was full of what I felt were the really interesting questions. Why are we alive? Where do we go after death? Do we live on several planes of existence at once? What is happening in other galaxies? If there are x million Catholics and even more Buddhists and Hindus, how come they are all Wrong and Damned and a few thousand members of the Free Church of Scotland are Right and Saved?

And what would happen if you unwrapped an Egyptian mummy? And I wonder if I could make a shrunken head like the Jivaro Indians? And why did people paint pictures on cave walls thousands of years ago?

These were the issues which preoccupied me for years. No-one knew about them except my maternal grandfather. He had spent time taming wild horses alone in the middle of Argentina before World War 1, and in later life was the only Church of Scotland missionary to visit ill or injured foreign sailors of all religions in the local island hospital, despite the disapproval of the Free Church. 'We are all God's children', he would say firmly to his critics – and to me. He died when I was eleven, after which I spoke to no-one until I grew up and left home about anything which really mattered.

Pluto – revisiting the family past

As Pluto squared 12th-house Venus, Moon and Sun, then crossed the IC conjunct South Node from 1993-95, what was left of my family of origin fell apart in a particularly painful and tragic way. I had to make choices in order to protect myself from the destructive urges of other family members which involved separation from loved ones (which is probably permanent). The major decision I made during those years was that the blood tie does not give others the right to destroy your life. I was indeed fortunate in having an astrological framework which helped to provide a meaningful context for the pain.

As part of trying to process what was happening, I decided to compile a family history, returning to my native island to collect some oral material from old people who knew my family back a couple of generations. The day I sat down to write it up, transiting Pluto was exactly conjunct the South Node, within half a degree of the IC. During the same week, I looked back through some old writings of my own, finding two unpublished pieces.

Neptune on the IC (1)

The first was written in July 1970, six months after the start of Neptune transiting the IC. I had no knowledge of astrology then.

My sister and I decided to take the dog and walk from our house, just outside the town, to a beach very exposed to the sea, well beyond the harbour. It would be a long walk, but it was a beautiful briskly windy sunny day – snatched from the usual bleak incessant rains of a Hebridean July.

We took a curving route through the town, then via an outlying district overlooking the navigation beacon. This landmark had winked its electric eye reassuringly at the mouth of the harbour for as long as I could remember. Approaching the district cemetery, my sister walked on by, but I slowed down, never having passed through its gates. Only men attended funerals in the Outer Hebrides when I was growing up.

'The sun is shining on the dead today!' I called to my sister. 'Let's go and pay our respects.' She wasn't too keen. 'Have you ever visited Granddad and Granny's grave?' I asked.

'No,' she said.' I suppose we could do that.'

We pushed open the heavy creaking gate. The graveyard, beautifully tended, sloped gently down to within a few hundred yards of the sea. I realised that I did not know where my father's parents lay.

'I remember where Daddy said it was,' my sister said. 'Follow me. With our English name, it shouldn't be difficult to find.'

Our paternal grandfather had been posted to the Outer Hebrides before the First World War, meeting our grandmother on his first trip ashore. English gentlemen were a great rarity in these parts; very desirable 'catches' to aspiring island girls like Granny, who had by all accounts been a handsome, strong and wilful young woman. He was well and truly caught; apart from a period of war service he remained in the Outer Isles for the rest of his long life.

His death devastated my grandmother. They had been married for fifty-two years. I remember sitting with her in her bedroom, she who had always turned herself out so elegantly propped up in bed, an old singlet of my grandfather's failing to conceal her droopy, withered breasts from my young eyes. Up to then I had never known the desolation of not being able to console another human being – or that old people ever cried. She wept and wailed and moaned, repeating: 'I don't want to live any more. What's the use, what's the use now he's away?'

Live on she did, doggedly, for nine years, lightened only by a late addition to the family. I was fifteen when my brother was born. Granny was eighty-two, and half-way senile. The child was called Frederick, after Granddad; as the novelty wore off Granny slipped into senility, a querulous fractious husk, and finally just a husk, and a medical miracle, carried off at eighty-six with her fourth bout of pneumonia.

I was at university when she died, having become so distant from her by then that I felt nothing but a vague sense of relief ...

'I've found it!'

I had fallen behind my sister in my reverie. She was standing about twenty yards away; I hurried to the spot. It was a plain, simple grave. A low railing ran round it. The headstone was in sandstone, with only the facts of their births and deaths etched on it in gold lettering. Noting with satisfaction (which my grandmother would have shared) the absence of 'fancy versification', I stood and looked at the grave.

Without any warning, for I had felt quiet and composed, there was a rush and a roar in a deep silent centre of my being; a torrent of desolation and grief swept through me. I wept and wept and wept, quite uncontrolled.

There they were, half my being. Where had it all gone? The passion of their early love; the conception of their children; her sweat and blood and pain as she thrust my father into the world; their quarrels, silences, love, laughter, loneliness and grief; their shared and separate lives? And this was it. On a hot beautiful day with the sea lapping on the shore and the seabirds wheeling and diving, a few bits of cloth and bone under the earth, an iron railing and a stone above.

I was not weeping just for them. Overwhelmed by total awareness of my own mortality and that of all human beings before and after me, I had never felt so stricken, so vulnerable, so alone.' [5]

NEPTUNE ON THE IC (II)

The second piece, however, written in the autumn of 1971, at the end of the Neptune transit to the IC, whilst Neptune was at 0° Sagittarius, shows that something else was now emerging from the underworld which would offer me inspiration and support.

(*The 'pibroch' referred to below is the music of lament played on the Scottish bagpipes*)

It was a clear autumn evening. Peter called just after seven; he was going out to practice some pibroch. Would I like to come along? It was a rare time of balance – in the weather, in the satisfaction of work which was still new enough to be stimulating, in the fact that Peter and I were falling in love.

Peter drove several miles out of town, winding slowly up deserted country roads to a hill above a small village. Taking out the pipes he began to blow them up, and after much tinkering began to play. To avoid distracting him, I strolled slowly down the road. Peter was

---

5   This and the second extract in this piece were published together and separately in several articles in the USA, the UK and Australia during the 1990s, e.g., in 'Of Cerberus and Blackest Midnight Born' which appeared in the UK's *The Astrological Journal*, 1996, and was then reprinted in *Considerations* magazine (USA) in the same year. The title 'Of Cerberus and Blackest Midnight Born' is a quote from the first line of 'L'Allegro' by the English poet John Milton (1608-1674).

standing on a bank of grass at the top of the hill; on his left was a little wood. On the other side of the road was a ditch thick with whin bushes.

Beyond the ditch was a rusty, sagging fence; on the far side of the fence, smooth, mossy moorland dotted with whins, their vivid yellow colour fading into the deepening dusk. In the distance I could just see the Highland hills, purple and rust, gathering shadows in the autumnal twilight.

A myriad of stars, taking their lead from Venus, was growing bright with increasing intensity. A mellow harvest moon was slowly rising, casting a glow on the hills. The air held a hint of cold. I could feel the melancholy music of the bagpipes flowing through me like a magical current.

Reaching the foot of the hill, surrendering myself completely to the intensity of the moment, I lay down in the middle of the road. Spreading out my arms, I gazed up at the stars.

A gentle breeze blew over my body, soughing through the reedy grass. Drifting with the music through the night sky, slipping away from awareness of myself or the present, I was a timeless spirit of the air, travelling the vastness of space on the notes of the pibroch. An unobtrusive rhythm, a pulse, began to beat; growing more and more steady, it became a whispering message in my mind:

'There is nothing to fear,' it said. 'There is nothing to fear.'

An image of my lying dead, under the earth, came to me. Such images, occurring at other times, had filled me with panic and disgust. Now, there was none of that. I could gladly have died at that moment; my flesh would return to the earth and nourish it; my spirit would soar to infinity. The pulse continued, flooding me with its light:

'There is nothing to fear, nothing to fear, nothing to fear … '

At that point of spiritual ecstasy, I felt the absolute reality of my soul.

Such a moment might have lasted a second, an hour, or a hundred thousand years; but the music ceased, and the chill which was gradually taking over my body drew me back gently into the present. [See footnote]

The knowledge that such a vitalising sense of connectedness was possible, glimpsed during the above experience, kept me going through the long struggle to believe that life had an overall meaning, and to find my own way of offering my energy creatively in the years which were to follow.

URANUS ZAPS THE IC – ENTER ASTROLOGY!

When Uranus crossed the South Node/IC in 1980/81, I began to study astrology, thereby fulfilling a prediction made by an astrologer I had casually encountered in a launderette in Bath in England in the early 1970s.

I also met, moved in with and later married my partner – his Scorpio Moon is conjunct my IC and South Node, and he has an Aquarian Sun and Venus. All very appropriate symbolism for the timing of the Uranus IC transit!

His steadfast support, combined with the deep awareness of teleology which many years' practice of astrology brings, have been vital for my personal and professional growth and development from the time Uranus crossed the IC until now, (i.e., end of 1995/early 1996) as Pluto moves off that point.

When Pluto was still transiting the IC, but from Sagittarius, I applied and was accepted for a major astrological study course. The very day that Pluto was exactly on the South Node and about to cross the IC for the last time saw me beginning the first year of study. I felt a powerful sense of standing on firm inner ground after the turbulence and trauma of the last few years – of being in the right place at the right time, of having done what I could, for now, with my family inheritance – of being ready to move on to the next growth cycle.

Now that the outer planets have crossed the IC and moved into the Western hemisphere of my horoscope, I feel liberated from much of the pathology of the past, and more able to use directly in the world the undoubted creativity inherited with it. Nor do I need any longer to make bargains with the shadowy figures who emerge when the light of day is dimming.

Astrodienst

June 2017

Cusps, Houses, Twins:
Top Topics for Beginners' Questions

There are some topics which come up repeatedly in an astrologer's life, especially if that astrologer has taken on the role of introducing beginners to our great subject.

Here are my three top favourites: house cusps, the fraught question of house division and the equally challenging question of how astrology explains twins in general – and their differences in particular. All three articles were published on my 'Astrology: Questions and Answers' blog, with the one on houses republished, I think, on The Mountain Astrologer *magazine's blog a few years ago.*

I feel sure my astrological colleagues will agree that those three are perennial head-scratchers for students new to astrology.

Rian's question: born on the cusp: which sign am I?

QUESTION: 'Could you talk a little bit about cusps? How much does a person with their Sun at 29.5 degrees take on the next sign? Or is it black and white? I think it might be a fade-out/fade-in, but I've never found anything written about this. Thank you.' – Rian

ANNE'S ANSWER: I'm glad you asked this question, Rian. It's one that astrologers are asked a lot. I'll answer it in two stages. Firstly, let's imagine someone out there is due to give birth mid-to-late June 2013 in Glasgow, UK, and is wondering whether their baby will have the Sun in Gemini or Cancer.

At midnight GMT on 21 June (1:00 a.m. British Summer Time), the Sun is at the very end of Gemini: 29°48'. By midnight GMT on 22 June (1:00 a.m. BST), the Sun has moved to the next sign and occupies the very beginning of Cancer: 0°45'. Thus, our imaginary child arriving on 21 June 2013 sometime after midnight GMT in Glasgow, would in popular terms be born on the cusp.

However, as anyone who takes their interest in astrology beyond Sun signs very quickly will realise, there is a lot more to astrology than its popular media face would suggest. With an accurately calculated horoscope which uses the date, place and vital time of birth, an astrologer (or, these days, anyone with access to a reasonable computer program) can work out to the minute where the Sun is on that child's birthday.

To illustrate this, let us look at the chart of an imaginary cusp Baby X [opposite] born in Glasgow at 6:00 a.m. BST (5:00 am GMT) on Friday, 21 June 2013, he/she will have the Sun in Gemini – at 29°59'. If this child is born only five minutes later, however, he/she will have the Sun in Cancer – at 0°00'.

Thus, strictly speaking, there is no such thing as 'born on the cusp'.

Baby X chart

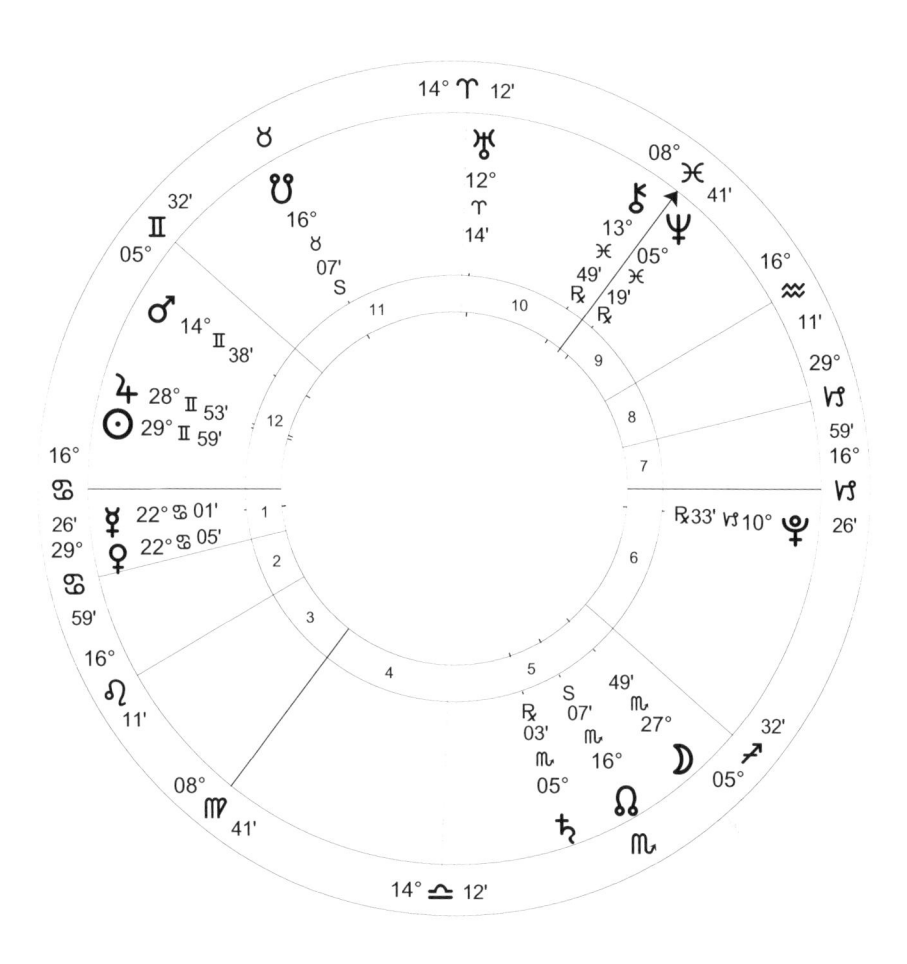

Our Baby X horoscope accurately calculated is either – in Sun sign terms – a Gemini or a Cancer.

However, Rian, your guess was quite correct. Someone born with the Sun at the very beginning of the 30 degrees of any zodiac sign has a stronger, more vivid and obvious 'charge' of the sign's energy than someone born at the very end.

Imagine that you are standing in a favourite room which you have occupied for a long time. You are becoming a little bored, jaded with what that room may have to offer. Suddenly, a door you'd never noticed before opens slightly. A shaft of new light streams through from another room. You step forward, intrigued. Could this be a new adventure? Or, to conclude our analogy: the Sun in fickle, restless Gemini is becoming stale – the prospect of entry into a journey through another sign, watery mysterious Cancer, beckons …

The second stage of my answer, though, brings in a little of the more complex picture which more in-depth astrology has to offer.

Even those of you with very little knowledge of astrology should be able to imagine the 36co-degree zodiac circle before you as a stage. Stand in the centre and look around the circle.

You will see various symbols, representing the planets. Humans have been standing on Earth, looking out into the night sky, plotting the planets' positions against an imaginary 360-degree great circle, the zodiac, for more than six thousand years. That view has never changed, despite our knowledge for several centuries that the Sun, not Earth, is the centre of our solar system. We still look out from the same Earth to the same celestial view.

On the left of the circle, just above and below the horizontal black line, fall the sectors of Gemini and Cancer. Our Baby X may be a Sun Gemini – only just! – but very close to that Sun is Jupiter (a desire to connect to the big picture) and not far away is Mars (action). This gives our Baby X a very strong emphasis on the Gemini theme.

However, the horizontal black line is his/her Ascendant or rising sign, revealing the way s/he will appear to the world in general. This is in the sign of Cancer. Just below this point, squashed together on 22° Cancer, are Venus (urge to relate) and Mercury (drive toward communication, expression). Thus, Baby X will have five out of the ten planets (or characters on the stage), and rising sign, occupying only two of the twelve signs of the zodiac.

This places a very strong emphasis on the signs of Gemini and Cancer, rational air and emotional water. Therefore, at a very simple level (full interpretation has to take all the characters, their locations and interactions on the zodiac stage into account) Baby X will have the gifts and pains of that classic Shakespearean clash between reason and passion, to wrestle with and reconcile and be driven by for as long as s/he lives.

Well, Rian, a long answer for a short question! But I do hope it sheds some light – and reveals in the process a deeper astrology beyond the Sun signs. Do let me know what you think.

anne-whitaker.com

How does astrology explain twins?

This is a very frequent question. How does it work when you do a birth chart for twins? Or two babies born the same minute at the same hospital? Can two people have the same horoscope?

It is important at this point to emphasise to readers who are familiar only with Sun signs that to get beyond them requires an individual's horoscope to be drawn up for the date, place *and* time of birth. Human beings are complex and contradictory. It's not possible to approach any satisfying symbolic exploration of that complexity through the Sun (or 'star') sign alone.

A number of years ago, I decided to address the typical questions students asked about twins via one of the tutorial classes I ran for my more advanced students, all of whom had a good grasp of the basics of astrology, and some of whom were already practitioners in their own right.

One student – let's call her Anna – was the devoted aunt to a set of twins in their mid-teens, a boy and a girl – let's call them Angus and Miriam. These two had been born less than fifteen minutes apart and had almost identical horoscopes.

I had formulated a theory about twins and astrology which I wanted to test out, so I obtained permission via Anna from Angus and Miriam's parents as well as the twins themselves, to calculate their horoscopes and discuss them anonymously in class.

My method was to put up on the board only one horoscope since there was so little difference between the twins' horoscopes and ask the students to take an hour to prepare along with me a basic outline of the key characteristics revealed by this one horoscope. We did the preparation as though we were preparing a birth chart for just one person.

The class knew nothing about either of the twins, and I asked Anna to observe us, but not to make any comments at all.

Once we had written up the outline, we spent the next hour discussing our findings with Anna who knew her nephew and niece well.

I am writing this after a gap of about twenty years and no longer have the notes for detailed reference, so can only give a summary of the essence of what emerged from our discussion.

Anna found our summary from the one horoscope of the basic characteristics of both her nephew and niece to be highly accurate. Very clear was that certain traits were held in common, but that the rest were, as it were, divided up between the twins. To put it simply, looking at a range of traits, 1, 2, 3 and 4 were recognisable in both, Miriam manifested traits 5, 6 and 10 whilst Angus lived out traits 7, 8 and 9.

This interesting and enlightening experiment does not of course constitute any kind of proof. But it bore out my impressions from reading about the similarities and differences in the lives of twins about whom I had read, as well as my own observations of twins I had come across from my own experience, as well as the few horoscope readings I had done for individuals who were twins.

What was this impression? Coming back to the analogy of the horoscope revealing the characters poised on life's stage, waiting for the moment of birth to kick start the action of the play, it seemed that twins unconsciously chose which characters on their shared stage they were going to live out jointly – and the ones which they were going to live out separately.

The experiment which I did all those years ago with my students, Anna and her nephew and niece certainly bore out my theory.

After writing this piece I googled 'astrology and twins' to see what came up, and was pleased to find on my favourite astrology site, Astrodienst at astro.com, that other astrologers including Dr Liz Greene had come to much the same conclusion.

As far as two people born at the same time in the same place is concerned, yes, they would in effect have the same horoscopes. You would certainly see considerable similarities if you studied both their lives over time. But each character on the stage at a given moment in time has a range of possible modes of expression. Thus, the influence of different family circumstances and different opportunities etc. would call forth a range of possible responses from the same basic character.

To read much more on this topic, do go over to the [late] master astrologer Donna Cunningham's excellent blog Sky Writer where she has an excellent piece on the astrology of twins. Then come back and let me know what you think!

The Mountain Astrologer blog
December 2013

Astrological Houses: Placidus, equal – or what?

Sooner or later, it dawns on the student or budding astrologer that the method of dividing the inner space in a horoscope into twelve sectors or spheres of life, known as houses, poses some problems ...

Firstly, since there are a number of different house systems, which should you choose? Secondly, to a varying degree depending on your chart, planets can move house. In my chart, for instance, by Equal House, I have no less than six planets in the 12th house. When I first saw my horoscope in Placidus houses, one planet, my ruler Mercury, had migrated to the 11th. 'Oh joy! I need all the help I can get here,' I thought then. But, as you will soon see, it's not as simple as that.

Then there is a further problem. In Placidus, the MC-IC axis always defines the cusp of the 10th/ 4th houses. If you use Equal House, the MC-IC axis can fall through any pair of houses from the 8th/2nd to the 11th/5th. How do you deal with that?

I have worked with only two systems over the years, i.e., the most commonly used ones in the UK – Equal and Placidus. I used Equal House from the early 1980s perfectly happily, finding that the system worked well for me. Then I changed to Placidus in 1995. I didn't choose it for any carefully thought through philosophical or practice reasons; it was simply the system used on the diploma course I was doing. Now, in 2015, I am moving back to using Equal again. For philosophical reasons this time, as you will see shortly.

A CLASS EXPERIMENT

Ever since a small group of my 'old' students persuaded me to run a refresher class for them starting last August (2014), I have really enjoyed returning to astrology teaching. Those students were all very rusty and wanted to cover the basics again. Inevitably, the question of house division came up. Having covered the core meanings of the houses in an introductory class, we recently spent a whole tutorial looking in more detail at the issue of house division.

The methods I adopted on this occasion were twofold. Firstly, I gave the class copies of their charts in Equal House to compare with their existing Placidus charts. Then I drew up a grid of which we all had a copy. This listed all the planets, Chiron and the North Node as well as the pair of houses through which the Equal House MC-IC axis ran. Thus, we could see at a glance those features which stayed the same in both systems and which ones changed. In some charts many features changed. In others' e.g., mine, there was very little difference.

I have always taught astrology with every student having a copy of everyone else's horoscopes, including mine. With permissions always asked and given before the start of a course, and appropriate emphasis on confidentiality, this way of working has been very effective. It creates each class as a kind of mini qualitative research laboratory where astrological theory can be tested out there and then, observing to what extent it manifests accurately in the nuts and bolts of the everyday lives of those present. It is a model which makes for very lively teaching.

We worked our way round everyone in the small group, including me, discussing how interpretations might change, and most importantly, how much that mattered by potentially altering the emphasis on key horoscope themes.

For instance, the Moon in one student's horoscope changed from the Placidus 9th house (a location she really liked for her Moon, being both a teacher and an education junkie) to the 10th by Equal House which emphasised the importance of her vocational/career life but not the dimensions of teaching and learning which are both 9th-house concerns. However, we pointed out to her that this didn't really matter in terms of overall accuracy of interpretation; she really was very well endowed with Jupiterian energy anyway, given her Moon's trine to Jupiter in Aries, as well as her Sun's square to Jupiter.

This was just one example in which, whatever shift we saw of planets from one house to another, there was invariably an underlying strong theme in the birth chart, so that the emphasis being slightly shifted in one context made little if any difference to the overall accuracy of interpretation of the whole horoscope. Interestingly, more than half of our small group, despite my having worked with all students with Placidus from 1995, said that they preferred the relative simplicity of the Equal House system.

In my own case, although ruling planet Mercury moved from the sociable, group-oriented Placidus 11th house to join five other planets in the reclusive 12th by Equal House, I have an exact semi-square from Mercury to 10th-house Uranus in both systems, Uranus also strongly aspects the Sun and Moon, so the Aquarian/Uranian/11th-house 'tone' remains strongly emphasised. That Mercury energy also flows from the 12th house to an exact sextile to Neptune, and a square to 3rd-house Jupiter in both systems. So, any reclusive tendencies brought by the move are well and truly restrained by other horoscope factors!

The students could see from our small experiment something which is fundamental to the accurate reading of any horoscope: strong themes will shine through, whatever way you divide up the circle. As U.K astrologer Robin Heath so memorably observed a number of years ago: 'Astrology appears more and more to behave like a hologram. You can perform almost any technique with the data, turn the chart inside out or slice it up, and still the symbolic pictures remain.'[6] Both this statement and our class experiment bore out the conclusion at which I had arrived some time ago. It doesn't really matter much what system you use. What you get is the same overall picture.

HORSES (HOUSES!) FOR COURSES ...

I went onto outline the way some astrologers use different house systems for different purposes. Since the Equal House system is based on the Ascendant/Descendant axis (which is the axis of 'Here I am in relation to you'), this system can be used when the client in their reading wishes

---

6   *The Mountain Astrologer*, Issue 78, April/May 1998, Letters, p. 11.

specifically to address matters pertaining to relationship.

Since the IC-MC axis can be seen as an arrow flowing from the person's deepest self and origins (IC) to their future direction (MC), then issues of roots, vocation and life direction are most appropriately contemplated (some astrologers think) via the Placidus lens because that system can be seen to emphasise the MC-IC.

Also, although I have never worked with the Koch system myself, I know that some astrologers swear by the accuracy of its house cusps in plotting transits and progressions.

The Equal House MC-IC 'Problem'

The placing of quote marks above gives you a clue that I do not see the shifting placement of the MC-IC axis in the Equal House system as a problem at all. Quite the opposite. I think that working with the MC-IC axis against the backdrop of either the 2nd/8th, 3rd/9th, 4th/10th or the 5th/11th adds a layer of richness to the interpretation of the MC-IC which of course should remain just as focal and important in the Equal House system as in any other where the MC/IC is always the cusp of the 10th/4th houses.

For example, I have often encountered clients or students with 2nd/8th backdrops in professions involving finance and collective money. Those with 4th/10th backdrops have their strong life focus on career/vocation emphasised. With 5th/11th emphasised, you often find 'creative' types who work co-operatively and collaboratively in the pursuit of their careers. And in my own case, the 3rd/9th backdrop is highly appropriate since writing and higher education have been central to all the diverse vocational paths I have pursued throughout my working life.

Equal House: the return

In conclusion, the students were very keen to know why I had decided to return to working with Equal House. For giving me the final shove in that direction I have to thank Phoebe Wyss and her excellent recent book

Inside the Cosmic Mind which I would urge any astrology student or practitioner to read – if they are inclined, as I am, to perceive astrology as a 'top down' art whose practice and interpretation reveals us as expressing in micro form, the shifting macro patterns of the whole cosmos.

In Phoebe Wyss' own words:

> *'Archetypal astrology is an approach to astrological chart interpretation that is based on this cosmological view. The meanings of the chart factors such as zodiac signs, houses, and planets are then seen to derive from the twelve basic categories of meaning associated with the astrological archetypes. These fundamental cosmic principles and their inter-relationships are symbolised in the geometry of the zodiac ... '*[7]

Wyss' book – which builds on the recent work of Richard Tarnas, Kieron Le Grice and other pioneers in the field of archetypal cosmology – has taken me back and re-grounded me in the basic geometry of sacred numbers whose symbolism reflects the core shaping principles or archetypes governing the movement of energy throughout the whole cosmos. The number twelve is one of those sacred numbers.

From that symbolic, geometric perspective, dividing the inner space of the horoscope symbolically into twelve equal parts seems more appropriate than using any other house system, including Placidus, whose devising arises purely from measurements limited by the view from planet Earth in relation to the solar system in our tiny corner of space/time.

The Mountain Astrologer blog
November 2015

---

[7]   *Inside the Cosmic Mind*, Phoebe Wyss, Floris Books, 2014, p. 93.

Cycles:

'History fancies itself linear – but yields to a cyclical temptation.'

– Criss Jami, *Healology*

Large or small, I love them all – cycles. Not bi-cycles; planetary cycles. As I wrote in a recent article in The Mountain Astrologer *magazine:*

Whether the cycle is huge, like the five-hundred-year Neptune-Pluto one, or small, like that of the monthly Sun-Moon, the same basic stages apply: seeding, germinating, sprouting, flowering, ripening, harvesting, dying back in preparation for the new. Those stages describe developmental processes from gnats to galaxies: we can thus apply the basic template of what we see enacted above us in the heavens every month to the ebb and flow to everything, including cultural phases and the rise and fall of whole civilisations. – 'Waning and Waxing Crescents: Windows to the Future … the Jupiter-Saturn Cycles', TMA, Dec 2020/Jan 2021

I hope you enjoy the range of perspectives on this fascinating topic. I've left the three pieces on the formidable Saturn-Pluto cycle, highly active during 2019/20, not concluding until 2053, until the end of this section.

Incidentally, the last section of this book, 'PS', combines two of my favourite obsessions: cycles and Mary Shelley, with Greta Thunberg as her companion. Please forgive some necessary repetition of material: regard any such as my astro-motifs.

The attraction of new horizons ... the Jupiter cycle

WHAT IS THE JUPITER CYCLE?

As ever, it is important at the outset of a general article to stress that one can only really judge in detail what the essence of any planetary shift is likely to be from consideration of the whole horoscope or birth chart. However, it is certainly possible to sketch out a broad picture that can offer some perspective: both to readers with some astrological knowledge and to those of you with none who are curious to know more.

Each of the planets, travelling through the twelve signs of the zodiac as viewed from Earth, has a cycle of differing length. Pluto, currently in Capricorn [as of 2021], will take 248 years to traverse the 360 zodiacal degrees, returning to that sign long after we are all dead and gone. Saturn's cycle, on the other hand, is a much shorter 29-30 years. Currently in Scorpio (when this article was first written), dredging up all kinds of sexual scandal from its previous traverse of that sign in the 1980s, it is offering the collective the famous Saturn return experience, when Saturn returns to the place it occupied at our birth when we are 29-30 years of age and again at 59-60, inviting us all to grow up.

Jupiter and Saturn together form a symbolic, complementary whole: as Saturn's cycle unfolds, it helps us to be realistic and to set limits without which no maturation or growth can take place. Jupiter creates contrast and balance to this. It energises that optimistic, expansive part of us that reaches out to the pleasure of new experience, new learning and understanding. Its natural exuberance can make life a fun, joyful experience.

It can also cause us to over-reach our limits and expect more than life can realistically deliver. That facet needs to be watched carefully when Jupiter is very active in our lives.

Jupiter's cycle is 11-12 years: 11.6 years to be exact. It's an easy one to track, being accessible both to those of you who know some astrology and those of you who don't. Everyone can track through their lives, measuring the Jupiter cycles: Jupiter returns to its location in your birth horoscope at 11-12 years of age, 23-24, 35-36, 47-48, 59-60, 71-72, 83-84 in a currently average lifetime.

What do we look for in the Jupiter cycle? In essence, the start of each cycle represents the opening out of a whole new learning period whose archetypal purpose is to expose us to new experience and new learning, and to all kinds of travelling within both inner and outer life.

REAL LIFE FLESH ON SYMBOLIC BONES

These experiences vary hugely from one person to another, taking their flavour from the zodiacal sign and house in which Jupiter was located at birth.

At 23-24 (Jupiter in Sagittarius in the 9th house), you might take off to Australia to do a postgraduate diploma in Adult Education. Your friend (Jupiter in Capricorn in the 6th house) might not travel anywhere but concentrate on mastering a new skill like carpentry which enables him, after a few years' apprenticeship, to set up his own business. In the meantime, my neighbour down the street (Jupiter in Cancer in the 5th house) might marry at 23-24 and have three children in rapid succession before the age of 30. In a real-life example, Alexa said: 'My second Jupiter return, at age 24. coincided with me buying a house. Natal Jupiter was in Cancer, which is appropriate, of course, and the house was bigger (Jupiter) than we needed for just the two of us, so we could have space for lodgers.'

These are very different branches of experience based on Jupiter being in different signs and houses of the zodiac at birth, but they have the same underlying principle of expansion and the growth of experience; of understanding. And (hopefully!) some wisdom shines through them all.

You can also detect the archetypal lifelong themes provided via Jupiter's placement by sign and house in your personal horoscope, as you follow the Jupiter cycle unfolding throughout your lifetime. For example, I have natal Jupiter in Scorpio in the 3rd house. It's not hard to work out from this (and Jupiter's strong links to most of the planets in that horoscope) that an intense preoccupation with gathering and sharing all kinds of information (while placing it in contexts that expand one's understanding of life's deeper meanings) might be rather important to me.

The Jupiter cycle: unfolding in one lifetime

At age 11-12, I passed the 'Quali' (the long defunct Scottish entrance exam to determine one's level of entry to secondary education). At 23-24, I completed a post-graduate Diploma in Education, having already been an adult education teacher for two years. At 35-36, I studied for and passed my first astrology qualification, the Certificate of the Faculty of Astrological Studies (UK), prior to beginning a career as an astrologer.

At 47-48, I began the Diploma in Psychological Astrology course, studying with Liz Greene and the late Charles Harvey at the Centre for Psychological Astrology in London. In completing this course, I commuted by plane for three years, earning myself the nickname of 'The Flying Scot'. The year after the age 59-60 Jupiter return, I stepped into cyberspace via my main blog, 'Writing from the Twelfth House'. My first book, a research study called *Jupiter Meets Uranus*, was published the following year.

Perhaps this personal account will encourage you to track through your Jupiter cycles and see that there is indeed a thematic unfolding of a specific kind of experience.

Fate, freewill ... or what?

The question of what the balance is between fate and freewill has preoccupied humans for millennia and remains unresolved. However, as an astrologer, it is important to have a viewpoint regarding this ageless question. Decades of astrological practice, combined with much reading that has included what I can grasp of probability theory and chaos theory, and my own efforts to become a more conscious person, have led me to the view (not original at all – many astrologers take this standpoint) that there are certain givens in this life, as shown by the characters standing on a person's life stage when the horoscope is drawn up. Those characters, namely the planets, shown in the horoscope's symbolic, archetypal patterns, are ours for life.

However, the evidence of observation and experience appears to suggest this vital point: the more conscious we become of our motivations and drives, and how they impact our inner and external life, the wider becomes the range of possible avenues of expression to which we can have access while choosing how to make our particular life's drama as positive and creative as possible.

Bearing this in mind, let's return to the Jupiter cycle and see how we might work creatively and consciously with its 11/12-year periods.

Working with cycles

All life cycles, whether we are looking at a gnat, a human or a galaxy go through the same process: seeding, germinating, sprouting, flowering, ripening, harvesting and dying back in preparation for the new. So it is with the planetary cycles.

Think of the tiny monthly cycle of the Sun and Moon. The New Moon takes place in darkness. Only when that first magical Waxing Crescent appears after two-to-three days does the energy of the cycle begin to build. After a week, at the First Quarter Moon, things are taking shape. At the Full Moon, the cycle's energy is in full light, at its most obvious. A week later, on the Waning Square, the Moon is shrinking, the month's energy on the wane. Then the last, Waning Crescent, precedes Moondark (i.e., Balsamic), those two-to-three days in which the energy of the completed cycle sinks back into the void, waiting for the energy of the next New Moon to arise.

Applying the same template to the 11/12-year cycle of Jupiter, it takes about a year or more for the initial upsurge of desire for new expansive challenges to stabilise and take definite form.

Jupiter in action: a real-life example
Let's use the person with Jupiter in Sagittarius in the 9th house as our example. At the age of 23, off she goes to Australia, completes her diploma and obtains a good teaching job in Melbourne. She works there for a couple of years, then relocates to Sydney (first quarter phase, Jupiter now in Pisces), since she wants to take up sailing and she has a friend there who runs a sailing school.

Three years later (Full Moon phase, Jupiter in Gemini) she agrees to take on a teaching job at the sailing school where she has been a student. Another three years go by and she begins to feel dissatisfied and critical (last quarter phase, Jupiter now in Virgo). She has become bogged down in admin and paperwork. Not her style!

She puts less and less commitment into her job, and after over ten years in Australia, she has itchy feet again (Moondark). Nearly twelve years after arriving, full of enthusiasm, she is off to work in the Greek Islands. She has fallen in love with a Greek Australian and decides to return with him to his home island of Rhodes. She is nearly thirty-six years old. A new Jupiter cycle is about to begin.

Working with our Jupiter cycles
I've always found that astrology students and clients are fascinated when I unfold their major cycles with them; they find it so helpful in understanding the unfolding pattern of their lives. The Jupiter cycle is a particularly easy one to connect to. The rhythm of the cycle, looking back, can usually be tracked. In the last year or two before a new 11/12-year period begins, one can generally perceive a certain dissatisfaction, boredom, loss of any great interest and a desire for a new challenge in the sphere of life indicated by the sign and house placement of natal Jupiter. (If Jupiter is a very strongly placed and emphasised 'character on the stage', the overall effect is, of course, amplified.)

With Jupiter in Scorpio in the 3rd house, I clearly recall my boredom, restlessness and desire for a new educational project towards the end of my fourth Jupiter cycle when I was 46 or 47. Alexa, with her Jupiter in Cancer, bought a house at the start of the second Jupiter cycle when she was twenty-four, that was 'bigger (Jupiter) than we needed for just the two of us, so we could have space for lodgers.'

Are you a year or two into a new Jupiter cycle? Or three years into it? After five or six years, the cycle is at its Full Moon phase, its peak of energy. By nine years, impetus generally is on the wane, and restlessness is setting in. By the Moondark phase of the cycle, it really feels like time for a new project, a new venture. But you know – if you become familiar with this cycle's rhythm – that it will probably be another couple of years before the new idea has taken shape and translated itself into a fresh, exciting direction.

One of the great gifts of astrological knowledge is the help it offers in setting our sails, metaphorically speaking, to the prevailing winds of our lives. It is useful to get to know your Jupiter cycle in planning those times in life when your spirit is calling you to open up your life to new experience. I do hope this introductory article has given you some useful food for reflection and an impetus to action.

The Mountain Astrologer
June/July 2015

The Saturn cycles – forging the 'diamond soul'

'Just as water flows downhill, the tendency in all of nature is to take the easiest path. That direction, however, is not the path of personal growth.' [8]

'Saturn's heat and pressure are needed in order that we can develop what Buddhists call the 'diamond soul'.' [9]

I like both of these quotes very much. The first conveys a basic realisation about life that needs to dawn by the first Saturn return, so that in terms of personal growth, we can gain real benefit from the unfolding of Saturn's second cycle. The second quote contains a marvellous image of what the rewards can be during the second Saturn cycle as we grapple with the stern demands of the Saturn archetype.

During the first cycle, the major task is to find a place to stand in our lives and perceive a few reliable landmarks from which to take bearings, so that we can face life more than retreat from it. Then from age 29-30 onward, we can begin to extend and deepen the various possibilities that our lives contain – a process culminating in the second Saturn return at the age of 58-59. After this point of stocktaking, the third and final cycle begins. However, before being able to define clearly what the psychological changes and challenges of the three cycles are, it is necessary to define the essence of what the Saturn archetype brings into our personal lives.

I find it beautifully symbolic that the cycle of the progressed Moon runs closely with the Saturn cycle. The progressed Moon talks about

---

8   Alexander Ruperti, *Cycles of Becoming: The Planetary Pattern of Growth*, CRCS Publications, 1978, p. 56; reprint edition by Earthwalk School of Astrology Publishing, 2005.

9   Stephen Arroyo, *Astrology, Karma & Transformation: The Inner Dimensions of the Birth Chart*, CRCS Publications, 1978, p. 73; reprint edition, 2013.

our inextricable connection with the rhythms of life – its cycles and its limits. It describes the necessity of separating out and moving on from one period of experience to another if we are to develop texture and complexity. But it also explains our drive to be safe and secure and to keep ourselves in familiar territory. The progressed Sun challenges the latter need, pushing us to differentiate, to take risks, to 'follow our bliss.'

The Saturn archetype, however, contains both dimensions of this inner soli-lunar dynamic described by the progressed Sun and Moon, and it can be seen as their external worldly agent. Saturn, as life's challenging, defining and shaping principle, clearly says to each newly born individual: 'Anything you can achieve in your life is confined by the inevitability of your mortality and by the givens described in your birth chart. In terms of complete Saturn cycles, you have three to work with at the most. Now get on with it – see how far you can go!'

At the start of life, all is potential. As the Saturn cycles unfold, they describe how that potential gradually crystallises, concretises, until by the end there is nothing left to develop in this lifetime. The challenges presented by Saturn have at their core the demand that we become who we are and who we can be as fully as possible by separating from that which we are not and could never be.

There are important differences in the developmental demands of the stages symbolised by the three major cycles of Saturn. The first, from birth to age 29-30, is the thesis stage. It is the most intensely physical and energetic and the least conscious cycle. It is about building the platform on which to stand in life.

The second cycle, from age 29-30 to 58-59, is the antithesis stage. The initial structure is tested and challenged to grow; awareness and consciousness are more fully developed; life's goals are pursued and hopefully achieved to a sufficient degree in order to bring at least a tolerable level of satisfaction.

In the synthesis stage, culminating at age 87-88, ideally there is a bringing together and summing-up of what one's life has meant, and a shifting of emphasis from worldly achievement to reflection and spiritual maturing. There is an acceptance of, and preparation for, the inevitable physical decline that ends in the death of the physical body.

I find the Saturn archetype profoundly paradoxical. On the one hand, Saturn represents that which nails us to the cross of matter and holds us in the world of form. On the other hand, when Saturn's challenges have been patiently and honestly worked with, and a mature realism arrived at, the sense of freedom of spirit that can then be released is immense – full of the potential for satisfaction and joy. This sense of freedom is unconfined because it does not relate to matter at all. I am sure this is what the Buddhists mean when they talk about the 'diamond soul'.

First Saturn return cycle

We all arrive at the first Saturn return at the age of 29-30. Whether we know we're having one or not, the broad determinants are the same. My metaphor for this return is the recollection I have of a science class where I was fascinated to observe the growth of a copper sulphate crystal which, over a period of weeks, emerged from clear blue water into a highly defined, beautiful, crystalline shape. At the first Saturn return, the crystalline shape that must emerge is that of realism. In a developmentally healthy person, the purity of that crystal of realism is not overly tainted by bitterness, cynicism or disillusionment, all of which corrode the soul and limit the potential for further growth. As the crystal of realism emerges, it may well carry with it some pain, grief and depression. This is healthy and normal enough as part of the process of getting through the 27-to-30-year period. We know from observation of the lives of others, and our own, that this period is critical.

To an astrologer's perception, this age range's critical nature is emphasised by the knowledge that ages 27 to 30 bring four major symbolic patterns that are all about differentiation, individuation and the facing and purging of illusions that hold us back from realising our full potential. These patterns are the following: the second transit of the North Node to the natal South Node's position at age 27; the progressed Moon's return around age 27; transiting Pluto to natal

Neptune between ages 27 and 29 [10]; and, of course, the Saturn return at age 29-30 which seems to focus the three other patterns.

Letting go of the illusions and defenses that buffer us from the poundings of life, but which also limit our becoming what we may most fully be, can be desperately painful. During this period, I was forced to give up my long-cherished illusion of being a writer. It gave me a secret sense of superiority over the rest of the world and met my profound need to be special and different. When put to the test between ages 27 and 30, this illusion crumbled. I realised that I had writing talent for which I received some public recognition, but I also discovered that I lacked the single-minded drive that keeps one at it full-time. Without shedding my illusion and moving on, I would never have been able to develop my other gifts and talents which began to take shape from my Saturn return onward.

The development of an internal 'locus of evaluation' – a sound sense of one's own worth that is not overly dependent on the approval of parents, colleagues, partners or peers – is another psychological change that should be happening to a reasonably substantial degree by the first Saturn return. This marks the point in life where we are no longer seen as children or even very young adults by the larger world. We are expected to take responsibility for our own actions and to be effective in the world as workers, partners, parents and friends, with no excuses or allowances having to be made for our youth and immaturity.

Ideally, we should also have developed a sense of what the boundary is between our parents and ourselves – between their demands of us and ours of them – and how to respond to them in a mature fashion without falling prey to old childlike patterns of behaviour. If our parents have not been mature enough to let go of us, we should be well on the way

---

10   This pattern is confined to an approximate 100-year period that has the following criteria: (1) the Neptune-Pluto sextile which moved into orb in the early 1940s and continues well into the 21st century; and (2) Pluto's current rate of passage through the zodiac signs. This pattern begins with people born around 1920 and ends for those who will be born after 2015.

toward having the maturity to draw our own boundaries.

Although there is a common core to the rites of passage that we all face, birth charts show that there are as many different Saturn returns as there are individuals. With Saturn in a fire sign, one's core challenge is to find faith in life which, in turn, fuels the struggle to establish an unshakable sense of self-worth and of the special nature of one's contributions to the world. The Saturn-in-water person's major task is to come to terms with the inevitability that we are all separate and alone, no matter how much we may love other people or be loved by them. For Saturn in air, developing mental discipline, establishing intellectual credibility and contributing worthwhile ideas to collective life are key formative tasks. The Saturn-in-earth person, to a greater extent than the other three elements, must form a sound relationship with the world of everyday reality and honour the physical and material dimensions of life in order to feel at peace within. Each will have a different journey through the first formative Saturn cycle.

The sign and house position of Saturn (as well as whether it is angular or not), the lunar nodes, Chiron, and other planetary connections provide the fine-tuning that shows the relationship between the archetypal forces present in all of life and the many differing ways they may manifest individually.

Whether a person is functioning in a healthy way by the first Saturn return is dependent psychologically on how well he or she has negotiated the first three stages of the cycle. For example, those who have been unable to effectively separate from their mothers at the waxing square at age 7-8 may still be locked into a dependent relationship at age 29-30, and this will distort their development as the second cycle begins. Those without long-term partners, unable as yet to mature from the challenges of the first opposition at age 14-15, may not see that being alone is better than being in an unfulfilling partnership, and are likely to carry some self-destructive relationship patterns into the next cycle. And finally, those who have failed to negotiate effective entry into the adult working world at the waning square of age 21-22 are likely to have even more difficulty as their thirties advance, unless they can begin to see what self-defeating patterns are blocking their path.

Everyone has their distortions, their failures and their blind spots. The gift of the first Saturn return is that the pressures it inevitably applies bring a great opportunity for us to look at those very aspects we have hitherto been unable to face. Saturn turns up the heat and pressure so much that the price of continued avoidance usually becomes higher than we are prepared to pay. Thus, realising at a heart and soul level that 'the easiest path is not the path of personal growth' has been the major turning point of many a life.

I find it very satisfying to work with clients who are either in the 27-to-30-year phase or have been through the first Saturn return and are taking stock at the beginning of the second cycle. It is here that the gifts of astrology are at their most potent, but only if people are willing to face who they are and be open to exploring some possible avenues of development that a good astrology reading can provide.

Clients who are strongly plugged into the energies symbolised by Uranus, Neptune and/or Pluto can take a very long time to bring these connections into consciousness. The usual pattern is to be battered and buffeted by these forces right up until the age of 30 and beyond. It usually takes at least this long for such individuals to begin to comprehend their relationship with those great impersonal forces. Then they can consciously begin to align the personal with the impersonal in a more aware, less fearful and therefore more creative way.

Until age 30, life's energy is waxing. The first Saturn return could be seen as the Full Moon point of life. Thereafter, the body starts to die, energy to wane; and our ability to recover from self-inflicted punishment and the batterings of life begins to diminish. Consequently, the margin for serious errors – from which one can recover and even benefit – grows inexorably narrower. The development of self-awareness and a realistic appreciation of both one's gifts and limitations become ever more important.

Second Saturn return cycle

Saturn is the planet of strict justice. Blind, stubborn, arrogant or fearful refusal to face certain basic realities in life, as the second Saturn cycle unfolds, skews the life path further and further away from who we could become, were we able to acknowledge and accept who we actually are rather than try to be who we are not. This brings increasing pain, dissatisfaction, emptiness, depression and perhaps despair, as the second Saturn return approaches.

By the second Saturn return, we can see what our lives have become – and we can see what it is too late to change. This is one of the most fundamental differences in perspective between the first and second return. At age 30, we have probably still to sow the most productive seeds of our lives – what we have already sown is still only germinating. But by the approach of 60, we are reaping the harvest and are confronted with the stark biblical words, 'As you sow, so shall you reap'.

At one end of the spectrum are those who arrive at this stage feeling that their time on this Earth has not been wasted. They have very few regrets and are prepared to face the final cycle of life with equanimity, perhaps rooted in great spiritual depth. These people usually retain a great zest for life and its remaining possibilities. At the other end are those who have sown meanly, poorly or fearfully and are reaping a harvest of regret, bitterness, loneliness, physical ill health and fear of the waning of physical power and attractiveness in the inevitable decline toward death.

Most of us will arrive somewhere in the middle range, satisfied with some aspects of our achievement and disappointed by our areas of failure – or those things that fate appears to have denied us without our having had much option for negotiation. I see the main challenges of this stage as follows: first, to value what we have been able to do; second, to come to terms with and accept those failures or disappointments that it is now too late to change; and third, to find within the limitations and constraints, imposed by our state of mind, body, spirit and bank balance, some further goals that are realistically achievable, which can bring a sense of meaning and enjoyment to whatever time we have left.

To end on a personal note, I agree with Jung's dictum that a major task for the second half of life is preparation for the end of it – this is not morbid but full of wisdom. I intend to start specifically, rather than tangentially, to prepare for the end of my life by the time I get through the second Saturn return, if I live that long. Whether I will take it as far as the 16th century poet John Donne, who practised for his death by lying in his coffin on a daily basis in the latter years of his life, I don't know. But with an exact Saturn-Pluto conjunction, also conjunct Mercury, Venus, the Moon and the Sun, I can't pretend that the idea doesn't appeal to me!

2016 POSTSCRIPT

Well, I have lived that long, and without as yet feeling the need to indulge in the John Donne option. A friend of mine remarked recently, with grim humour, that after the age of 60 anyone not in pain from one thing or another is probably dead. Another older friend also remarked, 'Growing old is not for softies.'

They are right, up to a point. There are many positives to being an elder, but let's get the minuses out of the way first. Nothing works as well as it once did – from joints to the digestive system to memory (for people's names or what you did yesterday or even five minutes ago). Some of us have to live with debilitating conditions like arthritis, hearing loss, eyesight problems or diabetes. Juggling responsibilities between grandchildren and increasingly frail elderly parents is a major challenge for many. Money is often tighter than it was. There is the stark realisation, during the final Saturn cycle, that we are moving toward the end of our time on Earth.

Despite those realities, I can honestly report feeling freer and more at peace now than ever before. From my experience, and that of friends, family and clients who are well into the third Saturn cycle, the key is to embrace being an elder, facing as best we can the challenges laid out in the latter part of the above article. In sum, what I have learned since I wrote it twenty years ago is as follows: the best way to prepare for the end of life is to live out what time is left as fully and authentically as possible.

One of my delights in returning to the teaching and practice of astrology, after a very long Neptunian absence, has been the re-encountering of clients and students who, thanks to the Internet and social media, have found me again for horoscope updates, more classes or both, in the last four years. Cheeringly, most of the clients I last saw when in their 30s and 40s, now in their 60s or older, are coping with the process of ageing pretty well, finding new freedoms and satisfactions.

Some typical observations have been: 'I am more me than I have ever been'; 'I do what I want to do far more than when I was younger'; 'I no longer care much, if at all, what anyone thinks'; and 'I have got rid of the hangers-on and hung onto my real friends'. Three members of my astrology tutorial class are women in their 60s, and they are such fun to teach. They are warm, witty, wise and very sharp. Working with them and enjoying their insights is a real gift.

The happiest elders I know have important things in common. One, they are aware of life's fragility and do not pretend otherwise: they choose to live in the moment as much as possible, taking pleasure in life's many gifts, no matter how small. Two, they are glad to offer time and experience to help both younger and older folks in their various communities. And three, they have varied but deeply rooted spiritual beliefs.

They have tried their best, given the inevitable frailties and limitations, to honour Saturn. And Saturn, dispenser of strict justice, is thus far returning the compliment.

BIBLIOGRAPHY
Arroyo, Stephen, and Liz Greene. *New Insights in Modern Astrology.* CRCS Publications, 1991.
Greene, Liz. 'Puer and Senex', from *The Development of the Personality, Seminars in Psychological Astrology,* Vol. 1, by Liz Greene & Howard Sasportas. Samuel Weiser, Inc., 1987, pp. 225-313.
Greene, Liz. *Saturn: A New Look at an Old Devil.* Samuel Weiser Inc., 1976; reprint edition, 2011.

The Astrological Journal, November/December 1996.
The Mountain Astrologer, 1998 re-published 2015.

Cycles end, new ones begin. On being 'liminal'

I always seem to have a favourite word. Maybe that's one of the hallmarks of being a writer. It's probably tiresome for other people when I cram it into conversations. By now, I'm sure you are quite desperate to know what the damn word is this time.

OK, it's 'liminal'. From the Latin *limen*, meaning 'threshold', it refers to that stage in life when one is hovering … departing from what is in the past: not quite at home here in the present; not quite arrived there in the future. It's an uncomfortable, fluid state to be in, but highly creative and full of potential.

How about this contemporary definition from Wikipedia: 'More recently, usage of the term has broadened to describe political and cultural change … During liminal periods of all kinds, social hierarchies may be reversed or temporarily dissolved, continuity of tradition may become uncertain, and future outcomes once taken for granted may be thrown into doubt.'

I don't know about you, but this to me sounds just like where we are collectively on planet Earth at present. Let's hope in the long run – which we Baby-Boomers likely won't live to see – we end up with something better than the mess we have now.

'As above, so below': no contemporary astrologer has come up with a pithier definition of the essence of our art than did fabled Ancient Egyptian sage Hermes Trismegistus in the equally fabled Emerald Tablet. Hermes was conceived as apparently hovering between the divine and human worlds.

Down here in that all-too-human world, thinking about Hermes in relation to the word 'liminal', this is providing me with some inspiration; much needed in my case, as I hover uncomfortably and uncertainly between the end of one 12-year Jupiter cycle and the beginning of a new one.

Jupiter cycles have always been a big deal for me, since 3rd-house Jupiter at 19°07' Scorpio squares all six of my Leo 11th-/12th-house planets. I wrote about the dubious but transformative delights of this astro-lineup in my very first column for *Dell*.

This idea of hovering between the divine and human worlds might be of some comfort and inspiration also to those of you readers who are ending one cycle at present, without being able to see how the energy of the next one is going to form. Standing in this liminal place, one cannot bully, cajole or entreat the new order to reveal itself. There is divine time, and there is human time.

This may sound pretty mystical, but my feeling – from both personal and professional experience – is that the deeper wisdom of our soul knows the direction in which we need to proceed in order to become all we can be, and how long it may take to get there.

The astrological cycles can put us in touch with that spark of divinity within each of us, offering profound insights into what a waning cycle has been about, and what the newly forming one might bring. They also teach us that 'To every thing there is a season, and a time to every purpose under the heaven:' [11]

Our egos, located in human, ordinary time, can often rail against this when we don't like what we see of the shape of things to come, or how long a particular transitional period is going to take. Try consulting your ephemeris. As I did at the end of 1998 and realised that I was about to have a series of 6th-house Neptune oppositions to 12th-house planets lasting from 1999 to 2012, as well as the ending/beginning of five major cycles.

It was some immersion I can tell you. Did my ego rail against it? You bet. I had to quit my career in 2002, and did not begin to surface, via writing on the Web at first, until 2008, not returning to consulting and teaching until 2012.

But guess what? I now look back on that period – when I felt liminal approximately twenty-four hours a day for years – as the most soul-enriching of my entire life.

---

[11] Ecclesiastes 3:1-8 King James Version (KJV).

One of the many lessons I took from that period was to pay close attention especially to the feelings of restlessness, dissatisfaction and uncertainty which herald the end of, for example, the 29/30-year cycle of Saturn which we all share. Many of us recall – or are experiencing now! – the turbulence and pain of the end of our twenties, from which most of us emerged or will emerge by around the age of thirty-three with a much clearer idea of who we are, and most importantly, who we are not.

Those difficult feelings and experiences occurring in the 12th-house phase of any major cycle are part of the dissolution of the old order of that part of our lives. An ending must take place – so that new energy may arise, taking us forward to the next stage of our unfolding.

Astrology's great gift is to show us that we are not random butterflies pinned to the board of Fate. We each have our small, meaningful strand to weave into life's vast tapestry.

In the end, it was consent to my tough and frightening period of liminality, patient waiting, the love and support I was fortunate to have and trust in the wisdom of the Unseen that got me through.

So, my liminal fellow-travellers, take heart. The old order may be waning, but something fresh and new is surely arising.

Dell Horoscope
May/June 2018

Cycles: a Saturn-Pluto trio (1)
A vandalised ephemeris – Saturn-Pluto strikes?

Having been born under an exact Saturn-Pluto conjunction, also conjunct Mercury, Venus, Moon and Sun – fortunately with the whole lot squared by persistently optimistic Jupiter and softened by a sextile to Neptune – it should hardly be a surprise that I have done my fair share of musing on that rather fearsome planetary combination over the years. And I am still here, folks. Here are three contrasting offerings, differing perspectives, on that same challenging combination, as a new cycle which began on 12 January 2020 slowly takes form; it does not conclude until 2053. Our world community will be in a very different place by then.

Pondering on Saturn-Pluto and its challenges reminded me of a column I wrote for the UK's *The Astrological Journal* a while ago which described a striking incident evoking Saturn-Pluto. Here is what I wrote:

Something oddly unsettling happened to me on 1 June 2016. Not a surprise, you might say, with the Sun that day conjunct Mercury in Gemini square Jupiter in Virgo square Saturn in Sagittarius square Neptune in Pisces – all churning between 10-15 degrees of the mutables: my Ascendant/Descendant plus Mercury tossed and turned within this restless brew.

I was peacefully preparing some notes for an especially interesting-looking client booked in for that afternoon. I like noting when clients' progressed planets change signs or turn retrograde/direct as their life pattern unfolds. This offers good material for enlightening contemplation and discussion. But it's not something you can quickly and easily do using a computer.

So – I reached for my 20th century midnight ephemeris, turned to the 1990s and made an unpleasant discovery. Someone had torn out pages from the 1990s. But not random pages. The whole of 1993 and 1994. Nothing else was damaged.

There were two possibilities, given that I had purchased this ephemeris secondhand on moving into my current office in January 2015. One – someone with keys to my office had come in and torn out specific pages at some point in the last year or so. (You'd never spot my Mercury-Saturn-Pluto lineup here, surely … .)

Or two – the more credible – whoever sold the ephemeris had hated those two years so much that he/she had taken their revenge via this act of mercurial vandalism. It was odd, however, that I had not noticed the damage earlier.

What to do now that I had a maimed ephemeris? Every client from now to forever, I thought, is *bound* to be born in the 1990s or have key life events happening then which require close symbolic examination and elucidation. With the passage of decades, one becomes fully cognisant of Sod's frequently malign intentions.

Ephemeris diaries 1993/4

Whilst reluctantly concluding, therefore, that a new ephemeris was probably required, a sudden memory lit up my grumpy, puzzled, somewhat paranoid mental processes. During the 1990s, I had made up my own ephemeris for each year. Perhaps I could use two of those to cover the missing years? Had those ephemerides survived one of my periodic purges?

They had! Their distinctive, colourful covers impressed me. How arty I was, briefly, in the 1990s. Included with the photocopied ephemeris pages were lined sheets of yellow paper for notes; these were full of astrological significators linked with personal and mundane events for 1991 to 1996. Why had I stopped then? No idea.

A morning was spent browsing through those notes, focusing especially on the two missing years of 1993-4; what a harrowing read! Staggering out semi-traumatised into gorgeous sunshine, I restored balance by basking outside my favourite boho cafe. Sipping delicious coffee and feasting on sandwiches followed by jammy creamy fruit scones, I reflected on our – fortunately – well-developed capacity to forget grim events. How unpleasant and upsetting it is to be reminded.

These were awful, turbulent times: not only at a macro level, but also in our small personal worlds: many of us who were plugged into the same degrees as the major planetary patterns of those years suffered very considerably. I often found myself talking to clients about family traumas which in many cases closely mirrored my own.

From my notes, January 1993: 'The start of a momentous year, with a triple conjunction of Uranus-Neptune at 18/19 degrees Capricorn in February, August and October, AND a triple meeting between Saturn in Aquarius square Pluto in Scorpio from 24-27 degrees of their respective signs in March and October 1993, then January 1994 ... world situation incredibly unstable, turbulent and cruel throughout 1992 as exactitudes approached.'

The notes went onto describe planetary links to major oil spills, earthquakes, mudslides, volcanic eruptions ... and that was just January and February 1993! There followed, as many of us will remember, ongoing IRA bombings on the UK mainland, the first attack on the World Trade Center, attempts to stop a genocidal war in the Balkans and horrific genocide in Ruanda. Worth quoting from the UK's *The Sunday Times* for 22 August 1993, two days after the second exact Uranus-Neptune conjunction: 'Islamic fundamentalism, if it remains unchecked, could destabilise Egypt, Sudan, Africa, Middle East – the whole world community.' Grimly prescient.

I now understood why that mysterious reader had torn out 1993 and 1994. Feeling very reflective, and grateful that life had eventually reached calmer waters in recent times, I headed off home. There in the mail was a letter: the first for many years from a close relative – from whom I was forced to cut off contact in 1993/4.

As a famous scientist once observed, life is not only stranger than we suppose, it is stranger than we *can* suppose.

astrologyquestionsandanswers.com 27 January 2018, incorporating work first published in *The Astrological Journal* July/August 2016

Cycles: a Saturn-Pluto trio (2)
'in my end is my beginning': paradox and the Saturn-Pluto cycle

Cycles: beginnings – and endings

In *East Coker*, the second of T.S. Eliot's *Four Quartets*, he begins that section with, 'In my beginning is my end' and ends it, 'in my end is my beginning'. This rather paradoxical juxtaposition bookends the whole of life. Every beginning carries the seeds of its ending, every ending, potential for new beginnings. However, generally speaking, you don't find much astrological musing on the topic of cycles' endings – or their slow beginnings. Especially in this particular Western cultural phase. Expedited by faster and faster broadband speeds and ever more sophisticated technology, the emphasis is on satisfying the wants (often as opposed to the needs) of *now*.

The problem with this, however, is that Life on our planet continues in its ancient, cyclic way, to which humans are still physically, emotionally and spiritually bound. Chronic disregard for this reality is now throwing up huge problems for us from the state of the planet to the increasingly fragile state of some of our young folks' mental and physical health.

Here is an example, from a recent issue of *The Week* which compiles 'the best of the British and international media': in a hard-hitting piece entitled 'Deaths of despair: why Americans are dying young', Joel Achenbach in *The Washington Post* writes: 'Whether as a result of economic hardship, stress, the lack of universal healthcare, loneliness or family breakdown, people just aren't looking after themselves properly, and are making destructive life choices … .'

The importance of paying attention

So – in my (it is alleged) contrarian way, I am here to muse on the endings, or balsamic phases, of cycles and the great importance of paying attention to them, especially as we approach the ending/new beginning of a whole 37-year Saturn-Pluto cycle. As everyone must be aware by now, astrologers or no, we are not living in a particularly easy, light-hearted time either collectively or individually. To put it mildly.

That excellent astrological writer Dana Gerhardt observed some time ago in relation to the balsamic phase of, for example, the 29-year progressed New Moon cycle:

'When will it end?' is everybody's first question on learning they've entered a progressed Balsamic phase. No matter how colourfully I paint its virtues, they peer beyond to a bleaker landscape, to a three-to-four-year sentence of all loss and no gain. I can see it in their eyes … I tell them this is the richest spiritual time. I tell them when my own progressed Balsamic phase was over, I had nostalgia for it. I cheer: 'You will too!' But it's a tough sell.

I would certainly endorse this from my own experience some years ago, of beginning a new phase in my career journey when no less than four major cycles were coming to an end over a period of almost a decade. I should have taken astrology's advice, not that of my own ego! The consequence was a long period of enforced retreat, triggered by a long family crisis and my subsequent energy burnout – an enriching and deepening time, but very tough whilst it was happening, until the progressed New Moon told me it was time to emerge and begin again.

Trying to do things differently

Looking over my last few posts, I can see my preoccupation with cycles generally and this Saturn-Pluto one in particular. Hardly surprising, being so plugged into it from birth myself. In 'Some Notes on Cycles in a Time of Crises' published recently on Astrodienst, I offered this very brief summary of Saturn-Pluto's challenges:

In essence, Saturn-Pluto lets us off with nothing, either personally or collectively. We are forced into increasingly tight corners, whilst the pressure is ramped up on us to face and deal with the present consequences of past decisions, some of which might not be of our direct making. The environmental crisis which has become so vivid this year with the nodal axis joining the dance of Saturn-Pluto throughout 2019 is a case in point.

As I write today, on 4 January 2020, Australia is ablaze. And on USA President Trump's directive – apparently without running the plan through Congress first – Qasem Soleimani, top general and one of the most powerful men in Iran, was killed in a drone strike at Baghdad airport early today. His deputy was also killed. According to US Secretary of State Mike Pompeo the airstrikes disrupted an 'imminent attack' in the region that put American lives at risk. Iran's Supreme Leader Ayatollah Ali Khamenei vows for 'harsh revenge.'

Collectively, Saturn-Pluto equals warfare of one kind or another. Relentless consistency every time. Our political masters worldwide should study history via the planetary cycles, see if they can just for once learn something from them. It would make a change to be making war on the issues that really matter e.g., climate change, increasing social and fiscal inequality, widespread homelessness, equal rights for women worldwide, inadequate healthcare – to name just a few contemporary problems urgently in need of war being waged upon them. Wouldn't it be great if most of our countries in the world weren't being run by narcissistic psychopaths?

Personal power and insightful choices

It is one of Life's great ironies, pointed out by Carl Jung, that as individuals we probably have more control and choice over how collective energies manifest than e.g., nations do. In order to exercise that control and choice, however, we need to work towards more conscious awareness of what our personal issues are – and how we go about making choices in relation to what Life throws at us. This is where astrology can be such an enlightening help.

Working with awareness, we can see patterns shaping up, get some idea from our first encounter with them, such as Saturn-Pluto opposing/conjoining/squaring our personal planet(s). We may learn what challenges they are offering – then with some reflection and perhaps therapeutic/astrological help when necessary, we work out what the planetary gods in question are asking of us over the several years in which long-term transits/progressions are in operation as they slowly apply, become exact and separate.

To quote Dr Liz Greene from one of her 1990s seminars at London's Centre for Psychological Astrology: 'You have to give the god what the god wants ... and if it's Mars, don't offer a bunch of flowers!'

I've never forgotten this sage advice and have passed it on many times both to clients and students. However, like all good advice, most of us to our detriment fail sometimes on the good advice front. As I admitted earlier, I failed to pay attention to what the planetary cycles were telling me, with very harsh results.

The wisdom offered by planetary cycles:
a general overview

In nearly forty years of working with clients, students, and with my own process, I have found that sharing wisdom offered by the planetary cycles has been very useful in helping to set Life's sails to go with the prevailing winds at any given time. I routinely take people through the 11/12-year Jupiter cycle, the 7/8-year stages of the 29/30-year Saturn cycles, and the progressed Sun/Moon cycle. Depending on the lunar phase at which a person was born, a progressed New Moon can fall in any year of life, such as at age four. You can then see that in 29/30 years' time, another progressed New Moon in a new sign, usually a new house, and making different aspects to the natal planets, is describing the early start of a new life phase.

I recall a recent client who experienced progressed New Moons at those very ages. She could see how a whole challenging process had arisen as a result of a significant event at the time of her first progressed New Moon when she was four years old, and how life changes at her second progressed New Moon in the next sign had symbolised a new start – feeling like an important stage along the road of freeing herself from old negative patterns.

It is really moving, and powerful, to see how the theme of opening up to new adventures of mind, body and spirit develops as clients' and students' Jupiter cycles unfold: age 11/12, then 23/4, then 35/6 and so on, depending on the person's age at the time of a reading, or in a class when we are doing some qualitative research within the group.

A great gift of astrology, perhaps its greatest gift, is this: it shows us that we are part of something vast and meaningful, not mere random accidents in space/time. That knowledge offers a great challenge: to take our tiny 'chip' of that vast energy field as revealed though the symbols in our horoscopes, with its pains as well as its gifts, and strive to leave the world a slightly better place on our exit than it was when we came in. Grand achievements are not mandatory. Just being better, more fulfilled human beings as a result of having an extra, symbolic, source of potential insight is quite enough.

The degree to which a person's life responds to the promptings of Jupiter, Saturn, Uranus, Neptune and Pluto transits and cycles – and the 18.6-year cycle of the Moon's nodes – depends very much upon how strongly that person is 'plugged in' to that particular planet or point, its transits and its cycles. It is also very important in contemplating the planetary cycles, to realise that each cycle carries the same basic developmental template within it: seeding, germinating, sprouting, flowering, ripening, harvesting, dying back in preparation for the new.

So – as any cycle comes to an end, typical feelings are: restlessness and ennui; lower energy available to put into the key areas of life/activities governed by that cycle; dissatisfaction with what once seemed to work quite well, but now does not. In the case of the larger cycles' endings, such as those of Saturn-Pluto, Uranus-Pluto, Uranus-Neptune, life can sometimes plunge us into circumstances of extreme difficulty or pain, through upheavals and hurts not directly related to our actions or choices. Some might prefer to call this the action of Fate.

However, it is also most important to note, as that wise poet T.S. Eliot observed, 'in my end is my beginning'.

Germinating, hidden below the churned-up earth of cycles' endings, are also the delicate seeds of new beginnings. I have always found it helpful for myself, students and clients to relate this to our solar system's tiny monthly cycle of the sun and moon, clearly observable in the heavens above us. The delicate sliver of the Waning Crescent Moon, which we can sometimes see if the skies are clear, indicates that an old cycle is in its dying days. Then nothing is visible for another couple of days. It's important to remember that the New Moon, and a new cycle beginning, takes place in the dark.

Think of the moment of conception of a new human or a new animal. Without the very sophisticated technology of IVF, a very recent phenomenon in terms of our technological progress, this cannot be observed – although it may well be sensed, especially by a child's mother. Similarly, some of us may sense, at that liminal point, that something has changed, something new may be emerging. And then – that beautiful slender silver crescent of the waxing New Moon appears in the sky, two or three days after its total absence. We are on a new journey.

We can apply that basic template both to individual planetary cycles, such as the famous 29/30-year Saturn one and to the cycles of planets in combination, for example, the 172-year Uranus-Neptune cycle or the vast 500-year Neptune-Pluto cycle. The latter began in the 1890s, and we are still only moving off from the first sextile 130 years later … an average human life will only encompass two full Saturn-Pluto cycles, and perhaps part of a third one.

Saturn-Pluto in particular

What can we do as individuals to navigate this significant Saturn-Pluto ending/new beginning with some degree of useful awareness? What I write here can only be of general guidance. How things work out for you in particular depends on your personal horoscope and its patterns. However, the more strongly this combination occurs in your natal chart, then by transit/progression as your life unfolds, the more potent the challenge is going to be. It's also helpful to note the houses/angles/nodes that are ruled by Saturn and Pluto.

For instance, I have Saturn-Pluto in the 12th house conjunct Mercury, Venus, Moon and Sun, all in Leo; Saturn rules the 5th house, Pluto and the IC/South Node conjunction. All my major life challenges have circled round children (others', not mine), home and roots – and how to extricate and direct my powerful creative energies and vocational drives from the mire of family fate and from the consequences of unwise choices, often not made by me.

The first piece of advice – and I do realise that it may well not be to your liking since it certainly wasn't to mine – is to have patience. This is a pretty long cycle of ending and beginning, so things are likely to have been difficult for you one way or another, along the lines of what I outlined earlier, for around a couple of years, perhaps more. Similarly, it is likely to take around that amount of time for the energies of the new cycle to take form and focus so that you can see the way ahead more clearly.

There is no point in pretending that the combination of Saturn and Pluto is not tough. I used to find with my classes that the aspects from which new students recoiled the most, and the transits they most feared the more they learned, were those of Saturn and Pluto, both separately and in combination through their cycle. Pluto manifests the raw creative and destructive power of the life force; Saturn tries to shape, control and focus that power. This dynamic in our collective lives has always produced life or death struggle of one kind or another. Individuals plugged in have a 'chip', as it were, of that powerful energy pattern to wrestle with, and hopefully learn to channel wisely and constructively throughout their lives.

As I said at the outset of this essay, 'In essence, Saturn-Pluto lets us off with nothing, either personally or collectively. We are forced into increasingly tight corners whilst the pressure is ramped up on us to face and deal with the present consequences of past decisions, some of which might not be of our direct making.'

The next piece of advice is this: try to get some perspective on what the challenges are now, and how you might best deal with them as the new cycle starts to unfold. To do this, go back to the beginning of this cycle, note the dates and check out what was going on in your life then. Then note the dates of the waxing square, then the opposition, then the waning square. There are of course the other aspects as the cycle waxes and wanes. But let's stick with the biggies for now.

Those of you young folk who have not yet lived through a whole cycle, take especial note of the nearest of the biggies to your birth date. Some of you older readers will be able to go further back – it is worth making the effort to do so: both for the life insights it may well give you, but also regarding your family history in many cases, since Pluto usually seems to have connections to issues of family fate and its consequences which have woven into the fabric of the present time. Some of that material, and its influences on your life, can be usefully recognised, mined and processed during Saturn-Pluto periods.

Let's do it now

The first Saturn-Pluto conjunction of the last century occurred in October 1914 at 2° Cancer, and May 1915 at 1° Cancer. The second followed on 11 August 1947 at 13° Leo. You can look up the first squares, opposition points and waning squares of both those cycles in a 20th century ephemeris – or Google them!

The last Saturn-Pluto exact conjunction occurred – once – in November 1982 at 27° Libra, applying for a year before, separating for a year afterwards. The waxing square was exact in March 1993 at 25° Aquarius/Scorpio, then again at 24° Aquarius/Scorpio in October 1993, and finally at 27° Aquarius/Scorpio in January 1994. The opposition was first exact in August 2001 at 13° Gemini/Sagittarius, then in November 2001 at 14° Gemini/Sagittarius, lastly in May 2002 at 16° Gemini/Sagittarius. The waning square was exact in November 2009 at 2° Libra/Capricorn, then in January 2010 at 4° Libra/Capricorn, then finally in August 2010 at 3° Libra/Capricorn.

The end of the 1982/2020 cycle occurs – with the new Saturn-Pluto cycle starting slowly to form – on 12 January 2020 at 23° Capricorn

– a much anticipated, feared and discussed planetary event as a new decade begins (or an old one ends, depending on your stance on the matter). If you care to do so, you can go forward in the 21st century ephemeris to plot the waxing square, opposition, waning square and ending dates of this new cycle.

A PERSONAL EXAMPLE

As the Saturn-Pluto cycle begun in 1947 drew to a close in 1980/82, little did I know that a whole phase of my personal and vocational life was also ending, and a new one was set to begin. I knew nothing then of astrological cycles and their significance. I met my husband in 1980, marrying him a few months before November 1982 and the start of the Libran Saturn-Pluto cycle. I also began studying astrology in 1980, commencing serious work for the Certificate of the Faculty of Astrological Studies in November 1982.

Each of the four key stages of that unfolding cycle from 1982 up to the present time have brought very challenging, painful and difficult issues of a family of origin nature for me to cope with, as well as with my husband's family since I took on a stepparent role with our marriage. These times also represented key stages in the development and unfolding of my parallel careers as a social worker, trainer and private practising therapist, along with developing an astrology consulting, writing and teaching practice.

However, as the cycle has moved towards its slow conclusion from the waning square in 2010, I have been aware of an increasing feeling of deep satisfaction with how an initially tough life pattern has turned out, beginning with my birth seven weeks prematurely and an expectation that I would not survive. I am experiencing the long-term rewards from hanging on in there, at times having to struggle very hard to deal with and free myself from old family complexes as much as possible which were getting in the way of my professional and relationship lives.

Our marriage has survived and deepened, my Aquarian husband having provided unwavering support both personally and professionally.

Through some tough and at times tragic family challenges, I have slowly and gradually learned something which I believe only Saturn-Pluto could have pushed me to learn, but which growing older with less life force to waste has helped along: to focus and channel my leonine creative energies as much as possible into constructive vocational pursuits, thereby honouring my path. And most importantly, not to waste that life force on those who are unwilling or unable to benefit from my efforts. Learning the very hard way that you can't make anyone do anything for what you see as their own good if they don't wish to – or can't – is an excellent lesson for a Saturn-Pluto control freak!

I still love astrology as much as ever. The difference, though, as this cycle closes and a new one arises, is this: my desire to work directly with clients has waned, as has my desire to have any public role other than through my writing and a limited amount of teaching and mentoring. However, my awareness of the need to claim and honour the role of elder, to offer as much support as I can to the next able generation of astrologers arising, especially in my local area, is growing.

Beyond being aware of the gifts and limitations that come with ageing, and of the importance of living as much as possible in a soulful way in the present moment, sharing whatever time we may have left with my husband, close family members and friends, I have little idea of what new creative challenges/opportunities the new Saturn-Pluto cycle may bring. I'm not too worried about that, feeling freer in spirit now than I have ever felt – despite the dismal state of the world at present as we grapple with unprecedented turbulence and a planet under threat.

In conclusion

To paraphrase Jung's point, mentioned earlier: individuals working in a conscious way can have more power to shift the balance of a difficult planetary pattern in a positive direction than collectives do. I have long believed that if we want to change the world, we need to start with ourselves and work outwards.

We are currently experiencing the end of an important, powerful, challenging and formative planetary cycle, and wondering what this next Saturn-Pluto phase will bring. It is my hope, therefore, that my musings in this essay may offer some pointers regarding how to approach and understand the phase that is passing – and to gain some perspective which will help in facing the upcoming Saturn-Pluto cycle with greater understanding and insight.

Astrodienst
March 2020

Cycles: a Saturn-Pluto trio: 3
wall – what wall?

As 2019 gets into its stride, wall stories are high profile. On New Year's Day 2019, one million Indian women did a remarkable thing – they created a wall of protest by forming a 620 km human chain across the length of the southern state of Kerala. They were asserting their right to enter the Sabarimala Temple, following a ruling by the Indian Supreme Court in September 2018. This forced the Temple's doors open to women of all ages in a sensational blow to religious tradition.

The biggest wall story, of course, is taking place in the USA as President Trump struggles to extract $5.7 billion from Congress to build a wall along the U.S./Mexico border. As I revise this column on 2 February 2019, the longest US Government shutdown in history caused by refusal to give into this demand is over. Trump has caved in, at least for now.

What planetary combo suggests walls, especially big walls, more than any other? Yes, that's right. Saturn-Pluto combinations.

In 2002/3, we had a Saturn-Pluto opposition. Its combination with the Moon's nodal axis at 17 degrees Gemini/Sagittarius in June 2002 saw the beginning of another now notorious wall built by Israel's government, 'a separation barrier' comprising fences and walls running alongside and into the West Bank and Jerusalem. Israelis call this the security barrier and Palestinians the separation or apartheid wall. It was a controversial project and the International Court of Justice ruled in 2004 that it violated international law as it infringed on the rights of Palestinians.

The currently applying Saturn-Pluto conjunction in Capricorn, exact at 22.5° on 12 January 2020, meets with the Moon's nodal axis during April and May 2019. We can expect especially crucial developments concerning barriers of various kinds – physical, political, cultural, psychological – around that time. My research study *The Moon's Nodes in Action* shows that both in collective and personal life, the nodes meeting Pluto bring events of an especially testing, life-changing nature.

Until wall observation got me going, I had been resisting writing about Saturn-Pluto for some months. Believe me, resistance is a big key word when it comes to talking about this formidable combination of planetary energies. I should know, having been born with an exact conjunction of those two, also conjunct my ruling planet Mercury. Fortunately for those around me, this lineup is closely sextile Neptune, and squared by a 3rd-house Jupiter which cheers things up quite considerably!

I have never forgotten my beloved mentor, the late great mundane astrologer Charles Harvey – sadly missed still by so many of us – casually winding me up over lunchtime during my student years at the Centre for Psychological Astrology in London in the 1990s. 'Well, Anne, what's it to be today? Mass murderer or deeply searching scientist?' He was referring to my Saturn-Pluto conjunction, and that astrology classic *The Combination of Stellar Influences* (or COSI, for short) by Reinhold Ebertin who did not hold back on potentially snowflake sensibilities when he was writing this famous book in the 1940s. His take on the extremes of negative and positive potential for the Saturn-Pluto combination was precisely as Charles had humorously offered me. Just as well Saturn-Pluto goes with a black sense of humour.

Ebertin and other astrologers agree that this combination is indeed tough. The image of a wall, especially, sums up its essential meaning. Saturn puts up barriers, to keep Pluto – that dangerous, potentially murderous but often imaginary Other – out. People with Saturn-Pluto combinations have to take care not to become over-defensive and paranoid. The famous French mundane astrologer André Barbault pointed out that the build-up toward Saturn-Pluto conjunctions, which happen around every thirty-five years, coincides with a rise of the Right and with Fascism. The rise of Adolf Hitler and Nazism during the 1930s is a case in point.

We are seeing similar patterns of polarisation now in Europe, the UK and the USA where the politics of division and hatred have been increasing steadily in recent years: two noticeable drivers being the UK's voting to leave the European Union in June 2016 … and the divisive election of Donald Trump as USA President in November 2016 with the consequences which have flowed from that.

However, Saturn-Pluto is not all bad. Every planetary combination describes a range of potential expressions from the very negative to the very positive. If you want someone with you in a grim crisis who will do what has to be done without flinching or giving in, then choose someone with a strong Saturn-Pluto signature in their horoscope. If what is required are long hours of persistent application, such as to conduct a complex research project (in my case, No to the mass murder, definitely Yes to in-depth research) then no aspect is more useful than, say, Mercury combined with Saturn-Pluto.

Unflinching self-honesty arising from a deep commitment to be true to oneself and to use one's power to be scrupulously fair to others, no matter what the cost, are the best qualities to be mined from this challenging combination. As the Saturn-Pluto conjunction of 2020 closes in, let's hope some of those qualities can emerge from the collective and personal pressure we will increasingly be feeling as 2019 unfolds.

After all, extreme pressure is what creates diamonds – eventually.

Dell Horoscope
May/June 2019

Ethics & practice:
where we must take care

I consider that the vitally important issues of what our professional ethics are, and how we conduct the practice of astrology in a compassionate and responsible manner, are questions which should be revisited and reappraised by astrologers on a regular basis. Here are some of my thoughts on those essential topics.

I really appreciate the questions and comments offered via my Astrology: Questions and Answers blog for prodding me into action in writing about matters which should be of deep concern to all of us.

An astrologer's job description

Every so often, someone asks me what I think my job as an astrologer is. It's a good question – it makes me 'return to base', as it were, and set out the basics again, both for the questioner – and for my own benefit.

Here goes!

My job as an astrologer is to help other people understand themselves more clearly. I don't know what the balance is between fate and freewill any more than anyone else does. But the birth chart or horoscope suggests strongly that we come into this world, not as tabulae rasae (blank slates) but with certain characters on the stage poised to live out a complex drama as the process of our life unfolds from birth to death.

What astrologers cannot do is describe the whole range of possibilities of expression which arise from each core character on the stage. There appears to be a dynamic relationship between what you have been given through family physical and psychological inheritance (the Old Norse word for fate also means genitals!), location, social status and your own choices in what you do with those givens.

I think that effective astrologers in consultation are poised on the interface between fate and freewill – on the one hand helping clients to confirm who they are, which they probably already know if they are honest with themselves; but on the other hand, helping them to see, and to broaden, the range of possible expression of the energies with which they have been born.

The astrologer's ego should have a minimal influence on the process of reading another person's horoscope. It's impossible to keep ego completely out of it. It's impossible to be completely objective, to avoid making mistakes; but what the person takes away should be as much theirs, and as little the astrologers', as is possible.

To maximise this outcome, I feel it is very important to have my work regularly supervised by an experienced and well-qualified colleague. I am fortunate in this to have the support of a very experienced astrologer who is also a psychodynamic psychotherapist and writer. She has known me, my foibles, my weaknesses and my strengths over a very long period of time.

I look at the relationship between the patterns present in clients' natal horoscopes and how that relates to the here-and-now patterns of the planets in the heavens. I'm also very interested in setting clients' lives in the context of the unfolding stages of the 11/12-year Jupiter cycles and the 29/30-year Saturn cycles, as well as the progressed New Moons which also occur in 30-year periods. My experience is that setting their lives in the context of the bigger pictures, and taking guidance from that, is both comforting, supportive and helpful to people who consult me.

I'm only interested in working with clients who are prepared to take responsibility for themselves in relation to the way in which their inner world is connected to the unfolding of their outer life. Astrology, appropriately used, should enhance the sense of personal responsibility – not take it away and hang it on the planets or even worse, on the astrologer.

In my view it is important for people not to become too dependent on a symbolic context. Astrology and astrologers, like relationships, drugs, sex, alcohol or the National Lottery can become highly addictive. The great symbolic arts, such as astrology, tarot, palmistry and I Ching, should be consulted with deep respect, and with considerable restraint.

In sum – I think it is my job is to send people away feeling more able to operate constructively and honestly in their world than when they came in, by supporting their courage and confidence to lead their own lives – using their own judgement.

anne-whitaker.com, 2019

Answering a challenge: 'is it true that real astrologers do not charge for their services?'

One of the delights of running a regular astrology site – especially one called Astrology: Questions and Answers – is the ensuing dialogue with emailers and commenters. Some of it can be quite testing, such as this recent enquiry: 'Is it true that REAL astrologers do not charge for their services as it is against the code to take profit out of a gift from God to help people? I read this and saw a medium on telly say it. In these circles it is donations given based on good work. Is this true at all?'

My reply:

Dear Ms/Mr X,

This interesting question strongly suggests that you associate the practice of astrology with the practice of mediumship. They are two separate activities. Thus, a comment on how mediums operate cannot usefully be applied to the practice of astrology. Before getting down to discussing the issue of payment of fees for any professional service, be that professional an experienced lawyer, doctor, accountant or astrologer, it might be useful for you to know, very broadly speaking, what astrology is.

Popular star sign or Sun sign astrology is the most well-known kind. Perhaps that is the type you had in mind? This astrology functions largely as popular entertainment in which the point of reference is the twelve Sun or star signs under which individuals are born, depending upon the time of year, whether Scorpio, Aries, Leo, etc. The predictions offered on the basis of this limited focus entertain millions of people across the world on a daily basis.

However, popular astrology can only give a general picture. It's like trying to tell the story of a complex play with reference to only one character on the stage, in this instance, your Sun sign. To get a view of all the characters on the stage of your life, you need a map which an astrologer draws of the heavens for the particular time and place as well as the day of your birth. This map, horoscope or birth chart can then be used via the position of all the planets on that day as a tool to describe, as lucidly as possible, the different characters on the stage of your life and how they interact with one another.

The key thing people gain from an astrology reading, in my view, is confirmation of who they actually are, along with their strengths and weaknesses, their difficulties – and their gifts. It gives them more confidence and courage to be themselves. It is a very powerful and potentially spiritual experience to have a stranger, who knows nothing of you, describe your essential qualities accurately from a map drawn of the heavens for the moment you entered this world. This helps you to see that we are all interconnected and part of the One, whatever name you choose to give that vast, indescribable mystery.

Regarding qualifications and training, I have a university degree and three post-graduate diplomas, the third of which involved three years' travel to and from London in order to meet the stringent requirements required to obtain my Diploma in Psychological Astrology in 1998. This included one year of mandatory personal therapy in order to have the experience of being a client myself.

I am not alone in having made considerable efforts and allocated a great deal of time and money to becoming skilled and competent at my profession. Whilst not wishing to speak for my colleagues, all the astrologers with whom I associate are well-educated people of considerable intelligence and integrity who share the same core values as I do regarding the importance of treating our fellow human beings with sensitivity and compassion. We owe this to those who come looking for help and clarification, often at turning points in their lives. Their experience, and mine, is that an astrology reading can be of considerable assistance.

And now, about money.

In the process of being useful people in the world, astrologers, like anyone else, need to eat, put a roof over their heads and bring up their families. We also need to pay for our office rent, professional indemnity insurance, professional supervision and organisational memberships – as well as the many other expenses involved in running a professional practice.

Dear Ms/Mr X, are you suggesting that we should live in this world and practice our profession without charging realistic fees to cover our living costs like everyone else? I do hope not. In conclusion, thank you very much for asking your question. It has provided me with an opportunity to give readers a window into how responsible, professional astrologers actually operate.

The Astrological Journal
May/June 2016

The ethics of astrological practice: a question needing an answer

I like it when the day throws up a compelling hot topic for my blog first thing – even if I am still half asleep at the time. A particular exchange of questions and answers recently with two commenters on my Astrology: Questions and Answers Facebook Page woke me up very quickly. (Names have been changed.)

ANGELA: Do you do astrology? I would love to have mine done sometime but I don't know who does it? Any ideas?

RYAN: I've stumbled upon dozens of bloggers who give readings, you just have to look.

ME: Ryan, it may well be the case that one can stumble upon lots of bloggers doing readings, but Angela needs to be careful to choose someone who is well experienced and qualified, preferably with their work insured and supervised, with an adequate degree of experience in reading horoscopes, counselling training, and a well-developed sense of awareness of the power and responsibility that is taken on by virtue of reading people's horoscopes.

Donna Cunningham, if you care to visit her excellent Sky Writer blog, has written about the negative and irresponsible things that some people can say when reading their fellow citizens' charts. It would be instructive for anyone contemplating booking a reading to go over to Donna's blog and read about some of this alarming material, which by its existence emphasises the importance of prospective clients choosing carefully if they wish their charts to be read constructively and responsibly.

Here is a short quote from Donna Cunningham's 4 December 2014 post [which supports my response to Angela and to Ryan]:

'For many years, I had a monthly advice column in Dell Horoscope *magazine, a Dear Abby-type column in which readers wrote their problems and I answered based on their astrology charts. Part of the job description for that column seemed to be putting out fires that other astrologers have set, for I got many letters from readers who were devastated by the way their chart reading was handled. These letters pointed to the need for true and responsible professional training in our field and the need, especially, for a certain amount of counselling training. Like it or not, counselling is what an astrologer does each time a client comes for a reading.'*

– From 'Awful Things Astrologers Say to their Clients'

I have been an astrology practitioner, teacher and writer for over thirty years now. However, I remain awestruck by the power that astrology holds, when used responsibly with compassion and sensitivity, to offer creative and constructive guidance to clients as their lives unfold.

It is incredibly affirming to be able to say – either directly or by inference, depending on what that particular client needs at that time – 'Here is your unique little chip of the cosmos into which you were born. Use the energies therein as best you can, given the gifts and limitations we are all handed at the outset – which I will try to convey to you as honestly and constructively as possible. Try to work with those energies well enough to be able to hand your chip back with a little more light shining through it at the end of your days.'

A sense of connection to an unfolding, meaningful energy weave where each of us has a thread to contribute is a wonderful antidote to the feelings of anomie, disconnectedness and woundedness which so many people seem to be feeling at this time of great turbulence and upheaval.

However, the task of placing another person's life in a context for them which makes their life's current challenges easier to bear, helping them to work with often very painful circumstances as constructively as possible (how many people come for astrology readings when life is bowling smoothly along? Not many, in my experience!) is not straightforward, easy or to be embarked upon lightly. It should *not* be embarked upon lightly or casually.

I can still recall, in the early days of my astrology practice, being extremely grateful that I had had a number of years of social work, psychiatric work and counselling practice in which to ground myself. There is nothing quite like having to face the limitations of your capacity to help other people, which is a major dimension of social work, to ground you and keep you humble when taking upon yourself the power that being an astrologer brings.

I was fortunate enough to have been a student of Liz Greene's for most of the 1990s. An entry requirement to study for the Diploma in Psychological Astrology, which I completed in 1998, was that all students be in therapy for a year. It was made clear to us, in Liz Greene's inimitable way, that we should not take upon ourselves the responsibility of being astrological practitioners without having the experience of a long seat in the client's chair ourselves.

So, Ryan, I do hope that my response to your casual comment, with which no doubt you meant no harm, has not left you feeling too winded! And I thank you for making it, thereby giving me the opportunity to put forward my own thoughts regarding the great capacity for doing ill as well as good that astrologers take on when they read their fellow citizens' horoscopes. 'At least do no harm' is the bottom line of the medical profession. It should be ours too.

Angela, if you are reading this, do not be too put off. There are many competent, compassionate, realistic, empathic astrologers out there. Just take your sweet time to make sure you seek out a good one!

anne-whitaker.com

2019

On becoming a responsible astrologer: how do you get there?

That post [previous essay] on the ethics of astrological practice, a topic to which all astrological practitioners should return from time to time in my opinion, generated a great deal of interest over at my Astrology: Questions and Answers' Facebook page. My dialogue there with thoughtful astrologer Sellieve Ezra Neptune (her real name, used here with her permission) made it clear to me that the question of responsible astrological practice needed to be pursued further. She has given me permission to quote from our discussion.

Sellieve: 'I do have a question for you, Anne. If you tell people that they should only get a reading from an astrologer who has lots of experience reading charts, how does someone get that experience if someone inexperienced isn't worthy of giving readings yet? It's that same Catch-22 of, 'Can't get a job without experience, can't get experience without a job'. I am an aspiring professional astrologer with a decade of learning under me, but the number of professional readings I have given is not too many ... .'

Me: This is a very fair question, Sellieve, and it does indeed look as though I've presented a Catch-22. The last thing I want to do is discourage potentially effective astrologers like yourself from ending up as serious professional practitioners. There are a number of ways from which to approach this question, and I do not claim to have all the answers – a brief post can only cover a few key bases. However, here goes! I should state at the outset that I am based in the UK, so am not very familiar with the specifics of what constitutes professional regulation in other countries.

Mainstream vs. Maverick

The advantage of belonging to one of the traditional professions recognised by mainstream society (such as medicine, the law, teaching, accountancy, etc.) is that one has to go through rigorous training and professional licensing in order to be able to practice. This does not rule out bad practice, but it does mean it is kept to a minimum and offers legal redress to people who have been on the receiving end of such practice. However, astrologers – especially in this reductionist age – are very much *not* regarded as being in the mainstream of professional practice, and it is possible for anyone to set themselves up as an astrologer with no training, regulation or background counselling experience whatsoever. In an ideal world, it should not be possible for people to do this. But as we all know the world that we live in is far from ideal. I think the reality is that it is never going to be possible fully to prevent people from abusing their fellow citizens, as described by Donna Cunningham in my earlier post re: 'Awful Things Astrologers Say to their Clients'.

Increasing public awareness

However, it is my hope that the public is more aware these days of the difference between responsible, quality astrologers and dangerous amateurs. In recent years, much progress has been made in training and monitoring astrologers through such reputable bodies as the APAI in the UK, and OPA, ISAR, NCGR and the AFA in the USA, where very high standards are set for what is expected of practising astrologers. Likewise, The Mayo School of Astrology, The London School of Astrology, Mercury Internet School of Psychological Astrology, the Faculty of Astrological Studies and the Centre for Psychological Astrology in the UK. I studied with both the last two bodies and am a member of the Association of Professional Astrologers International to whose ethical codes I subscribe. In order to protect ourselves legally, the APAI advises its members thus in dealing with clients:

- Explain briefly and in general what astrology is and what astrologers do.
- Explain the limitations of the techniques employed, for example: astrology is a symbolic language and offers a balance of probabilities rather than specific certainties.

- Describe the service(s) to be provided, for example: character analysis, compatibility assessment – and the scale of fees.
- Emphasise that astrology is not scientifically proven and that no reading can be 100% accurate.
- Explain, nevertheless, that APAI astrologers will work to the best of their knowledge and abilities in the preparation and delivery of the services to be provided.

How we begin

Most of us who end up as astrologers have a similar route. First, we encounter astrology in a range of different ways depending on who we are and what our context is, this encounter leading us to being fascinated and compelled to take our interest further. In my case, I encountered a couple in a launderette in Bath, England, in the 1970s who took me home with them, did my chart and told me I was likely to end up studying astrology or something very like it in seven years' time. At that time, I was both engaged in another professional life, and a dismisser of astrology from the dismissers' standard base of knowing nothing at all about it. However, that couple were right. Then we practice, on friends, family, anyone who would like their chart read – hopefully sticking to the basics of Sun, Moon, Saturn, Ascendant and Midheaven, and even more hopefully, having some awareness of when one is getting out of one's depth – not going too far into wounding other people through our own lack of expertise and knowledge.

From amateur to professional

It should take quite a while of doing this before one's thoughts turn to whether becoming a professional astrologer is a realistic possibility. In a follow-up comment to her original question, Sellieve partially answers it herself, by pointing out the following:

> *'Not everyone comes to an astrologer looking for serious advice, sometimes they want a theatrical presentation of their personality, or they find astrology interesting but don't want to study it themselves ... In this such case I think it is better to refer these kinds of clients to less experienced professional astrologers, people like me and other millennials. If someone wants to see an astrologer for counselling, if they want light brought onto a difficult situation, then it is best to refer them to a psychological astrologer, or someone with more impressive credentials than me ... '*

In the end, how much one gradually realises, through this process of initial dabbling, the amount of power and responsibility one is taking on by reading people's charts is dependent upon the degree of self-awareness, experience and maturity one has acquired by this point. Personal integrity, which no-one can teach, is also a major factor in determining the path people take when they realise they wish to practise as professional astrologers.

ETHICAL FRAMEWORKS AND GUIDELINES

I think that the best possible start for a would-be astrologer is to place themselves at the outset within a clear framework of ethics and guidelines which all the reputable training and monitoring bodies provide and follow those guidelines to the best of their ability. An excellent recent book to acquire in helping this process along, is OPA's (the Organization for Professional Astrology) *The Professional Astrologer* which is a comprehensive guide to all aspects of setting up an astrology practice. Do acquire this book, Sellieve, as soon as possible! Master astrologer Donna Cunningham's *Counseling Principles for Astrologers* is also an excellent guide for astrologers at this very important stage of their careers. One of the best books I know which covers the practical, ethical, moral, psychological and spiritual dimensions of being an astrologer is

The Astrologer, the Counsellor and the Priest by Liz Greene and Juliet Sharman-Burke, based on a seminar given at the Centre for Psychological Astrology in 1996, which I had the good fortune to attend, and which was comprehensive, practical, and thought provoking.

Setting up a practice – some practicalities
Sellieve also added some more comments regarding how to go about setting up an astrology practice to which I responded as follows.

I think that you probably need to look around a few astrologers' consultation/tuition Web pages – you are welcome to look at mine for some ideas – and set up a professional Web page stating your approach, what you do and don't do, qualifications, background relevant experience and fees. And join a reputable professional organisation (as listed above) if you haven't already. And set up a professional email only to be used for your practice. You will also need to think about how you wish to be contacted initially, where you are going to practise with attendant privacy, recording policy, and so forth.

If you set a context for yourself so that you know clearly what you are doing, whom you wish to draw to you by way of clientele, and what your professional boundaries are, then get out there doing a few talks and maybe offering a small beginners' class for starters, all that will help.

I set boundaries by saying to people who want me to comment on their charts, that I only do that within the boundaries of a professional consultation. It's a sacred art, after all, so it should be practised with appropriate respect for both yourself, your client and astrology. If people want a reading, they can go to your page, then get back to you. That saves a lot of time and energy. And of course, if people are enthusiastic and open-minded without trying to get bits of a reading from you informally, then talk astrology with as many people as wish to hear about the real deal as opposed to playing 'Guess my sign!'. Something I never do, incidentally.

Disclaimer – or not?

One of Sellieve's later comments concerned the question of adding a disclaimer to one's publicity, advising that astrology is 'for entertainment purposes only', something which she found disquieting in the same way that I or anyone else would who considers that what they do as astrologers goes into a considerable degree of depth and cannot be described as entertainment. Here, I can only speak for myself: I would never add such a disclaimer to my publicity, since I consider a high standard of practice to be my greatest protection against any likelihood of legal action.

She adds: 'Astrologers could potentially find themselves in a predicament when a client takes an astrological prediction very seriously and it doesn't come true, or if the astrologer gives advice about what to do in a relationship: the client can hold the astrologer responsible for anything that goes wrong … .'

Here we come slap up against the reason why, in my view, anyone wishing to take themselves seriously as an astrologer, or be taken seriously by members of the public as a responsible person, needs to get themselves at the very least some counselling skills training (if full counselling training is not at first a realistic option for whatever reason, often financial) as well as having the experience of being in the client's seat themselves. Many counselling/therapy training courses will offer cut-price counselling sessions with trainees in supervision. In this way, counselling or therapy of a satisfactory standard can often be obtained without too great a financial outlay.

An important part of an astrologer's job is to combine the natal horoscope with transits, progressions and other directions in the heavens at the time of the consultation to help clients clarify situations in which they find themselves, so that they can then make their *own* decisions regarding what to do. Making definite or definitive predictions and advising people what to do diminishes clients' freewill and confidence in themselves, although in the short run it might afford them some temporary relief to hand over those choices to the astrologer – upon whom they can later dump the blame and perhaps threaten legal action when things do not turn out according to either predictions or advice given.

In conclusion

This is but a brief sketch. I hope readers will flesh it out for themselves – starting with the suggestions made for organisations to join and reading to do, enabling them to become clearer about what taking the first steps to becoming responsible professional astrologers involves. There is far more support available now for the Millennial generation of emerging astrologers like Sellieve than there was when we Baby-Boomers started out. That's great, and how it should be. One of my great pleasures at this stage in my life is to pass on some of what I know and have learned – usually the hard way! – to the generation of talented young folk now arising. And – thanks so much to Sellieve Ezra Neptune for prodding me into action on this most important topic.

anne-whitaker.com
2019

Fate

'The power of fate is a wonder, dark, terrible wonder – neither wealth nor armies towered walls nor ships' black hulls lashed by the salt can save us from that force.'

– The choral songs of Antigone, from Sophocles' *Antigone*.

'Tell me a story … ' Why do we humans never tire of stories? I have been reflecting on this recently, and on stories where fate seems to weave a powerful cross thread into the pattern of a person's life, changing that life's direction forever. The first piece here shows how personal and family fate can intersect most powerfully – offering one the choice of repeating the past or stepping beyond it. The second is, quite simply, one of the most striking stories of fate's apparent intervention I have ever heard.

I have also been reflecting yet again on that age-old fate/freewill question, probably as a consequence of recently spending a great deal of time reading and reviewing a fascinating book The Astrological World of Jung's Liber Novus *by Dr Liz Greene, well-known and respected Jungian psychologist, astrologer, teacher and writer on the topic of Jung's deeply personal 'soul journey' during the years 1913-1932. In evidence throughout Greene's account of that journey is Jung's fascination with* heimarmene *or fate. My review of this book, published on Astrodienst in February 2019, is included here.*

The most striking encounter I have had with fate's intervening and changing my life is one by now familiar to my family, friends, students and some of my readers – not everyone can say they first encountered in-depth astrology as a consequence of a chance encounter in a launderette. In Bath. So, of course, it has also to be included – in the last piece.

And finally – no section on fate would be complete without some musings on prediction. Here are my thoughts on that fraught and weighty topic, concluding with a more detailed account and analysis of what happened in that famous launderette in the summer of 1974.

A tale of Saturn, Capricorn, nodes and family history

My Aquarian husband loves mountains. His ruling planet Mercury, and Mars, reside resolutely in Capricorn. He has climbed all 284 mountains in Scotland over 3000 feet – named Munros, after the first person to map them, Sir Hugh Munro, born with Saturn, Capricorn's ruler, square his Aries North Node. Reader, here is a clue regarding this column: it's about the long reach of family fate, centred on the signs of Aries and Capricorn.

Picture this scene. My maternal grandfather Calum, with Capricorn Sun square the 10th-house North Node in Aries, was a true adventurer. In his young days he was employed as a sheep herder in the Cascade Mountains in Canada. Dropping in on Patagonia, he fetched up eventually as a cattle rancher in Argentina, South America. Returning briefly home to marry the comely, dark-haired Mary Ann, he left her to bring up their first child in her parents' home in a remote village on the Isle of Lewis, Scotland.

At last, he returned, bursting with excitement. 'Mary Ann, Mary Ann, we have a wonderful opportunity to make our fortune!'

'And what would that be, Calum?' she enquired.

'I have done so well with the cattle ranching that my employer has offered me a senior position on his ranch, with my own land and a herd of cattle thrown in. You and our son will love Argentina! What do you say?'

There was a long pause before my grandmother Mary Ann finally spoke. 'I will come with you, Calum,' she said slowly and deliberately, 'as long as we bring my coffin along too.'

That was the end of our South American connection.

My mother, their last child, was born with the Sun in Aries exactly square her Capricorn Moon. For most of us, drawing up family charts is a compelling early step in the astrological adventure. When I saw my mother's chart my heart turned over the vivid family story that

I have just related leaping out of the symbolism. Calum saying 'Yes!' and Mary Ann saying a mournful 'No': both clearly encoded in that Sun/Moon square.

My father had an Aries Sun, too, trine Saturn: he combined a responsible professional life as a senior local government officer with being the most notorious poacher our island community had seen for many years. My mother's attitude to his exploits was summed up in her Capricorn Moon square both their Aries Suns.

Eventually, I married. With my family history and a fiery Sun-Moon conjunction linked with Saturn, I was in no hurry. When husband Ian's progressed Sun entered Aries, he took up serious mountaineering, and I took up serious worrying about him. However, I don't have a 10th-house Mars-Uranus conjunction for nothing. He went up North to do mountains, I went down South to study astrology with Liz Greene. This kept everything in balance for years; not everyone's solution, but it worked for us.

Fast forward to 11 April 2018. Most of us that week were feeling pressured one way or another, as Mars separated from Saturn, advancing towards Pluto in Capricorn. Saturn retrograding, Chiron entering Aries and the Aries New Moon would all occur the following week. Not very relaxing.

We were due to set off to Switzerland on 22 April, the day Pluto would turn retrograde in Capricorn. Mars would be transiting Pluto for the whole trip. Our goal? My husband loves trains and mountains: venturing to the highest railway station in Europe near the top of the Jungfrau mountain had been his aim for many years.

The previous autumn, he'd been knocked down by a cyclist in our local park and struck his head. Dealing with the consequences of this had taken up the whole winter and spring. He was probably well enough now to withstand all the rail travel involved from Scotland via London and Strasbourg until we eventually got to Switzerland. But I was seriously worried. Then, on Wednesday, 11 April, he injured his back, always a weak point.

Sitting at our kitchen table in tears, I now wanted to cancel the trip – but knew how devastated he would be. Then something dawned. This day was my late mother's birthday. Her Sun was at 21 degrees Aries, her Moon at 21 degrees Capricorn. Pluto, sitting by transit exactly on her Moon, was being triggered by the Sun at 21 degrees Aries.

I was being faced, in essence, by my grandparents' life-changing dilemma. Ian desperately wanted to go on a longed-for adventure. Being fearful, I wanted to stop him. The power of this realisation was astonishing. Would I repeat family history whose consequences had profoundly shaped my grandparents' and then my parents' marriages? Or would I let go of intense fear – trusting to fate that Ian would fulfil his dream and we would be OK?

I stopped crying and offered the situation up to the Divine. Jupiter, who rises at 18° Virgo in our composite chart, was linking both our natal charts to currently transiting Jupiter at 21.5° Scorpio sextile Pluto at 21° Capricorn. Amidst all the really challenging energies of this time, my core feeling, beneath the fear, was that Ian would be fine. He was. We had a fantastic trip.

Being able to decode and confront a significant piece of my family inheritance via the medium of astrological symbolism was deeply moving and awe-inspiring. For those of us who have been given both challenging horoscopes and a willingness to examine ourselves and our motives with as much honesty as we dare to muster, I have long felt that a significant task in this life is to try to redeem some of the pain and limitation which our ancestors have unwittingly handed on to us, along with their gifts, talents and strengths.

By saying 'Yes' to my husband, despite the fear, I like to think that, in a small way, a painful part of that family past was honoured – and partly redeemed.

Dell Horoscope
November/December 2018

Encountering fate – in the middle of nowhere

The most recent encounter I had with a striking tale of fate's intervention came, of all places, when I was flat on my face on an osteopath's couch, having a back problem treated. Being a typical writer, rather than chatting about the weather or what I was doing for the weekend, I indulged my curiosity about other folks' endlessly fascinating lives by finding out something about the well-respected osteopath who was treating me, Mr. James Sneddon. [12]

His clinic, along with the team of therapists who work with him, is one of the longest established and most highly regarded in the city of Glasgow, Scotland, UK. I found out that Mr. Sneddon had taken over the clinic from his father, James Russell Sneddon who had founded it over 80 years ago.

The poor unsuspecting man then made the mistake of asking me what I did. Taking a deep breath (probably not a bad thing to do under the face-down circumstances!) I summarised my varied, rather wayward career path as briefly as I could. 'My goodness,' he commented. 'That's so interesting – especially your story about that fated encounter. As a matter of fact, my own father had an encounter like that which certainly changed *his* life.'

Mr. Sneddon Snr. left school not long after the First World War without much formal education and was sent to sea by his parents. He had bronchial problems; his parents thought sea air might help his condition. Whilst in China, it was recommended that he visit a Chinese doctor in Shanghai who pierced various parts of his body with sharpened bamboo sticks (Mr. S Snr. had never heard of acupuncture at this point), took his various pulses and said he should not 'drink the juice of the cow.'

---

[12] Mr. James Sneddon gave me permission to use his real name, the clinic's real name and his father's birth date and place in this article.

Giving up milk and dairy products got rid of his bronchial problems. When he returned to Scotland on leave, a Western alternative practitioner gave him the same health advice. Amazed that he should have had the same verdict from both the exotic East and the familiar West, his interest in nutrition and the effects of food on the body was piqued and he began to investigate alternative medicine, which was more-or-less beyond the pale in Scotland in the 1920s.

Meanwhile, his mid-twenties found him in Alaska. One day, whilst they were on shore leave, the ship's captain invited him to come fishing. At that point a humble ship's engineer, James R Sneddon happily accepted. Both men set off on a rough track with their fishing rods, into 'the middle of nowhere', where the captain knew of a promising fishing loch.

Mr. Sneddon Snr. had some tobacco with him. When he saw an old Native American woman sitting by the track, smoking her pipe, he reached out to give her some. She grasped his hand, turned it palm up, examined it for a moment and said, 'You will leave the sea and take up a healing art that won't use knives.'

In due course, he did exactly that.

In the absence of a birth time, I have used a symbolic Noon/MC chart for James R Sneddon's horoscope [to be found at the end of this short essay], since we are considering his vocation and direction through life. This striking horoscope could have a post all to itself! However, I'll leave you to study it, dear readers, and confine myself to one or two key observations which are valid regardless of his time of birth.

Note the Sun-Jupiter conjunction in Taurus on the Noon Midheaven, opposite Mars in Scorpio conjunct the IC. This reveals an adventurous traveller, a restless seeker after higher knowledge, prepared to plumb the depths as he pursues his quest. The Taurus/Scorpio combination in the signs of physicality and in-depth transformation also speaks to us both of osteopathy and acupuncture as branches of expression from that core pairing.

James R Sneddon chart

13 May 1905, Sat
12:00 UT +0:00 Glasgow,
United Kingdom 55°N53'
004°W15' Geocentric
Tropical
Placidus
True Node

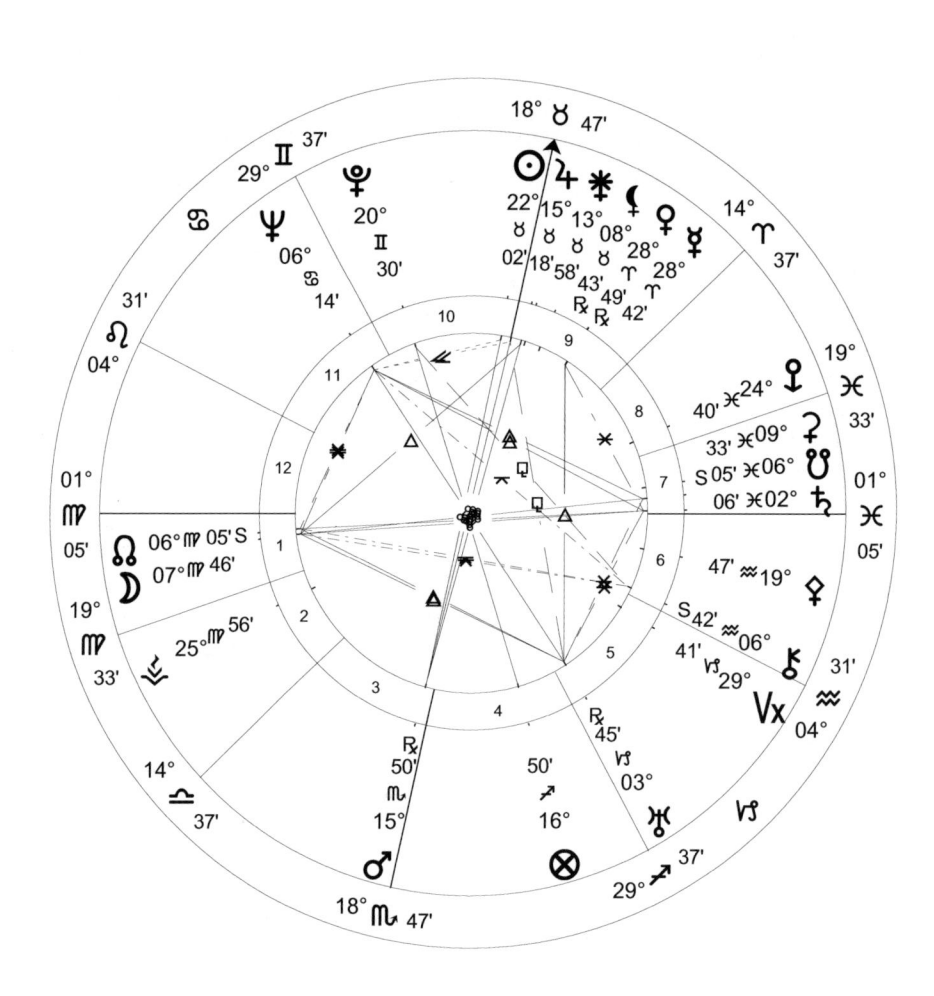

By a delightful piece of synchronicity, the Noon Ascendant of Mr. Sneddon Snr's chart is at 1° Virgo: the exact place where the 19 February 2019 Full Moon is due to fall as I share this remarkable story. Also, the Virgo Moon conjunct the North Node, opposite Saturn in Pisces on the South Node, is a very clear signature for working at healing through the body – and for preparedness for hard work and commitment to his future vocation.

In his mid-twenties James R Sneddon would have begun his third Jupiter cycle: Jupiter returns by transit to its own place in a birth horoscope every 11/12 years, at its best opening us up to new possibilities, bringing experiences our way which broaden our horizons. That certainly happened in a startling way to Mr. Sneddon Snr in the middle of nowhere in Alaska.

That encounter with the Chinese doctor when he was aged around 19/20 just after the North Node – the horoscope's North Star, compelling one towards one's destiny – returned to its natal position, 'set the scene' as it were, for his compelling encounter with the Native American fortune-teller. He returned home to Scotland, began studying in earnest and on his Saturn return (to the healer's sign of Pisces) in 1935, aged 30, opened the Buckingham Clinic which has been successfully treating generations of patients ever since.

As an interesting postscript which rounds off the tale nicely: James R Sneddon introduced acupuncture to his clinic in the mid-1960s – during his second Saturn return to the healer's sign of Pisces. By then, of course, he well understood what those sharpened bamboo sticks in Shanghai, so long ago, had been all about!

I loved hearing this story which took the compelling and intriguing ancient idea that Fate intervenes when we need a nudge in the direction in which we are meant to be going and placed it central stage in the life story of my osteopath's father.

I've never forgotten Dr Liz Greene, in one of her seminars at the Centre for Psychological Astrology during the 1990s, making a remark to the effect that it is truly astounding the lengths to which the Fates seem to be prepared to go to arrange life-changing encounters for people, sometimes right across continents.

Having mentioned Jung at the start of this tale, it seems appropriate to give him the last word here: 'Freewill is the ability to do gladly that which I must do.'

anne-whitaker.com

2019

Review of The Astrological World of Jung's Liber Novus – Daimons, Gods and the Planetary Journey *by Liz Greene*

The Astrological World of Jung's Liber Novus is a meticulous piece of scholarship in which Dr Liz Greene, a well-known and respected Jungian psychologist, astrologer, teacher and writer, provides an in-depth commentary on Carl Gustav Jung's *The Red Book*: *Liber Novus*, tracking especially the part which an extensive knowledge and use of astrology played in his deeply personal 'soul journey' during the years 1913-1932. He recorded this in a series of private diaries, *The Black Books*, which began at the time of his public break with Freud in 1913. *Liber Novus*, eventually published posthumously in 2009, was known as *The Red Book* because of its red leather binding.

> 'The years when I was pursuing my inner images were the most important in my life – in them everything essential was decided. It all began then; the later details are only supplements and clarifications of the material that burst forth from the unconscious, and at first swamped me. It was the prima materia for a lifetime's work ... .' – Carl Gustav Jung (pp. 1 & 2)

Liz Greene's grasp of her material is profound. Equally impressive is the clarity with which she has presented it, providing the reader with a golden thread with which to wander reasonably safely through the complex, often bewildering maze of Jung's deeply private inner experiences and encounters, a period which Greene describes as:

> 'Jung's journey from an inner state of alienation and depression to the restoration of his soul, through the long and painful process of integrating a seemingly irreconcilable conflict within his own nature ... also a prophetic narrative of the collective

> *human psyche ... on the eve of the passage from one great astrological Aion, that of Pisces, into the next, that of Aquarius ... .' (p. 2)*

As Greene makes clear, this journey was never seen by Jung purely as a personal affair. He also saw it as a metaphor for humanity's voyage toward a final goal of reconciliation of the dark and light forces of the universe, a chip of which challenge all we humans carry within us both at an individual and collective level – whether we recognise it or not:

> *'... he hoped that his inner work, undertaken in part from the desperation of attempting to resolve an intolerable inner conflict, might also result in an important contribution to the incipient chaos he feared was descending on the world around him. Jung insisted that it was on the shoulders of the individual that the fate of the collective ultimately rests ... .' (p. 185)*

THE EFFECT OF EVOCATION – OPENING UP THE BIG PICTURE

There already are highly academic, scholarly reviews of this immaculately researched volume. No doubt there will be more. However, reading this latest book of Liz Greene's – or rather, *engaging* with it – has for this reader been a powerful and altogether unexpected participatory experience as well as an intellectual challenge. Taking a purely rational, detached approach is partly to miss the point in my view. After all, *Liber Novus* is as much about evocation and invocation as it is about rational analysis.

I've therefore decided also to bring some personal elements to *The Astrological World of Jung's Liber Novus* in terms of what Jung's journey presented through the filter of Liz Greene's work has evoked for me.

OF LIONS AND MEN

Greene's writing calls forth a profound sense of the vast context within which Jung was locating his personal journey; I thus found myself drawn to reading, in tandem with *The Astrological World of Jung's Liber Novus,* the lavishly illustrated, wonderful *Living with the Gods* by Neil MacGregor, former director of the British Museum. Here he explores, across aeons of time and pluralities of cultures and their gods, how humans have attempted to create meaningful relationships with the great forces of the cosmos. I was reading about Jung's account of his transformation into the crucified lion-headed human figure who reconciles the opposites – an image from the Mithraic Mysteries – when I began MacGregor's book.

The first image I encountered was that of the famous Lion Man, a lion-headed human figure found in Stadel Cave, Baden-Württemberg, Germany – 40,000 years old, and the oldest known evidence of religious belief in the world. The synchronicity of this struck me quite forcefully – reinforcing my sense of the ancient context within which Jung's personal struggle was located. It also called forth astrological Jung, his Sun placed in the sign of Leo the Lion – a predictor for Jung's solar voyage toward individuation which was to follow as Liz Greene's account of *Liber Novus* opened out.

The Lion Man, an object with no known practical use, is estimated to have taken around 400 hours of meticulous craftsmanship by unknown Ice Age people for whom life would have been a constant struggle against all sorts of hazards from extreme weather to savage predators.

Its power lies in its reminding us that it has been of profound importance for humans for many millennia to grapple with and attempt to come into some kind of understanding of what the underlying forces might be giving rise to our cosmos – and alignment with what is perceived to be the Divine.

Inspiring figures

It could be said with some justification that Carl Jung's long and painful grapple during his version of that alignment, his soul-journey toward individuation, is one of the great inner voyages of the 20th century; he certainly had some illustrious forerunners to inspire him and illuminate his particular 'Dark Night of the Soul' as St John of the Cross so memorably put it. Dante was surely one of them, as Liz Greene makes clear:

> *'One of the most obvious literary parallels for the soul-journey of Liber Novus – and for many other artistic works that followed its completion in 1320 – is Dante's Divina Commedia ... .' (pp. 178/9)*

Dante's guide on his journey, Virgil the Roman poet, evoked for Jung his own psychopomp and soul guide, Philemon.

Jung also drew inspiration from subsequent mediaeval or Renaissance texts describing the archetypal journey of the soul, most notably the late 15th century work *Hypnerotomachia Poliphili,* attributed to Francesco Colonna. He commented that Colonna, whose work Linda Fierz-David viewed as having been given its core structure by Dante's *Divina Commedia,* was a 'perfect example of the course and the symbolism of the individuation process' (p. 178).

However, Greene's view is that Jung was more influenced by Colonna than Dante as his material in *Liber Novus* developed, the reason being that Dante's adopting of a Christian religious agenda, within an Aristotelian view of the cosmos, was rather too narrow to accommodate the older, pagan idea of planetary daimons, nor for 'an androgenous Orphic-Mithraic primal divinity, especially one with a lion's head' (p. 178).

WRITING ABOUT WHAT HURTS

I recall many years ago reading – I no longer recall where – a dictum of Jung's to the effect that if the unconscious doesn't come knocking on your door, don't you go looking for it. As I read Greene's account of that which hurt Jung sufficiently to compel and propel him toward his at times exhausting and terrifying encounter with the archetypal forces of the unconscious, it became very evident that the roots of that driving hurt could clearly be seen in symbolic form in Jung's horoscope.

Jung's fundamental conflict, in essence, was between the rational, detached scientist symbolised in his horoscope by the planet Saturn, the ruler of his horoscope, rising powerfully placed in Aquarius in the 1st house; and on the opposite side, setting in the 7th house in Leo, his Sun – square Neptune conjunct Chiron: vivid significators for his mystical leanings and the woundedness implicit therein. Added to this potent set of conflicts is the Moon conjunct Pluto, Lord of the Underworld, signifying his powerful attraction to matters occult, uncanny, paranormal.

Those opposites demanding reconciliation began to torment him from a very early age, as is clear from his later life memoir with Aniela Jaffe, *Memories, Dreams, Reflections*. It is also clear from this fascinating memoir that Philemon, his psychopomp and soul guide, and a major character in *Liber Novus*, began to make an appearance in his inner life from early on.

SCIENTISTS AND MYSTICS

By another apparent coincidence, whilst reflecting on Jung's scientist-versus-mystic conflict, essentially the fuel for *Liber Novus*, I remembered a fascinating book I'd read some years ago, *Deciphering the Cosmic Number* by Arthur I. Miller, also published in 2009. This is the tale of the extraordinary friendship – begun in 1932 when the eminent physicist Wolfgang Pauli became Jung's patient – between two equally brilliant yet very different men. It was, as Jung wrote, to lead both of them into 'the no-man's land between physics and the psychology of the unconscious … the most fascinating yet the darkest hunting ground of our times'. Both were obsessed with the far-reaching significance of the number 137 – a primal number that seemed to hint at the origins of the universe itself.

I was struck by the fact that this important relationship had begun in 1932, the year Jung completed *The Red Book*, and by the coincidence of Miller's book having been published in the same year as *The Red Book*.

Liz Greene's observation, in the Conclusion of her book, regarding the meaning of Jung's Pleroma, evoked one of my own long-term preoccupations, namely that of the 'no-man's land between physics and the psychology of the unconscious'. Greene quotes Jung:

> 'It is nothingness that is whole and continuous throughout. Only figuratively, therefore, do I speak of creation as part of the Pleroma. Because, actually, the Pleroma is nowhere divided, since it is nothingness. We are also the whole Pleroma, because, figuratively, the Pleroma is the smallest point in us, merely assumed, not existing, and the boundless firmament about us. But why then do we speak of the Pleroma at all, if it is everything and nothing!'. (pp. 178/9)

This quotation strongly reminded me of contemporary physicist – and some would say, mystic! – Brian Swimme's recent description of the vast energy field in which everything exists:

> 'The ground of the universe then is an empty fullness, a fecund nothingness ... The base of the universe seethes with creativity, so much so that physicists refer to the universe's ground state as 'space-time foam'.
>
> – Brian Swimme, *The Secret Heart of the Cosmos*, Orbis Books, 2003, p. 93

It appears to me from Liz Greene's account of Jung's 'night sea journey' – and from that highly revealing Pleroma quotation – that Jung, long before he met and had his long dialogues with Pauli, already understood that contemporary science, myth, astrology, alchemy, the tarot, the Kabbalah, the paranormal, magical practices and the psychology of the unconscious all occupied the same vast energetic 'territory'. Within this vastness, Jung's conflict between the scientist and the mystic had the potential to be resolved. Ultimately, both are gazing through their respective lenses at the same ground.

In recent years, the theories of contemporary science have informed us that only 4% of the universe appears to describe our 'normal' existence. The remaining 96% we know is there – but from reductionist perspectives we haven't a clue what it is – consists of 23% so-called dark matter and 73% so-called dark energy. It struck me some years ago, digesting this profoundly exciting and illuminating set of percentages, that Jung was really onto something: perhaps we can map consciousness onto the 4%, the unconscious onto the 23%, and the collective unconscious onto the 73%.

A COMPLEX WEAVE OF INFLUENCES
The breadth and depth of Jung's studies throughout his long life was extraordinary. The formulation of his concept of the collective unconscious substantially arose from his realisation that there were common archetypal patterns (energy fields) relating to the unfolding of human life from birth to death and beyond, belonging to the myths of all cultures across the globe. He was open to exploring any approach to the human psyche that opened up new fields of knowledge for him, and which assisted him in his work with both his own and his patients' inner worlds, including 'the apparently disreputable worlds of astrology, magic, spiritualism, Theosophy and ancient mystery cults ... ' (p. 4).

During the period in which Jung was creating the 'extraordinary visionary work' (p. 2) of *Liber Novus*, he was inspired by religious influences from, as Liz Greene points out, 'Gnostic, Hermetic, Platonic and Neoplatonic, Jewish, Orphic, Stoic, Mithraic – [which] hint at or directly describe a cosmos symbolised by, and infused with, celestial patterns' (p. 2).

Invaded during 1913-16 by ancestral voices and images from our deep past, the collective unconscious, he recorded those as they burst through. Jung also used what are essentially magical practices (which he later couched in the language of psychology as 'active imagination') to invoke these characters and grapple with setting them down on paper: both in words and in wonderfully detailed symbolic paintings, so that they could speak to generations both present and to come. Greene makes it clear that:

> 'The initial outpouring was genuinely spontaneous, although it was clearly impregnated, albeit unintentionally, with themes and images from the many mythological, philosophical and astrological texts Jung had been reading ... the more self-conscious aspects of the work, forming a kind of second 'layer', developed from 1916 onward, and it is here that specific astrological themes ... began to appear in a more constructed fashion, along with reflections on the psychological dimension of the visions.' (p. 6)

The dominant characters which emerged were Philemon, his soul guide, and Phanes. With his eventual arrival at Phanes, the bringer of the Sun, Jung concluded that his journey was done.

Roads to reconciliation: the structure of *The Astrological World of Jung's Liber Novus*

I found Liz Greene's method of setting out the appearances of all 22 major characters e.g., Siegfried the Hero, Salome, Izdubar/the Sun, the Fool, within broad groupings linked to astrological planetary symbols, to be a comprehensible way of following the essential lines of the unfolding pattern of *Liber Novus*.

She broadly links the first five chapters under the planetary archetypes of Mars, the Sun, the Moon, and two chapters under Saturn, the latter of those two being devoted to different facets of Philemon, Jung's soul guide: through those chapters one can track the gradual unfolding of the voyage towards Phanes, ' ... the great primal androgynous deity of Orphic cosmogonic myth' (p. 129).

Liz Greene describes this numinous encounter thus: 'In 1919, Jung painted a childlike figure whose body is composed of spherical shapes, wearing a harlequin costume patterned in black and white against a gold ground' (p. 129).

And – movingly – in Jung's own words:

> *'This is the image of the divine child. It means the completion of a long path. Just as the image was finished in April 1919, and work on the next image had already begun, the one who brought the Sun came, as [Philemon] had predicted to me. I called him [Phanes] because he is the newly appearing God.'* (p. 129)

Following this structure, in the final chapter, 'The Systema Munditotius and Jung's natal horoscope', one can see a movement towards containment of everything that has gone before within a bigger, cosmic pattern – that set out in the cosmological map known as the Systema. In Liz Greene's words:

> *'There is a long tradition of such pictorial representations of the cosmos in both Eastern and Western traditions ... All of them portray, through a particular cultural lens and a particular religious or philosophical worldview, the place of the human microcosm within the greater macrocosm. Jung was thoroughly familiar with these maps, which provided him with ample precedents for his Systema.'* (p. 144)

Here also can be seen the roots of Jung's key contributions to modern psychology, and the undoubted influence of his deep knowledge of astrology, although ...

> *'... the way in which Jung concealed, but did not remove, the astrological dimensions of the Systema's cosmology is a remarkable reflection of his understanding of the nature of symbols. ... the astrological material is there to be explored, it does not club the viewer over the head with one specific language.'* (p. 145)

Aion and the changing World Age

Liz Greene's view is that the Systema 'may also provide insights into the ways in which Jung understood his 'task' in the context of the new Aion he believed to be dawning' (p. 168).

Her writing on Jung's horoscope with his Aquarian Saturn and his Leo Sun – his self-described 'solar nature' – indicates that Jung apparently thought both his character and destiny to be linked with the new collective religious currents he identified as motifs of the World Age shifting from the Virgo/Pisces Age of the Fishes to the 'incoming Aion ... symbolised not only by Aquarius, but by the Aquarius/Leo polarity' (p. 168).

Jung believed that he had a vital role to play in working with individuals and thereby influencing future generations to 'facilitate the collective transition into an astrological Aion in which humans would be faced with the terrifying challenge of interiorising and integrating good and evil' (p 169).

In her conclusion to this challenging, remarkable book Liz Greene observes that 'As the 21st century progresses, whether or not it is indeed the time of entry into the Aquarian Aion, as Jung believed it to be, his perceptions seem to be proving entirely prophetic' (p185).

In conclusion

I've written many book reviews in my time, but never before had the kind of response I've had to this one. Entering and engaging with *The Astrological World of Jung's Liber Novus* made me realise quite quickly that, to get to grips with its essence, I had to let go of trying too hard to understand the material presented by Liz Greene from a purely rational perspective and allow myself at least partly to be drawn into the territory of the Imaginal, or the 96% we simply cannot explain or engage with from a purely rational perspective. Perhaps being a Leo with several planets including the Sun in the 12th house made that partial letting-go possible.

Throughout the weeks during which I was reading, note-making, reflecting, and immersing myself in this book, I had a powerful sense of Jung standing on that liminal border between the 4% and the 96%, driven there by the intensity and pain of his own internal contradictions, being buffeted by, and courageously invoking, the shape-shifting archetypal forms with which he worked for the rest of his life – thereby enriching the inner and outer lives of so many of us.

Liz Greene has given us a rich gift in this volume, by providing quality access to *Liber Novus*, Jung's deeply personal record of an astrological Leo's unique, heroic journey to the heart of his own darkness which eventually led to the light of the Sun. I found it inspiring – and personally very helpful in gaining a deeper understanding of my own contradictions and how to work with them. Jung's teaching, here via Liz Greene's writing, lives on.

Astrodienst
2019
The Astrological Journal
November/December 2020

Prediction and a personal story

The question of whether it is possible to foretell the future is one which has preoccupied humans ever since we evolved into self-conscious beings and began to conceptualise past, present and future – now thought to be around 80,000 years ago. Prediction has been around for a long time. Economists do it. Weather forecasters do it. Politicians do it. Physicists do it. Futurologists do it.

Most of the foregoing predictors direct scorn and derision at the people who have done it for longer than anyone else: astrologers.

There is several thousand years' worth of recorded empirical evidence – much of it stored on clay tablets, as yet undeciphered, in the basements of museums across the world – demonstrating that the movements of the planets in our solar system correlate with particular shifts in 'the affairs of men' (Shakespeare's term, not mine).

This empirical observation continues into the present day in the consulting rooms of astrologers across the world. For example, a number of politicians and economists consult astrologers regularly. They are mostly unwilling to admit it, though we astrologers know who they are!

WHAT WE CAN AND CANNOT DO

Both astrologers and astronomers, via planetary observation, can look at and correctly plot the unfolding pattern of energies through space-time. After that, astrologers step into a realm different from that of observation of the external, material, planetary world. By looking at a section of any points or moments of the past, present or future via a horoscope, they can examine the essence of that moment in terms of its meaning and speculate with moderate accuracy about what some of the branches manifesting in the wider world, or in individuals' lives, may be.

What they cannot do is to see exactly, and with consistency, how those branches are going to manifest. Historically, our track record on hindsight is much better than it is on foresight.

There have been some spectacularly accurate predictions made by astrologers in the public realm over the centuries; a famous one was made by Luc Gauricus in 1555 to the effect that King Henry II of France (then aged thirty-seven) was in danger of death in his forty-second year by a head injury incurred in single combat in an enclosed space. And five years later Henry duly died of a lance splinter which entered his eyes and pierced his brain. There have also been some spectacular failures, e.g., to predict that the Munich agreement of 1938 would lead to World War II.

A NEW MODEL SLOWLY EMERGING

We do much better at describing the essence of a pattern. But identifying the exact branches is much more hit and miss. Personally, this cheers me since it appears to suggest a creative balance between fate and freewill in the universe; chaos theory in contemporary physics also has strong parallels with the astrological paradigm. Both the language of astrology and the language of quantum physics tells us that not everything is pinned down.

Indeed, a view and a model are slowly emerging, despite considerable resistance from the diehard defenders of reductionism, which can demonstrate convincingly that the lenses of astrology and quantum physics are focusing on the same underlying, all-encompassing reality.

The perspectives offered by contemporary writers, astrologers, depth psychologists and scientists, such as Richard Tarnas, Liz Greene, the late Charles Harvey, Stanislav Grof, Brian Swimme, Rupert Sheldrake and others – including recent books by astrologers Armand Diaz, Kieron Le Grice and Bernadette Brady – have been of inestimable value to me. I urge any readers who are keen to expand their own perspectives to explore their work.

CONSCIOUSNESS HOLDS THE KEY

My view, based on my personal experiences and those of clients and students over 30 years, as well as extensive reading and study, is that the key dimension in determining how a particular planetary pattern will play out in a person's life is the level of consciousness at which they are operating at the time the inevitable challenges of life come their way.

Most astrologers have had the humbling experience of looking at the horoscope of a client which looks so difficult that the impending consultation feels very stressful, but upon encountering the client, they meet someone who has faced, dealt with, and grown through hard experiences that would have flattened a less aware person. We can never predict the level of awareness of a client we have never met, although we can have a good idea that, e.g., Mars conjunct Saturn conjunct Pluto square the Moon is going to be no walk in the park.

I am personally very hesitant about both the accuracy and the wisdom of predicting at all, especially for individuals, in any more than a 'describing the core and speculating about the branches' kind of way. Predicting that a specific branch will manifest may well close down possibilities rather than open them up, which also takes us into the realm of self-fulfilling prophecy.

For example, when Uranus was about to cross my Pisces Descendant in 2005, beginning its seven or so years' traverse of my 7th house, I became concerned about what this might mean for my marriage. The rather problematic implications of Uranus' impact on the relationship realm that practising astrologers see every day in their students' and clients' lives, as well as their own, worried me.

However, a profound, totally unexpected spiritual experience on my husband's part linked both our spiritual journeys into walking the same path at the same time. This has had a supportive, deepening effect on our marriage and not one I could possibly have envisaged before Uranus crossed my Descendant.

My personal prediction story and the launderette

Having just made what I hope is a coherent case for specific prediction being a practice of dubious merit and only intermittent accuracy, here is my own striking experience of being on the receiving end of a specific prediction I never asked for, at a time when I was a typical astrology dismisser: I considered that astrology was rubbish without ever having taken the trouble to study it.

Bath, Somerset, England, June 1974: I was engrossed in the Sunday evening chore of doing washing in the launderette on the London Road, near where I lived. It was a liminal time in my life. After having resigned from a lecturing job, I was preparing to leave Bath. A return to the Outer Hebrides was imminent.

A strange looking couple came in, accompanied by a little girl of about five years old. The woman was tall, slender, with long dark hair, a very scruffy Afghan coat, and a distinct look of Cher (of Sonny and Cher fame). The man was smaller than she, slight, with unruly greying hair and a mischievous face.

I carried on with my laundry. The little girl was chatty. Soon, she was putting money into the dryer for me, I was telling her stories, and we had become great friends. I met her parents. They were both artists and astrologers. (Note for below: Seamus and Gloria are fictitious names.)

'Not the kind who do that stuff you see in the papers,' said Seamus scornfully, having noted the fleeting look of disdain which crossed my face at the mention of the word astrology. (I had given one of my mature students a very hard time a couple of years before for her public devotion to what seemed to me a subject unworthy of someone of her intelligence.) Seamus said, 'We are the real thing.'

Twenty minutes later, I was sitting in their cramped basement kitchen, drinking tea, and being charmed by Seamus. His combination of erudition, intensity, conviction, humour and blarney was irresistible.

'Do you know your birth time?' he asked. 'Yes,' I replied. 'Why are you interested in that?' 'Because I am going to draw up your horoscope', he replied. Whether I wanted such a procedure embarked upon or not was of no consequence to him. So slain was I by his charm that I didn't offer any resistance.

As I watched, interested in spite of myself, Gloria and Seamus assembled a hefty tome, a slim pamphlet, blank sheets of paper, a calculator, a fountain pen, and a newly sharpened pencil. The tome was an ephemeris, they informed me – a list of the planets' placements every day at noon for the whole of the 20th century.

Seamus took a blank sheet, carefully drawing a circle freehand in its centre. He then proceeded with great rapidity and fluency to insert squiggles – 'Planets!' – and numbers around the inner edge of the circle. He then drew lines within a smaller inner circle – 'Aspects or links between the planets at the time you were born.' He and Gloria then sat back, gazing with silent preoccupation at the image they had created.

Seamus, looking at his drawing and only briefly at me, gave an astonishingly accurate description of my father's complex, domineering, idiosyncratic and wayward character. That was bad enough, not least because it reminded me of certain aspects of myself! Worse was to follow.

'You are a person rich with creative gifts,' he said. 'But you need to know and face more clearly the more difficult facets of your own nature. It's time to do that since you are approaching 30 and your Saturn return.' With that, he forensically summed up those parts of myself which I knew were there but had tried very hard to avoid facing or admitting to anyone – a very common and human failing that Saturn transits expose and challenge on a cyclic basis throughout our lives. I was feeling by this time as though I'd been hit on the side of the head with a sock full of sand.

Then, with true rhetorical skill, he delivered the punch line. 'You tell me you are a total sceptic now,' he said. 'But stop fooling yourself. You have a deeply spiritual nature which needs to find meaning and connection with something greater than yourself. Until you manage that, you will be driven by the same restlessness that still drives your father, and you will not find inner peace.'

There was a long pause.

'And I can see, from where the planets will be in about seven years' time, that the big picture is going to come seriously calling at your door. In your early thirties, you're going to end up either doing what I'm doing now or something very like it.'

I was utterly shocked. I had known those people for less than an hour, most of which had been spent walking back from the launderette to their flat and organising cups of tea. They knew nothing about me of any significance. How could they produce such specific and accurate material from marks on a piece of paper? I couldn't even begin to get my head round the prediction. It seemed beyond absurd. Slowly, I carried my laundry home. There was no way I could find to make sense of the experience I had just had. There was no file inside my head into which it could fit.

Seven years later

Seven years later, a friend gave me a copy of Alan Oken's *Complete Astrology*. I had no idea why but had enough respect for that friend and his opinions to begin reading. About three pages in, I had the strangest sensation of someone pulling me into the book, saying, 'Come here, you're for me … .' I still have this battered old copy with my signature on it — February 1981.

And my transits at the time? The Jupiter-Saturn conjunction in Libra exactly conjunct natal 2nd-house Neptune and exactly sextile natal 11th-house Mercury (my ruling planet); Uranus crossing the natal IC; Neptune beginning a long opposition to the natal 10th-house Uranus-Mars conjunction, and trine to the natal 12th-house Sun; Pluto trine natal Uranus and sextile natal Sun; North Node conjunct natal Mercury. A summons, pretty much.

In February 1981, that prediction, (which I had never quite forgotten), and the feeling of fascination, compulsion and exhilaration which Alan Oken's book triggered in me came together in a way that has profoundly shaped the whole of my subsequent life.

Concluding thoughts

It's good for us all – especially people like me, with seven planets in fixed signs! – to get jolted out of our positions now and then by experiences that don't fit our frames of reference. Hopefully, the jolt will have the effect of breaking down some of our old defences and letting new experience and new knowledge enter our lives.

I re-interpreted Seamus' prediction in the light of my own subsequent astrological knowledge; it was pretty obvious by then how he had got there, as was the timing of it.

I still think about the encounter with him, his child and partner over 40 years later. Did his prediction, at some subliminal level, point my life in a direction that it would not otherwise have gone? I will never know. But I do know, as a result of our encounter, that whatever my reservations are about the wisdom of offering such specific outcomes to people, astrologers sometimes have the power to do just that.

Whether they *should* do it is another issue altogether!

The Mountain Astrologer blog
August 2013

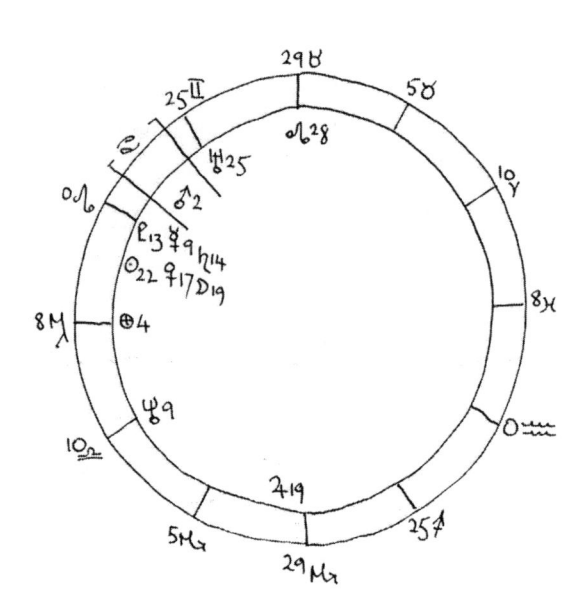

ANNE'S 'LAUNDERETTE HOROSCOPE'

Healing & wounding:
all arts have their shadow

'Astrology as a Healing and a Wounding Art' was written in 1999 for Issue 3 of Apollon, the Journal of Psychological Astrology *which featured a series of articles on healing. It had troubled me for some time that the issue of astrology's wounding potential for practitioners, students and clients did not seem to be addressed much in what I had read up until that time. This made me decide to tackle it. I hope you find the results, which include the thoughts and experiences of four of my long-term students, interesting and thought-provoking.*

By 2018, the year I wrote 'Reflecting on Chiron as his Aries Trip Begins', I had had plenty of time to observe Chiron, planetoid of healing and wounding, in my own horoscope and in the charts of my clients, students and astrology colleagues – as well as in people I knew informally as they each turned 50, the time of the Chiron return.

Interestingly, the North Node completed a full 18/19-year return from the time of writing the first, until I wrote the second. I have the North Node exactly conjunct my MC. So that cycle tends to follow me around, as far as my career is concerned.

The art of astrology: wounding, healing – or both?

*'Teach me your mood, o patient stars
who climb each night the ancient sky.
Leaving no space, no shade, no scars,
no trace of age, no fear to die.'*

– R.W. Emerson

We do not know why we are here. This could be said to be the primary wound of humankind. In order to assuage it, and in attempting to heal it, we have spun around ourselves a web of wonderful richness and intricacy, woven of many bright threads of myth, poetry, religious belief, art, sacred architecture, storytelling, music, adventurous quests of mind, body and spirit. Wars have been fought, and countless millions of lives destroyed, in the clash of differing religious beliefs and socio-political theories: all created in our attempts to heal that primary wound by creating a sense of meaning and order.

However, despite the best efforts of the greatest minds throughout the whole of our history, we still do not even know what consciousness is. Far less do we know why we tiny creatures, wonderfully creative and terrifyingly destructive, cling to planet Earth, an insignificant speck of planetary gravel hurtling through the vastness of infinite space.

Thus, we need teleological frameworks more than ever. This need is reflected in the proliferation of paths on the quest for meaning which seems to be opening up as this new millennium begins. The longest trodden of them all, about to enter its seventh millennium, is astrology. Not only has it survived the onslaught of contemporary science – but may even be seen in some quarters to be making alliances with it!

Wounding, healing – or both?

It is important at this point to stress that astrology itself neither heals nor wounds. Having arisen aeons ago from attempts to create a meaningful context to human life through observation of the physical movements of the planets in the heavens, whether such a framework is experienced as wounding or healing is heavily predicated upon the attitude of the individuals who choose to use it.

> *'The fault, dear Brutus, is not in our stars,*
> *But in ourselves, that we are underlings'*
>
> – Shakespeare, *Julius Caesar*, Act 1, Scene 2)

It is easy enough to talk about the positive healing benefits of an astrological framework, providing as it does a major defence against meaninglessness and insignificance. Feeling connected at a personal level to loved ones and friends is recognised as a major factor in promoting and maintaining physical, emotional and mental health and happiness. Feeling connected at a more cosmic level lets us see that we are not random accidents in time and space, but threads in the weave of a greater pattern – very small threads perhaps, but contributors, nevertheless. This awareness promotes a sense of spiritual wellbeing. There is also the sheer fun, excitement and intellectual discovery which the study of astrology brings.

The sense of wonder and significance (which comes with realising that one transiting aspect can and does produce a range of observable manifestations, all apparently different, which spring from the same core) never quite stops being thrilling no matter how long you have been a practitioner.

Saturn in Scorpio squared my Moon during the 1980s. I don't especially recall what the emotional challenges of the time were. But I still vividly remember that my favourite silver chain turned almost black for no reason at the start of the transit, resisting several jewellers' attempts to clean it up. It was dumped at the back of a drawer. Just after the transit was over, I came across it again – as sparkling bright as the day I got it.

Every bright light, however, has a dark shadow: in the promethean nature of our art lies its shadow, too. It is all very well to steal the gods' fire, with the noble intention of liberating humanity from some of its bonds, with the powerful enlightenment which that fire brings.

But fire burns. It is impossible to light up the darkness of our human limitations of perception without the hand that holds the illuminating fire being burned by it. It is not so easy to talk about that. But it does less than justice (in exploring the impact of the astrological model on human consciousness) to concentrate on the healing aspects of the interaction whilst glossing over the wounding dimensions. Exposure to the model brings both.

The client's view

Impetus in translating this essay from inner reflection to grounding in the actual world of people's lives came, fittingly enough, from a recent chance encounter with a former client, Lisa, now aged thirty-three. She was very excited about her imminent departure to live and work in California, and we talked about that. But then, quite unexpectedly, she brought up the subject of the one-off reading I had done for her eight years previously. In common with most astrologers, I am always interested in feedback from former clients, especially those with whom one only has a one-off encounter: I usually have no idea of what the impact of the experience over time has been for them.

What she had to say was so clearly expressed that I invited her to email me with her comments, which she did. Here they are.

> 'It must be about eight years since I came to you for a reading, but there are one or two things that stand out in my memory about that visit. The first was how accurately you were able to describe aspects of my character – I can't pretend to understand

it, but for some reason seeing it laid out in front of me was very reassuring. Perhaps because it gave validity to my personality. That was who I was, and you encouraged me to feel good and confident about that. However, I think that the main benefit of that visit was the discussion relating to my decision-making process. You said you imagined that I would find this quite difficult as there were three equally valid, and contradictory, aspects to my character. The outcome of that discussion was that I no longer got caught up in my inability to make a decision, something that used to cause me unnecessary stress. What I do now is to allow each of the viewpoints to surface until such time as the decision has to be made. It might seem like a simple thing, but it has had an enormous impact. Overall, I am less critical of myself. That's got to be a good thing.'

Lisa's feedback was pleasing and illuminating to have. If compared with feedback which other astrologers receive on the effect of their one-off sessions, I feel confident that the core of it would be similar, although of course individual clients as Lisa would also emphasise individual themes peculiar to their own horoscope. Competent and sensitive astrological work, one hopes, has an impact on clients' lives where the healing dimensions are very much to the forefront of their experience.

In trying to establish a general guideline for the interplay of healing and wounding in people's responses to exposure to the astrological model, one could use the simple images of light for healing and dark for wounding quite effectively. My feeling is, if we take a broad spectrum from very bright at one end to very dark at the other, then well-handled, one-off consultations with clients who are at the right point of readiness for the experience would occupy a position very close to the brightest end of that spectrum.

Where individuals find themselves, of course, depends on a number of factors such as age, experience, maturity, sensitivity or otherwise, degree of stoicism, capacity for joy and faith in life, predisposition to depression, and so on. There is also movement up and down the spectrum, depending on the same range of factors combined with what life chooses to dish up at various points. So, these images are only meant as a general reference tool.

However, experience and observation tell me that the more exposure there is to the astrological model, the more people's position begins to shift from bright to darker, as the promethean implications of involvement begin to emerge. As I write this I am thinking of a very bright and gifted male client, now in his mid-forties, who has been coming for astrological reviews every year or two for over a decade. His horoscope is rich and complex: at its heart lies a Grand Cross involving the Sun, Saturn, Neptune, Uranus and the Nodes. This complex pattern links in with both his brightest gifts and his deepest pains, and we have worked with that pattern on sufficient occasions now for him to have developed a clear understanding of the paradoxes it brings.

On balance, he feels that having the framework which astrology provides is more healing than wounding. But it doesn't stop him, for example, fearing his Saturn transits, at the same time as he knows intellectually that the upcoming challenge of each one is to define who he is in the world more clearly, whilst jettisoning ever more of the painful old baggage which slows him down. He now knows that the problem with accepting Prometheus' gift is that under no circumstances can one give it back, even if one feels too vulnerable at times to be able to cope with it very well.

The student/practitioner's view

In further pursuing the exploration which my chance encounter with Lisa had begun, I asked my ongoing students for their comments. I was particularly keen to receive feedback from those in my monthly study/supervision group who had been students and practitioners for seven to eight years or more, feeling that they would have a more rounded perspective to offer, based on going through many different stages in their relationship with astrology.

They were asked to reflect on the healing and wounding aspects of working within the astrological model from the viewpoint of the impact their involvement had had on their personal lives. Here is their feedback which I found rich, eloquent and varied.

Marie (52)

I came to astrology when you read my chart in May '87. Suddenly, after twenty-one years, old pain I had partly buried, partly learned to live with, resurfaced. I had to come to terms with it, heal it, if I were to live with myself. I had had a difficult time when I was nineteen. At the time of the consultation, Uranus was squaring the Uranus of those events in 1966, and Pluto was conjunct my Chiron – for me, astrology has always been a healing tool. More recently, it helped me through the period of my father's death in 1993 by enabling me to detach and accept by understanding the process. The Uranus-Neptune conjunction was exact, squaring his 19 Libra Sun. At the moment of his heart attack, the Ascendant was exactly conjunct my natal Chiron; Mercury was squaring my Chiron when he died.

For me, astrology is an invaluable tool. I trust more now in my own intuition, especially where the timing of events is concerned. I think we all subconsciously know when the time is right to take a decision, make a phone call, accept an offer or whatever. I regularly run up charts for significant moments and find the Ascendant reveals the flavour of the moment, the Moon the timing of the event, Mars the motivating force underlying it and Mercury often literally brings the message. An interesting example of this is when I began to realise that the house I lived in was playing a part in my healing process. Being convinced of the significance of certain moments in time, I ran up a chart for the exact moment my husband and I entered the house for the first time as owners. It was Hallowe'en 1984 and the Sun was at 8 Scorpio conjunct my Chiron. Not only that, the house's Chiron was conjunct my Moon and Node at 7 Gemini, the Moon was on my Ascendant and Venus on my MC. Even more incredible, the Ascendant of the house chart was 29 Cancer 27, which turned out to be the Jupiter of W.G. Morton, the artist who had had it built in 1912 – his Jupiter was 29 Cancer 30! Morton's ghost haunted the house; I felt I could help him let go and move on. My Pluto at 11 Leo is exactly conjunct his Moon and IC at 10 and 11 Leo.

These amazing synchronicities prove to me how finely tuned our lives are, and what a gift astrology is in helping me interpret the meaning of my life, face up to the dark side of my nature and co-operate as best I can with transits as they ebb and flow.

We don't always get what we expect. My Mum's Sun, Venus and Mars are at 2, 6 and 10 Sagittarius, respectively. With Pluto crossing these degrees and also opposing my Moon Node conjunction at 7 Gemini, I was scared I was going to lose her. She is 84; when I looked ahead to these Pluto transits, it seemed a likely outcome. I'm sure you would agree that projecting fear onto upcoming transits is one of the most obvious facets of the wounding side of astrology.

However, as Pluto stripped away all that was unnecessary in her life, she began to give away her money and her jewelry and to talk about her death in a very matter-of-fact way. How could she see us enjoy our inheritance if she'd gone? Better still, she began for the first time in my life to tell me she loved me and was proud of me, words I had waited for all my life. I no longer live in fear of her death, but accept all our time together now as a bonus. During this period, Chiron was also busy. On the day she gave me, out of the blue, a large sum of money, Chiron was 2 Sagittarius, conjunct her sun, and the IC of the moment!

I can only sum up by saying that whenever I feel I'm stumbling around in the dark, astrology restores my faith in life by reconnecting me to a sense of meaning and purpose.

Andrea (39)

On the whole, I've been very lucky with the astrologers I've met. Almost all have been good people, good astrologers and have definitely helped me on my way. From a personal viewpoint, astrology has helped me to open *my heart and my soul to a way of being centred on self-acceptance and love; I'm not sure I would have managed that otherwise. I've learned to treat myself with a bit more sympathy and understanding – and hopefully treat other people the same way. My experience of astrology has opened me to the deeper mysteries of life – even if I can't put that into words or fully understand it, I know it's there. That's such a healing experience, because the sense of awe makes me want to try harder to be responsible for my life, to live it in a positive way. Having said all that, for a while I didn't look at the ephemeris or any astrology. Partly, the reason for that is that astrology can turn me away from my own life. That seems a complete contradiction to what I've just said.*

Maybe, for me, this is the wounded/wounding side of astrology – being so busy reading astrology, looking at charts, thinking about aspects, looking at planets, transits, progressions or midpoints meant I was too busy to live my life in the present – I would be thinking about the past or looking to the future.

Recently, when looking at my transits, (which I hadn't looked at for months) I had a sharp intake of breath as I saw Saturn, Chiron, Uranus, Neptune, Pluto and progressed Moon all triggering off planets in my natal chart. The sense of trepidation was almost overwhelming. I have to work hard to just meet life as it comes. For me, that's a real challenge – astrology can help me to be more aware, but I have to resist the urge to think I know what it means before I get there.

CHARLOTTE (35)

I've never really been asked to consider the wounding aspects of astrology in such a direct way before. I did have a bit of a job focusing on the question without the more positive aspects coming up all the time! I think the serious study of astrology knocked me out of the idyllic vision I had had of my family background. I had to accept that my parents weren't perfect, and the overall effect of this was enlightening but also disappointing. It kind of knocked me into the real world and showed me things as they were which I found quite hard to come to terms with.

Seeing things in black and white on the astrological chart led to a lot of resentment on my part, raising a lot of difficult questions which I'm still working hard to understand. I think this can sometimes sidetrack me and stop me getting on with things, and lead to some disasters which might not have occurred otherwise – although I would say I do have a natural tendency to analyse things anyway. Astrology just provides more scope for this.

There is also the question: 'Why me? Why did I have to have this chart?', which may be quite childish, but did lead at one time to some resentment at the apparent unfairness of it all. Especially when you are grappling with hard Pluto and Saturn aspects. You know you have your work cut out for you, and that life is not going to be easy. The prospect of living your life with these aspects can be quite daunting and depressing, and lead to a lot of despondency at times.

Another factor that's hard to take on board is that you are responsible for yourself. You can't go around blaming other people for your misfortunes all the time. You have to take responsibility for your part in the drama. It's your stuff, and you're the only one who can deal with it. This can lead to a lot of self-criticism on my part, and a good deal of depression if things aren't working out.

Looking at it from a promethean point of view, Prometheus stole fire from the gods. He knew he would suffer for it, but he also, I think, knew on some intuitive level that he was doing the right thing. And in the end, he was released from his suffering. Personally, I couldn't not know. Otherwise, I wouldn't have pursued the subject as long as I have. I just hope it works out for me in the end, too.

Alice (35)

My first experience with 'real' as opposed to 'Sun sign' astrology was at night school. My birth chart was not what I had expected. I was a true Sagittarian, adventurous, lucky, fun loving and optimistic, wasn't I? Oh yes – I was pleased with my grand trine in fire. That made sense; but a meek, mild, service-seeking Virgo Ascendant was not exactly me.

Oh well, I suppose I could come across that way to some people. Then I see it – a small black glyph sitting right on top of my Ascendant. It must be a mistake. I feel like scrubbing it out. I don't want Pluto there on my lovely chart. I'm nothing like a Scorpion type – moody, emotional, secretive, jealous, controlling. My Venus sitting smugly in Capricorn does not enhance my frame of mind. I take small consolation from hearing it is earthy and loyal. I feel cheated and continue to long for Venus in Taurus.

Gradually over the term, astrology stripped me of my pre-conceptions of myself, and left me exposed to the facts. I could no longer carry on in blissful denial of the deeper, darker side of my nature.

A significant turning point came when I was asked to explain the types of things which had been happening to me, since I was experiencing my Saturn return at that point. I couldn't explain. I hadn't a clue what was going on. Where did I start? My teacher then summarised, in a couple of minutes the way I had been feeling and how it was all part of a process. The light had been switched on. It was an amazing experience. I felt understood, accepted and not alone.

The more I learned about the interacting energies within my chart, the more I could accept myself and stop having to put on an act. The energy I had previously been using to keep Pluto well at bay, could now be directed towards more constructive pursuits. I felt freed. The healing had begun.

THE 'BIG PICTURE'

I had hoped in asking for feedback from long-term students that they would provide a range of responses which illustrated the main themes regarding both the healing and the wounding dimensions of astrology – they did not disappoint me. Andrea's 'sense of awe' which inspires her to try harder to take responsibility for her life, live it in a positive way, is typical of the spiritual and soul healing which the study and practice of astrology can bring. This is well illustrated also by Marie's concluding comment that 'whenever I feel I'm stumbling around in the dark, astrology restores my faith in life by reconnecting me to a sense of meaning and purpose.'

However, there are also wounding dimensions to setting one's small individual life in the context of the big picture. The planetary energies are archetypal, and the further out you go, especially to the great collective powers of Uranus, Neptune and Pluto, the harder it is to hold onto any sense of personal identity, uniqueness. There is a cold inexorability to the unfolding of the planetary pattern through space and time, an utter impersonality. Being given a slice of that time and space as an image of one's all too fallible humanness can be less than comforting, in fact can be very threatening.

I sometimes get a gut sense of this whilst out walking in the Scottish hills, something I am addicted to doing, and will do under almost any weather conditions. Go to wild, remote places and you will become aware of the archetypal forces of nature, their potentially destructive power, even as your soul is being uplifted by marvellous landscape and the utter peace of being where the only sound is of the wind and of birdsong. In these beautiful, peaceful places I have occasionally had fear descend on me even on sunny days, accompanying an awareness of how implacably indifferent the landscape is to my existence. Its power could sweep my life away given a sudden change of weather, or one slip on a hillside could turn me into yet another fatality statistic. As Shakespeare put it in *King Lear*:

> 'As flies to wanton boys, are we to the gods;
> They kill us for their sport.'

Act 4, Scene 1

THE INDIVIDUAL CHART

One of the most potent pieces of healing that astrology has to offer was, I felt, well summed up by Lisa, the one-off client: 'How accurately you were able to describe aspects of my character – I can't pretend to understand it, but for some reason seeing it laid out in front of me was very reassuring. Perhaps because it gave validity to my personality. That was who I was.'

Over and over again, I have heard from clients that the most valuable thing about their astrology reading was just that validation commented on by Lisa. But Charlotte's question. 'Why me? Why did I have to have this chart?' clearly illustrates where all but the most blithe of us have surely been, as the harder realities of certain chart configurations began to dawn with our more sophisticated understanding of the implications of the natal horoscope.

Certain natal chart configurations may be wonderful opportunities for growth, but it's usually going to be bloody painful when they're triggered, and this is a lifetime's reality which even the sturdiest of us find hard to face and accept, especially in times of vulnerability. If there's anyone reading this who feels joyous at having been given an exact Saturn-Pluto conjunction linked with most of their personal planets (me!), could they please call me and reverse the charges!

The contrasts provided so humorously by Alice, who celebrated her Sagittarian energies as 'adventurous, lucky, fun loving and optimistic' but wanted to scrub out Pluto when she saw it sitting right on top of her Ascendant, who longed for Venus in Taurus whilst being decidedly lukewarm about her actual Venus in Capricorn, is so typical of most students' reactions to initial exposure to their natal chart.

I think it's also fairly typical of most astrologers' starting position in their developing relationship with their own horoscopes over time. Ideally, one comes to the point of enjoying and utilising, for example, one's Sun-Moon-Jupiter Grand Trine in fire without being too immodest about it, or too obviously pitying those lesser mortals not fortunate enough to have had this divine gift bestowed upon them.

If it is also possible to come to an acceptance of difficult energies such as Uranus-Pluto rising – notice that Alice forebore even to mention Pluto's close companion on her Ascendant! – combined with finding some positive outward channel for its disruptive, wayward and potentially destructive power: in this case, one is well on the way to living in a reasonably positive way with the unique challenges of the individual birth chart.

THE UNFOLDING PATTERN

The intricate weave of healing and wounding is very obvious in considering the responses to transits and progressions of those of us who have trodden the astrological path for a while. Trying to second guess the universe's response to our presence in it seems to be a favourite occupation of astrologers. This is trenchantly summed up by Andrea: 'I have to work hard to just meet life as it comes. For me, that's a real challenge – astrology can help me to be more aware, but I have to resist the urge to think I know what it means before I get there.'

Astrologers can be hubristic, arrogant and just plain wrong in their attempts to know what it means before they get there – damaging to their clients as well as themselves. Astrology is a very powerful aid to awareness. It is also very useful in mapping out the terrain in broad terms, and in offering accurate timings. But life reminds us often enough, through our mistakes and errors of judgement of the planetary pattern, that the unconscious, by definition, is precisely that. It is not notable for an inclination to reveal deeper intentions beyond the ego's access, just because some astrologer is standing somewhere near the entrance cave to its mysterious terrain waving an ephemeris, shouting 'I'm pretty sure this Venus-Uranus transit means … .'

Alice's and Marie's differing feedback on their response to transits, I think also sums up both ends of the healing/wounding continuum well, from a somewhat different perspective from that of Andrea. On the one hand we have Alice describing her teacher's clarifying what was going on at Alice's Saturn return: 'The light had been switched on. It was an amazing experience. I felt understood, accepted, and not alone.' Marie's reaction to recent transits affecting her elderly mother was a lot less positive: 'I was scared I was going to lose her. She is 84; when I looked ahead to these Pluto transits, it seemed a likely outcome. I'm sure you would agree that projecting fear onto upcoming transits is one of the most obvious facets of the wounding side of astrology.'

Yes, I certainly do agree! And we've all done it, no matter how spiritual, actualised, wise or mature we think we are. Most beginning students find their introduction to transits and progressions enlightening, productive of a powerful sense of meaningful connection to something greater than themselves, exhilarating – and scary.

As a teacher, I find I have to work hard to strike the right balance between giving information, setting a constructive context, offering honesty and realism, always trying to be aware of my own permanent and serious limitations by virtue of being human, avoiding projecting my own particular fears and bringing in the tempering influence of humour. I also have to realise that students must negotiate for themselves, after all that, what the balance is going to be for them between the healing and wounding facets of the study and practice of astrology.

I always point out to them when they start expressing fears about upcoming transits – Saturn and Pluto being the favourite raisers of fear – that 99.95% of the human race has got through the whole of our collective history without knowing anything about astrology, despite the fact that 100% of us have always had every kind of transit from the start of life till its end. This usually helps! It is very important not to give the impression that astrological knowledge can protect us from life. Its great healing gift is that it can help us greatly to make some sense of it.

Conclusion

I would like to conclude by wondering why so few people (having penetrated such a complex subject to the stage of acquiring a reasonable degree of fluency) seem to give up the practice of astrology, despite its having a wounding as well as a healing dimension. I suspect a major reason is that once virginity has been lost, it cannot be regained. For most of us, the price paid for that loss of innocence is worth it, for the more complex, and full (albeit more difficult) life that is opened up as a result. Once the gods' fire has been stolen, it cannot be returned. Moreover, as Charlotte put it: 'Personally, I couldn't not know. Otherwise, I wouldn't have pursued the subject as long as I have.' Trust a multiple Sagittarian to put that into words for the rest of us! There is an incurable curiosity in human beings, and a relentless drive to create meaning, perhaps in the hope that one day we will be able to heal the primary wound of not knowing why we are here. Once we have held the gods' stolen fire overhead, and seen the intriguing, flickering, chimeric shadows it throws up for us, we become addicted to the quest to find what the shapes behind those shadows might be.

Apollon: The Journal of Psychological Astrology
Issue 3, August 1999

Reflecting on Chiron as his Aries trip begins

What does Chiron mean to you? Have you experienced his symbolic energy as healing? Wounding? As the 'inconvenient benefic', kicking open doors to places you'd never have thought to go? Does he simply not register as any kind of recognisable influence in your life or those around you? Or have you simply not given him much thought as you work with your horoscope in relation to your life? Lots of questions. In this meditative 12th-house time just before the Pisces New Moon tomorrow, I am very much engaged with them, being all too aware of Chiron's approaching the end of his long 2010-18 sojourn in Pisces.

A LIMINAL TIME

Any time just before an important heavenly body shifts from one sign to another is a liminal time – a threshold time, a 12th-house time of final dissolution of the old cycle without the energies of the new yet being clearly evident. Chiron moves into Aries on 17 April 2018, dipping back into Pisces for a few months in the autumn of that year, settling into his journey through Aries on 18 February 2019, remaining there until 2026/7 when he shifts into Taurus.

Chiron's orbit is very irregular, and if you'd like to go into the detail of this, the Cafe Astrology website is the place to go for some very clear tables. However, Chiron's return cycle is a steady 50 years: we all have a Chiron return at that age. This return is especially significant since it represents the end of a whole 50-year period from 1968/9 when Chiron was last in Aries. A cycle is completing at the present time, and the shift from Pisces, the last sign of the zodiac, to Aries the first, is always more radical than any other – and fierier, more disruptive and far-reaching at a collective level.

Chiron in Aries – 20th century
Fifty years back from 1968/9 takes us to 1918/19 and the turbulent aftermath of the First World War. Some of us still vividly remember 1968/9 with the student riots in Europe, the protests in the USA against the Vietnam war and the assassinations of Robert Kennedy and Martin Luther King against the turbulent backdrop of the Civil Rights movement. We also remember that wonderfully pioneering event of the Moon landing, a stunning example of humanity's kicking open a door to a place no-one throughout our whole history until that moment thought we would go.

... and 21st ...
Early on in Chiron's transit through Aries, ruled by Mars, preparations for the first human mission to the Red Planet, envisaged for the 2030s, are well under way. The upcoming Mars 2020 rover mission will study the availability of Martian resources, including oxygen. This is a major step forward in the preparation process. Some of us Baby-Boomers, if we live a long life, may well see the first blast-off taking humans to (in Shakespeare's famous words about death) 'the undiscovered country from whose bourn No traveler returns' (*Hamlet*, Act 3 Scene 1). The Mars explorers know they will not return to their home planet.

No doubt there will be much more speculation across our various media outlets regarding what this shift may mean both collectively and individually. It has already begun, as a quick Google search will testify.

Back to first principles
However, I have found my reflections returning me to contemplation of first principles: the questions at the start of this post are in fact my own interrogations both of my experience of Chiron's symbolic energies in my personal life and my professional practice.

In response to those questions, on looking back, I can say that I have seen Chiron in his popular 'wounded healer' mode, most notably in colleagues and acquaintances with Chiron prominent in their charts, e.g., in the 2nd, 6th or 10th houses and/or strongly linked with planets, nodes and angles. They have found their way into caring, alternative healing or medical/nursing contexts, usually propelled there by family and/or personal wounding they were consciously or unconsciously seeking to assuage.

I have also seen situations where the wounding dimension was well to the fore and people struggled to see any healing in what they were experiencing – quite often at the Chiron return point, when the whole horoscope's Chiron aspects are triggered. This is where it is so vital that astrologers tread carefully in seeking to offer a context to deep pain and suffering which may offer some comfort and hope without raising unrealistic expectations – and to know when we are coming up against our own limitations, such as a lack in a specific expertise to deal with questions of health and healing.

Here, it is important to have a network of reputable and experienced practitioners in various healing modalities who might be able to offer some support which builds on what one has hopefully been able to clarify for the client.

Inconvenient but beneficial

It was the late astrologer A.L. Morrison who coined the term 'inconvenient benefic' as a facet of Chiron's actions – I can see his source for this interpretation on considering the placement of Chiron in our solar system. Chiron appeared in 1977 between the orbits of Saturn and Uranus. He can be seen as the one who unlocked the door between the safe boundaries of the known system contained by Saturn, lord of form and structure, security and stability, and the outer planetary realm of Uranus – lord of misrule; breaker of custom, known code and convention. It is very threatening to be kicked out of safe territory into the unpredictable and unknown. But often it is just what we need although we don't appreciate it at the time.

I have certainly seen this Chironian dimension in action by transit or progression with clients who turn up for readings after a long process where life has given them a good kicking (sound familiar, anyone?) but who emerge out the other end realising that the kicking was necessary to get them to move in a direction that they would not have been brave (or foolish!) enough to see held considerable positive benefits for them.

An amusing (in retrospect ...) and quite significant example of this 'inconvenient benefic' aspect of Chiron in action can be offered from my own life a long time ago. My husband developed mumps and had such a sore throat for several days that he could neither speak nor eat anything that wasn't liquidised, and certainly could not bear to smoke. Chiron was then transiting his Gemini Midheaven. He quit for good.

Chiron's return at midlife

It makes sense that Chiron doesn't feature very strongly in a person's life if not prominent by horoscope placement or by aspect. However, even in such cases, if Chiron directly transits any of the personal planets or angles, it is very unusual for there to be a dumb note struck. It also seems to me that the Chiron return at age 50 registers with everyone, but especially strongly when Chiron is a powerfully placed and aspected symbol.

A long time ago – I no longer have the chart or notes for reference but still remember the situation – a woman with Chiron conjunct her Moon consulted me not long after her 50th birthday. Chiron had recently returned to that natal conjunction. I recall that Saturn by transit was also probably involved. I asked her whether there was a difficult issue currently involving a key female in her life, and she said yes, that her mother-in-law – to whom she had been very close – had recently died and she was having difficulty getting over this loss; her deep grief seemed to her to be out of proportion.

I then asked if she had had a similar loss in the first year of her life. It turned out that her own mother had died when she was less than a year old, and that she had felt bereft of mothering until her mother-in-law came into her life, hence her great difficulty with the current situation. Both the client and I were deeply moved by how powerfully the Moon-Chiron symbolism had spoken on Chiron's return to its natal position. But realising this also helped the client to make more sense of the depth of her grief, and hopefully to process it more consciously.

CHIRON AND OUR DEEP ANCESTRAL WOUND

In approaching what Chiron's symbolic action may bring in our own and clients' horoscopes, it seems to me to make sense to hold those several facets I have described in this post in mind as we reflect. However, there is a deep layer which has meant more to me than any other, which I first came across in an article by Liz Greene called 'Wounding and the Will to Live' (in Issue 3 of *Apollon, the Journal of Psychological Astrology*, 1999). This article is now available on Astrodienst and I would strongly suggest that any readers interested in exploring Chiron's meaning at profound depth should read it. Here, Liz Greene points out, re: the centaur Chiron's unhealable wound, that 'the wound exists in the collective and is ancestral.'

My understanding of what she is saying is that where Chiron appears in our birth charts represents our 'chip' of the accumulated woundedness of humanity over the ages. It is not our fault that we have this particular 'chip' allocated to us, any more than it was the centaur Chiron's fault to be in the wrong place at the wrong time in the centaurs' battle with the Lapiths: he was grazed in the thigh by a poisoned arrow which would not heal because it was dipped in the blood of the Hydra.

We are not directly responsible for our personal share of humanity's wounding. But if we can work with as much honesty and humility, and as little bitterness as possible with that share as indicated by Chiron's placement in our natal chart, then we can begin to transform that woundedness into something which can be offered for the healing of others. This process can ultimately help us to grow sufficiently that our personal wound becomes an increasingly smaller part of who it is we are able to become.

I have used this understanding of Chiron in many client readings now. And I have found that it offers inspiration and consolation. Much of that healing flows from helping clients to accept that the wound is not our fault – but it is our responsibility to choose how we deal with it. No doubt the fact that I have found this deep message a consolation in my own work with ancestral wounding also communicates itself to my clients without my having to say a single word about my own process.

Astrodienst

2018

Astrology meets science:
differing lenses, same source

I've been deeply interested in science since childhood. Having grappled for years to get at least a tentative grasp of such subjects as quantum physics (check out the number of pop science books in my library to get some idea of the amount of effort put in!) I still fail to see why our culture should continue to be diminished by the polarisation which has arisen since the Scientific Revolution of the 17th century. This is the divide between symbolic and scientific ways of looking at our awe-inspiring universe. In my view, we need all the lenses we can get in that great human quest to comprehend the vast mystery in which we live, move and have our being.

As an astrologer with a love and fascination for science, the broad conclusion at which I have arrived, in essence, is this: we are part of a vast, shifting, changing, patterned energy field. Modern science has taught us that everything is energy. The lenses of science and of astrology are both trained on the same vast energy field, or Source if you prefer. Unfortunately, most modern scientists deeply object to the astrological approach of attaching meaning to the patterns that they see, based on at least six thousand years of observation of the heavens' correlations with both macro and micro life on Earth.

Some astrologers, however, are only too happy to be inspired by what science reveals, and to incorporate those insights into both our practice and our writings. I am happy to include myself in that group.

'Astrology is a load of rubbish!' Please, not that tedious old trope again

I know it's not like me to rant. Those of you good folk who call by my blog regularly, know that. However, I feel like a bit of a rant today. What about? Dismissers, that's what. Normally I view this response to astrology with weary resignation.

However, a recent airing of that tedious old 'astrology is a load of old rubbish' trope really got under my skin. How I wish that people would spend some time in studying subjects which have been a vital part of human experience for thousands of years, rather than displaying their profound ignorance of those very subjects in the public realm.

I know of what I speak, being a reformed dismisser myself. Readers of this blog may recall the tale of my being stopped in my tracks by a startling prediction – made as a result of an encounter with astrologers in a launderette in Bath, England – that I would in fact become an astrologer, too. You can find the full story in the Fate section of this book.

Moving from ignorant dismissal of a tradition going back at least six thousand years, to gradual acceptance of its validity based on study and experience, was one of the most profound and humbling processes of my entire life.

I used to like the word 'sceptical': for me, it meant not accepting anything on trust, but being prepared to consider the evidence, not just of accepted facts, but also of experiential evidence which to me and much of the world's population – including open-minded scientists like Professor Bernard Carr, Professor of Mathematics and Astronomy at London University and a Past President of the Society for Psychical Research – can have its own validity.

In a lecture some years ago, Professor Carr stated that there is a barrier which needs to be overcome between science and the rest. Those who consider only *experimental* evidence to be valid (i.e., conducted under strict laboratory conditions) clash with others who find well-researched *experiential* evidence to be of at least equal worth. I think he is absolutely right.

Unfortunately, the term 'sceptical' has now largely narrowed down to mean dismissing any body of knowledge, experience or practice which does not fall within the narrow terms of reference of reductionist, scientific procedures.

Astrology has never 'delivered' terribly convincingly when subjected to scientific approaches. Personally, I have not been the least surprised or upset by this. One cannot expect applying the procedures of one model of reality – say, reductionist science – to the practices of another – astrology – to produce much by way of validation.

My lifelong interest in science has not been diminished by the depressingly dominant reductionism of our era. A long-time preoccupation has been to bring together in my own mind contemporary insights flowing from the weird world of quantum physics with the ancient wisdom traditions and symbol systems centred round the Perennial Philosophy, including astrology.

Cosmos, Chaosmos and Astrology by Dr. Bernadette Brady has especially aided me recently. It's a book I have now read several times. Her highly stimulating rethink of the nature of astrology, taking us on an erudite journey from ancient myth to modern chaos and complexity theory, provides a convincing set of reasons why astrology (despite the increasingly dominant reductionism of 21st century culture) remains a lens of great value to look through in making sense of life. Even if, to quote Brady, 'the real result of … eighty years of research into the possibility of astrology being a science is the evidence that it is not.'

It belongs, Brady believes, to 'another worldview'. She offers us astrologer and author Garry Phillipson's opinion that astrology may work best when approached and practised as 'a sacred art'. From my own experience, I would agree with this. I heartily recommend Dr Brady's book to those of you who, like me, have respect for science when practised in an open-minded way but recognise that life offers more than one lens through which we may view the multi-faceted reality of which we are privileged to be a part. As the atomic physicist J. Robert Oppenheimer so wisely put it:

> 'These two ways of thinking, the ways of time and history and the way of eternity and timelessness, are both part of ... our ... efforts to comprehend the world in which ... we live ... Neither is comprehended in the other or reducible to it. They are, as we have learned to say in physics, complementary views, each supplementing the other, neither telling the whole story.'

In the end, we astrologers have each to find our own way of living with the dismissers. Maintaining both breadth and depth of study whilst striving for a high standard of professionalism in our teaching and practice is the most effective rebuttal of this kind of ignorance.

Having occupied more than one profession during my working lifetime, I have always found that integrity of action speaks much louder than any words can, although of course the latter have their place. Let the dismissers get on with being ill-informed and narrow-minded. Let us simply get on with our work.

Dell Horoscope
March 2017

Broken vows, genetics and astrology

Every so often, I take a vow not to buy any more books. As I left our excellent local charity bookstore in full vow mode a while ago, a book cover stopped me in my tracks. On the back, in large white letters on a dark blue background, it said: 'The realisation that an individual genetic code can result in multiple different outcomes is at the heart of epigenetics – the most exciting discipline in biology today.'

'Yes!!' I said, perhaps not entirely to myself judging from the pained look from a fellow browser next to me. Remembering the vow for a moment, I scanned the back page with my smartphone app. Then, feeling mean and irresponsible, I bought the book. Reader, it was worth it. By now you are probably wondering, 'Where on earth is she going with this?'

To in-depth astrology, that's where. Both the hard sciences, including genetics, and the symbolic arts, including astrology, are attempting to put comprehensible frameworks round a vast puzzle: why are we here and how can we best cope with the unpredictable and often brutal uncertainties of life? This being the case, I find it deeply dispiriting that they have increasingly been at odds with one another since the dawning of the Scientific Revolution. We need complementary disciplines, surely, to help us live as constructively as possible on our beautiful, fragile planet.

My excitement at the back cover quote from *The Epigenetics Revolution* therefore arose from the link it instantly made for me between the practices of both genetics and in-depth astrology. Most astrologers would agree that the complex patterns revealed in an individual's horoscope can express themselves in a range of possible manifestations from the same core. That quote regarding the genetic code struck me as being remarkably similar to what astrologers find in their practice.

In effect, two individuals with identical DNA can and do manifest both similar and different lives. In a chapter titled 'Why Aren't Identical

Twins Actually Identical?' author and geneticist Nessa Carey states that, 'The differences between identical twins have certainly captured the imaginations of creative people from all branches of the arts, but they have also completely captivated the world of science.'

This is certainly the most frequent question which students, clients, friends and the general public have thrown at me over the years. If identical twins born no more than a minute apart have identical horoscopes, how come there are usually significant differences both in their personalities and their life patterns, as well as undoubted similarities? Epigenetics would appear to provide the answer from a scientific point of view. (For an astrological perspective, check out the section in this book titled 'Cusps, Houses, Twins'.)

Nessa Carey is a very clear, entertaining writer. She uses vivid analogies from everyday life to illustrate an incredibly complex web of varied influences – both before and after birth – carried by infinitely subtle chemical messengers which modify our DNA epigenetically to produce, as she puts it, considerable variations on life's basic script.

Using Shakespeare's famous play *Romeo and Juliet* as one example, she points out that in the hands of two different directors, George Cukor in 1936 and Baz Luhrmann in 1996, 'both productions used Shakespeare's script, yet the two movies are entirely different.'

Theatrical analogy is also very useful to astrologers. Along with, no doubt, many of my astrologer colleagues, I invite my clients to think of their horoscopes as a stage with the planets representing the characters standing quietly on it, waiting for life's script to unfold from their birth moment.

I explain that I can certainly portray accurately the essence of each character illustrated by the ten planets, their 'style' as illustrated by the sign they occupy, and their location in terms of which houses are tenanted. I can also describe their dialogues and interactions, pointing out how different the conversation is between, say, Moon square Saturn and Mars sextile Uranus.

However, I tell them that I cannot describe with unfailing accuracy the whole range of possible branches which arise from each core character or archetype. I have seen, often enough, how for example one person's Moon square Saturn expresses very differently from another's – this is true of every other horoscope pattern. This is also true in observing clients' varying responses to the challenges and shaping influences of transits and progressions.

It can be difficult – if not impossible – to work out why one person emerges battered but strengthened from a lengthy Pluto transit to several planets whilst another of the same age, with a very similar horoscope, emerges battered and beaten. Neither has epigenetics, as yet, come up with a full explanation of why some genetic variations occur in some circumstances, but not in others of remarkable similarity.

I have long grappled to understand at least something of the essence of what quantum physics has revealed regarding the contradictory vastness of the energy field in which we exist, and the patterns arising therefrom which appear to interact to create the whole of life of which we are part. My conclusion is that practitioners of both the hard sciences and the symbolic arts are considering the same vast energy field and attempting to describe in different but essentially complementary ways, those mysterious patterns that shape our lives.

Wouldn't it be great if we could share our knowledge?

Dell Horoscope
September/October 2018

Scorpio's season, Hallowe'en, dark matter

Strange things delight me – for that I blame Jupiter in Scorpio (mainly). The other morning, I sat bolt upright in bed, almost spilling my tea, on hearing this: Hallowe'en is to be celebrated as Dark Matter Day. Such startling information triggered a whole stream of thoughts and reactions, so strongly that I have had to emerge briefly from my 3rd-house retro Venus in Scorpio retreat in order to share them. But where to start? Perhaps with dark matter. For those unfamiliar with the term, here is one definition:

> *'Dark matter is a huge part of the universe that scientists' calculations tell us exists, but that has never been observed. Yet, together with dark energy, scientists believe it makes up 95% of the total universe. What we can see, and the matter that scientists can account for, is just 5% of the universe, the rest is a mystery.'* – [From UK Research and Innovation]

Please pay great attention to that last sentence. Science can offer an explanation for just 5% of the universe. The rest, i.e., 23% dark matter and 72% dark energy, is a mystery. (Some accounts say it's 4%/96% – but what's 1% between friends?!) This being the case by modern science's own admission, I have been at a loss for decades to understand why, by and large, most scientists operate on the reductionist principle – loudly and vehemently declaimed by the likes of the UK's Professors Richard Dawkins and Brian Cox: that if it can't be seen, heard, smelled, tasted, touched or proved through the application of the procedures of contemporary science then it simply does not exist.

Here are just a few examples of the 'it' that does not exist or is of no credible value:

- All types of paranormal experience such as precognitive dreams, telepathy, premonitions, mediumship, seeing ghosts, mystical experience – well documented by a vast range of people and cultures throughout the world for millennia.
- The myths of all cultures throughout the ages – (the modern definition of a myth is 'an untrue story') – which through their symbolic stories have offered guidance to humans re: how best to navigate the complexities inherent in every facet of life.
- All religions, which no-one would deny have considerable flaws and deficiencies, but which have at least tried to address the unquantifiable facets of human experience and offer us teachings through which we might 'do as you would be done by'.
- The great symbolic arts, for example, astrology, the I Ching, palmistry and the tarot which have evolved over lengthy time periods for the guidance of us fallible humans as we try to make our way – all of which especially astrology have largely been dismissed as rubbish by scientists who have never taken the trouble to study in any depth that which they are only too happy to condemn.

It should be obvious to any reasonably sentient, rational person that a stance of ignorant dismissal of whole bodies of knowledge which have been embedded in human culture from the outset does not and should not command any respect whatsoever. I can imagine what Prof. Dawkins would say, were anyone to dismiss the whole of physics from a standpoint of wilful ignorance … .

Ooops! Must not fall into ranting … I can feel one coming on … .

I am in total awe of the magnificent achievements of science since the rise of the Age of Reason at around the middle of the 17th century and have been an avid reader of popular science books since my teens. This was part of a long attempt to understand the complexities thereof, especially those of quantum physics which have gradually revealed to us a universe at an energetic level which is paradoxical, deeply strange, and only partly predictable. I have also read widely and thought deeply – and practised – within those dimensions of life I have just listed which modern science largely dismiss as invalid and not worth taking seriously.

A view and model are slowly emerging, despite considerable resistance from the diehard defenders of reductionism, which can demonstrate convincingly that the lenses of astrology and quantum physics are focusing on the same all-encompassing energy field which generates our tiny existence on planet Earth.

Astrology maps this energy field in space/time through the movements of the planets in our solar system, a rational measuring process which is also conducted by mariners and astronomers. However, it goes much further than those disciplines by ascribing symbolic meaning to those planetary movements based on observations over millennia of the correspondences between life on Earth and the movements of the planets in their orbits.

My personal view is that both the scientific and the symbolic arts have their complementary roles to play in exploring and explicating the fundamental mystery of why we are here, and what we should do about it. We need all the help we can get, after all, and should be pooling our collective human knowledge for the benefit of us all. As the atomic physicist J. Robert Oppenheimer so wisely put it:

'These two ways of thinking, the ways of time and history and the way of eternity and timelessness, are both part of Man's efforts to comprehend the world in which he lives. Neither is comprehended in the other or reducible to it. They are, as we have learned to say in physics, complementary views, each supplementing the other, neither telling the whole story.' [13]

---

13 Stuart Holroyd, *The Arkana Dictionary of New Perspectives*, published by Arkana (Penguin Books Ltd), 1989, p. 154, quoting from Lawrence LeShan's book *The Medium, the Mystic and the Physicist*.

Dark matter meets Hallowe'en in the 96% field

Given the kind of prejudices I have been describing from a profoundly dominant and influential group of people, the scientific community, I was at first annoyed to see that 31 October (Hallowe'en) had been designated as Dark Matter Day, especially as its first event last year had been billed in some quarters as 'First Ever Dark Matter Day in Hallowe'en Takeover'. The implication in this headline is pretty clear: the choice of day represents an attempt by the scientific community yet again to attack and dismiss what they see as mere superstition which has no place in the contemporary world.

But on reflection, I realised that the scientific community could have unwittingly created a bridge between the two worlds of the non-rational and the rational by holding Dark Matter Day on Hallowe'en.

When I first came across the compelling notion of the division of the universe's energy, as far as science can ascertain, into 4% matter and the rest dark matter and dark energy, my immediate thought was this: 'Wow, so we only have direct access to a thin slice of reality. Then what goes on in the 96% we know is there but can't access via the methodologies of reductionist science?'

On further reflection, maybe the 4% could represent our conscious, practical relationship with the familiar world. Dark energy might be what Jung called the 'collective unconscious', home to those archetypal patterns shaping our myths, religious beliefs and cultural values as well as what we broadly call the realm of the paranormal. And – dark matter could represent individuals' personal unconscious, the liminal territory which acts as a filter through which images of all kinds from the collective unconscious make their way to the light of day ... the 4% that science can explain.

The 96% dark matter/dark energy 'field' could be the non-rational dimension, which is rich in creative energy of all kinds, energy giving rise (in partnership of course with the rational dimension of life represented by the 4%) to great art and music, and to those unquantifiable but essential attributes which represent the best of humanity, such as love, compassion, humour and kindness.

But, as we all know only too well from our collective and individual lives, there is a very dark shadow side to this non-rational dimension, one of whose manifestations is fear of the unknown, especially death. Historically, this has given rise to all kinds of superstitious beliefs and practices designed to ward off evil spirits and placate threatening supernatural beings – territory which is commemorated and engaged with each year in the shape of Hallowe'en.

We need constructive outlets for those dark fears and impulses, and Hallowe'en provides just that. I find it most interesting that, far from our reductionist-dominated culture stamping out all forms of irrationality, cultural practices such as Hallowe'en have become more mainstream in recent years.

Thinking about this, it calls to mind a brilliant – and brave – book written by the well-known UK journalist Bryan Appleyard. He risked all kinds of opprobrium by exhaustively researching and writing *Aliens: Why They Are Here*, a study of UFOs, which sets the whole thing in a long historical context. His conclusion, simply put, is this: if aliens didn't exist (and he remains personally agnostic on the topic despite extensive research) the human mind, needing irrationality to maintain some sort of balance, is such that it would need to invent them.

So, scientists, you have I think made the right decision in aligning your Dark Matter Day with Hallowe'en – although probably not for the reasons you had in mind! It could *only* happen in Scorpio's season.

anne-whitaker.com
2019

Pluto, the nodes – and a black hole revealed

> *'The combination of nodal activity with the foreground presence of outer planets, especially Pluto, points out that something really special is going on ... '*
>
> *– The Moon's Nodes in Action* by Anne Whitaker

Today, 10 April 2019, that 'something really special' was a giant leap forward in our understanding of our magnificent cosmos: the first ever image of a black hole, from the galaxy Messier 87. Or to quote *The New York Times*:

> *'At the center of our galaxy lies Sagittarius A*, a black hole as massive as four million suns: The black hole is obscured by thick dust and a bright haze of superheated gases. A network of eight telescopes called the Event Horizon Telescope tried to use radio waves to peer through the dust cloud and glimpse the edge of the black hole. After years of analysing data, the team did not release an image of Sagittarius A* on Wednesday. But it did catch a glimpse of something else: An even larger black hole, nearly 7 billion times the mass of the sun, sits at the heart of the nearby galaxy Messier 87.'*

From an astrologer's perspective

The astrology of this event is stunning, as you see from the horoscope [overleaf], set for the time the updated image was released to the public from Washington DC. There is much to be commented on in this remarkable chart, but I will confine myself for now to the major factors which leapt out on first sight.

First off, we see the Moon's South Node straddled by Pluto on one side, Saturn on the other, all in the 8th house of life's deepest and darkest mysteries. The nodal axis forms a dynamic t-square from the 11th house of the human collective, with the pioneering Aries Sun widely conjunct Eris, the battle goddess, and widely conjunct Uranus. To me this speaks of the vast destructive power of the energies involved, expressed vividly thus, to quote from *The New York Times* again: 'The images released today bolster the notion of violence perpetrated over cosmic scales,'

Black Hole chart

10 Apr 2019, Wed
10:13 EDT +4:00
Washington
38°N53'42" 077°W02'12"
Geocentric
Tropical
Placidus

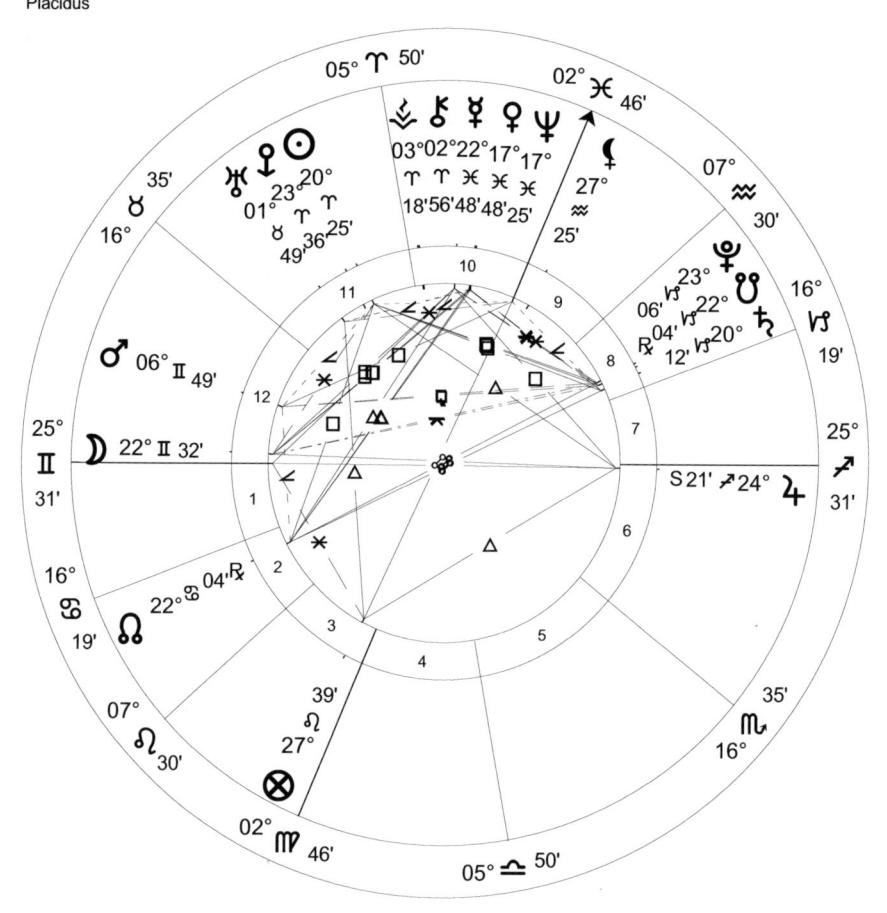

said Sera Markoff, an astrophysicist at the University of Amsterdam, and a member of the Event Horizon team. 'Black holes must be the most exotic major disrupters of cosmic order,' she said.'

Next up, just look at that Moon rising in the 12th house at 22°32' of Gemini, opposite Jupiter in Sagittarius, straddling the Ascendant-Descendant axis at 25°31' Gemini-Sagittarius. Not only does this pattern lie in the pair of signs connected to our endless quest for knowledge but is closely plugged into the planet Uranus' discovery degree, i.e., 24°27' Gemini (which I have written about in a piece included in this collection titled 'Fate, Uranus and the Astrologers' Degree').

Furthermore, the chart's ruling planet Mercury in the 10th house conjoins today's beautiful, ethereal Venus-Neptune conjunction – with Neptune ruling the horoscope's Pisces Midheaven, this line-up forming another t-square with the Moon-Ascendant-Jupiter-Descendant pattern.

I associate Pisces here on the MC, and its co-rulers Jupiter and Neptune, with our ancient human yearning to connect with those only dimly understood great forces of the universe which have held us in awe and stimulated our need to explore the farthest regions of both inner and outer space since the very beginning of human culture all those millennia ago.

Through the best efforts of human co-operation and pooling of knowledge shown by the 10th-house placement of the Mercury-Venus-Neptune line-up, and the 11th-house placement of the Sun, we have arrived at – *so far* – the deepest place of understanding of the immensity of forces at work in our cosmos.

This arrival is summed up in today's vivid visual image, a picture worth more than a thousand words: our first ever actual picture of one of the cosmos' most powerful, destructive and mysterious objects: a Black Hole.

anne-whitaker.com
2019

Red chair moment: a Saturn return tale

We have all had life-changing moments. Some, we only recognise retrospectively. Others hit us like lightning bolts, metaphorically pinning us to our seats. Literally, in my case. I remember it well, that scuffed red velvet chair in that rented room in a friend's scruffy flat. I was twenty-nine years old (Saturn return, anyone?), embarking on social work training. Navel-gazing, therefore, was the order of the day – in fact of that whole year.

There I was, seated on that chair, reading Carl Gustav Jung's *Memories, Dreams, Reflections.* Seven years previously, I had embarked on pondering how I could improve myself as a consequence of deciding to face up to the unsparingly honest comments of a good friend on aspects of my behaviour at that time.

Following that, at twenty-seven and an astrology dismisser, I had encountered astrologers, astrology and an initial dip into my horoscope which had shocked me with its accuracy – especially its uncomfortable ability to pinpoint pluses as well as those minuses in our character which so often get projected onto others.

The whole tenor of my self-challenging and self-learning at that stage was this: by gradually dragging into conscious awareness as much as possible about the difficult and dark sides of myself, I thought I could perhaps in time get rid of them, along with those contradictions in my character and behaviour which were causing me so much stress and pain.

This being the quest, I suppose it was inevitable that extensive reading should eventually bring me to Jung. Then, sitting comfortably on that red velvet chair, I read this:

> 'Therefore, the individual ... has need, first and foremost, of self-knowledge, that is, the utmost possible knowledge of his own wholeness. He must know relentlessly how much good

> *[that] he can do, and what crimes he is capable of, and must beware of regarding the one as real and the other as illusion. Both are elements within his nature, and both are bound to come to light in him, should he wish as he ought to live without self-deception or self-delusion.'*
>
> – 'Late Thoughts', last chapter of *Memories, Dreams, Reflections* by C. G. Jung

The lightning bolt was realising the futility of trying to cast my dark energies as 'bad' and trying to suppress them. In that truly life-changing moment I saw that the work ahead lay in creatively facing, owning and constructively channelling that vital energy which flows from sincere attempts to reconcile the opposites which are inherent in the whole of life.

Since we are each a tiny chip of Life's vital force – something which astrology illustrates wonderfully through the medium of our horoscopes – we need to own and work with the whole spectrum, not just the shiny end.

I have had a lifelong interest in science. I see it as one of many lenses through which to explore why we are here and what it may all mean. In an open-minded world, astrology and scientific exploration would go hand in hand. Happily, in some quarters now they actually do!

Being a person with many 12th-house planets, I've been driven all my life to set our tiny personal lives in the context of the big picture. Both science and astrology have provided huge help in this. It has struck me for a long time that contemplating the Big Bang, the best scientific theory currently available to us regarding how our universe began, is a wonderful starting point for work on reconciling the opposites.

That vast explosion which gave birth to everything we can conceive of was an event of monumental destructiveness. But it was also an event of monumental creativity without which we would not exist, nor would the glorious beauty of this world. Chaos theory has in its turn shown us that we live in a vast energy field, rippling with ever-repeating patterns from the vast down to the minute. This maps well onto astrology's archetypes: we can regard each planet as a mini energy field, each offering a range of possible manifestations arising from the same recognisable core.

Jung put the links between the vastness of universal energies and our tiny human existence very succinctly: 'Our psyche is set up in accord with the structure of the universe, and what happens in the macrocosm likewise happens in the infinitesimal and most subjective reaches of the psyche.' (From *Memories, Dreams, Reflections*.)

Contemplation of all this inextricable interweaving of what we culturally term 'positive' and 'negative' energies, via what I have understood both from science and from the teaching and practice of astrology, has helped me greatly in the never-ending process of reconciling and uniting my own opposites. I truly hope I have been able thus to offer out some inspiration via my vocational path, to clients, students, and readers over the years.

Here is an apt last word on the topic from 'Alice', taken from an article I wrote a long time ago titled 'Astrology as a Healing and a Wounding Art' (in which I asked students for feedback) – it's in Part 6 of this book, titled 'Healing and Wounding: All Arts have their Shadow':

> *'The more I learned about the interacting energies within my chart, the more I could accept myself and stop having to put on an act. The energy I had previously been using to keep Pluto well at bay, could now be directed towards more constructive pursuits. I felt freed. The healing had begun.'*

PS: I'd love to know what happened to that red velvet chair!

Dell Horoscope
March/April 2019

INTERVIEWS:

featuring the bacon sandwich motivational technique, plus other arcane delights

---

On the whole, shaping and focusing my ideas by writing them down in articles and essays is preferred to the spontaneity of interviews where I know I can have a tendency to ramble. This being the case, my ideal interview is the one in which I am sent the questions and can answer them in writing at leisure. Those were my criteria for the interviews included here.

The one between Victor Olliver and me is, of course, more a debate than an interview ... but it was such fun to spar with him that we felt it should definitely be included!

'20 Questions and a Selfie': a day in the life of 12th-house astrologer Anne Whitaker

This interview conducted a few years ago between me and that excellent writers' site Stuff Writers Like is one of the most enjoyable I have done to date. I have omitted the selfie. To see it in all its batty (or should I say 'hat-ty') glory, you can find it via a Google search at stuffwriterslike. com. Now, over to you, editor Gary Grimes ...

For this instalment of '20 Questions and a Selfie', we catch up with Anne Whitaker, astrologer, writer, teacher and mentor. Though the uninitiated may be intimidated by, if not downright sceptical of, the apparent mysticism of astrology, Anne's practical approach makes learning and interpreting the signs of the zodiac more accessible, even to a complete novice. Her qualitative research reveals fascinating and compelling correlations, if not causality, between planetary cycles and psychological, physiological and social change. 'Almost from the outset, I became utterly captivated by astrological symbolism. Captivated by its ability to reveal the relationship between that tiny, vital spark of an ordinary human life and those bigger pictures of family, nation, culture,' she writes. 'Realising the profound weave which exists between the symbolic and practical manifestations of every kind of life on Earth, I was awestruck.'

Our 20 questions with Anne start now:

1) **What is your full name?**
   Anne Whitaker

2) **What is your professional job title?**
   Writer, Teacher, Mentor, Astrologer

3) **Describe your organization.**
Writing from the Twelfth House is a one-woman band where I do all the things I love to do – and get paid!

4) **Describe your surroundings right now.**
Three floors up in a handsome Victorian red sandstone tenement, listening to the river flowing below us. Hand clutching teacup. Biscuit.

5) **What was your first paid writing gig?**
'How I was left on the shelf and found true happiness' for the *West Lothian Courier*'s Spring Brides feature. 'Unromantic' said the editor.

6) **What was the last thing you wrote?**
'How to travel without going anywhere … if Kant could do it, why not you?' for my website anne-whitaker.com.

7) **What is the next thing you plan to write?**
Immediate present: haven't a clue but will [know] by tomorrow. Long term plan: writing my fourth book, on the theme of descent and return.

[PS: December 2020. Well, that plan got derailed back then by a long bout of tendonitis probably caused by writing my third book, research study The Moon's Nodes in Action. *Although the problem appeared to clear up, any time I wrote anything of any length, it came back. So, sadly, I decided to give up on that idea and started writing one-off pieces instead: blogging, article writing and columning. I had no idea back then that these pieces of relative shortness would accumulate sufficiently to result in another book.]*

8) **Finish this sentence: The ideal way to start my day is …**
To wake up at 5:00 a.m., unable to sleep, so that I can get up and have two hours' peace and quiet, listening to the river and writing.

9) **Besides your computer, what is sitting on your desk right now?**
A brass Moon calendar carriage clock, a miniature of Rodin's Thinker, two digestive biscuits, mug of tea, box of tissues, heaps of clutter.

10) **So-called writer's block is no match for you! What is your antidote?**
A crispy bacon sandwich, lashings of butter, wrapped in foil, left to cool on my laptop overnight. Not allowed to open until 500 words written.

11) **Finish this sentence: I hate it when I read …**
Reductionist scientists banging on about how nothing can possibly exist outwith the remit of our five senses and the material world.

12) **What are the most important tools, programs and systems you use for your work?**
Up to date and synched laptop, iPad, iPhone. Social media especially Facebook and Twitter. Great backup from expert local web company.

13) **First book that comes to mind? Go!**
Stoner by novelist John Williams. Wonderfully well written, poignant, elegiac depiction of a quietly heroic life. Reading it just now.

14) **What are your favorite smartphone apps and why?**
iBooks to carry reading around and read anything, anywhere. The Night Sky to stretch my imagination. TimePassages to check daily planets.

15) **What have you always wanted to write?**
A book of people's experiences of the 'dark night of the soul' which links with ancient myths of descent and return, affirming myth's value.

16) **What is your advice for aspiring professional writers?**
Read widely and daily if possible. Write every day. Have a JFDI notice clearly displayed (Just F***ing Do It!). Keep a journal. Persevere!

17) **First famous writer who comes to mind? Go!**
Terry Pratchett. I love his mad *Discworld* for light relief reading – favourite character is the orangutan librarian at the Unseen University.

18) **Finish this sentence: My favorite thing about being a writer is …**
That the world of the imagination which I can enter whenever I like is totally uncluttered by the hassles, and limitations, of everyday life.

19) **Pencil versus pen – who wins and why?**
I just LOVE Faber-Castell pencils: the ones with rubbers that really work on the end are a delight to hold and are fabulous for writing!

20) **Finish this sentence: One word or phrase people will never read in my writing is …**
' … It is undoubtedly true that … .'

PS from editor Gary Grimes:
Thank you for sharing your answers, Anne. One of our favorite – or should I say favourite – 20 Qs yet. You better write a 'Bacon: The Ultimate Motivational Food' book before someone steals your idea!

From Anne Whitaker:
Thanks, Gary, pleased to hear that. Being a Leo, I love ANY praise! (Not that I set too much store by Sun sign astrology, of course.) And yes, I have always slavered to write a book about the motivational qualities of bacon. Unfortunately, Book 4, mentioned in the interview, 'Descent and Return – the dark night of the soul', must come first. Maybe I can work on being saved by a bacon sandwich in the Underworld.

My Favourite Interview Q & As

I have done quite a number of interviews over the years, in magazines and newspapers, and more recently on websites. Here are a few of my favourite interview questions and answers.

What transit always shows up for you in surprising ways?
They all do, especially the long-lasting ones. The deep challenges that force our growth lurk in the realms of the unconscious, just waiting to hitch a ride on the nearest really tough transit. For example, I didn't think that ten years of Neptune transits was going to involve an enforced descent into the Underworld for most of that period. However, the good news is that I emerged, much improved (unless you ask my husband ...).

What is your funniest transit or retrograde experience?
There are several, not all of which can be aired publicly. The one which comes immediately to mind is the occasion, in March 1985, when Saturn turned retrograde on my 28 Scorpio IC. In the middle of lunch with an old friend who at that time was a bank manager, without warning, I passed out. Just then, a friend of his, who was also a bank manager, was passing by the restaurant window. I came round and insisted on going home – very groggily, with a bank manager holding me up by each arm. Very Saturn in Scorpio, don't you think?

Would you rather be ruled by Uranus or Jupiter? Why?
What a question! Both those planets are strong in my horoscope, Uranus in the 10th house leading an Eastern bowl shape, with Jupiter in the 3rd closing the bowl, and the two in biquintile aspect. My Ascendant is also on the Jupiter-Uranus midpoint. However, if forced to choose I would go for Jupiter, provided the aspects weren't too difficult. My reasons are probably dictated by the stage I've got to in life: that disruptive, eccentric, unpredictable, stubborn individualism characteristic of a Uranus-ruled

life feels too tiring to contemplate now! Jupiter's boundless energy and optimism, ability to inspire others and be inspired by the more positive dimensions of life, and willingness to be open to a sense of meaningful connectedness to that which is greater than oneself, are especially attractive to me at this point.

What advice would you give to someone learning how to read their own chart?
One, there are dozens of ways of evading personal responsibility – resolve at the outset never to do so by blaming your horoscope or your transits for your difficulties in life.

Two, realise that objectivity is something to be aspired to, which can never be achieved by mere human beings. This being the case, try to recognise that you can be most objective and therefore most helpful by reading the horoscopes of strangers, provided you have appropriate training and supervision. When approaching your own horoscope, or those of your loved ones, you will inevitably colour the planetary picture before you with your own hopes and fears.

Three, the illuminating light which is gradually cast as your understanding of the symbols in your chart grows will be wonderfully helpful in shedding light on your gifts, pains, motivations and aspirations. But bear in mind that possessing astrological knowledge has a shadow side – for example, I have never known anyone including myself who didn't look at upcoming transits, especially of Saturn and Pluto, without a certain amount of fear. To help my astrology students with this, I point out that 99.9% of the human race from the beginning of time has managed to stagger through life without the aid of astrology! So – enjoy the fascination of deciphering the astrological map of your life. But don't get too precious about it – and be aware that this wonderful knowledge has a double edge.

anne-whitaker.com

2018

AFA interview: Jupiter, Uranus and the Purple People from Planet Zog

First of all, I am including this interview for the entirely frivolous reason that I truly love its title still. But also because of noticing recently that Jupiter will very soon be returning to the 5/6° Aquarius zodiacal power point of the 1997 Jupiter-Uranus conjunction, once again joining Uranus (at 6° Taurus this time) – in the waning square aspect of the 2010-11 conjunction in Pisces/Aries. I read on medium.com (on 18 December 2020) the headline, 'A Strange Signal is Emitting from the Milky Way' which scientists as yet cannot explain ... perhaps when this square is exact in mid-January 2021, we will find out. Or hear of some other left-field marvel!

I'm also including the interview because in the process of conducting the research I came up with some interesting affirmations of astrology's traditional claims. And finally – because I am still fascinated by the Jupiter-Uranus 14-year cycle of disruption, innovation and discovery, and think the material covered here is of continuing interest value. Now read on ...

In her new book published by the American Federation of Astrologers (April 2009), Scottish astrologer Anne Whitaker reveals the results of her extensive research project conducted during the 1997 Jupiter-Uranus conjunction in Aquarius. The book is titled *Jupiter meets Uranus – from Erotic Bathing to Star Gazing.* Her research includes mundane events and the conjunction's effects in individual lives, as she explains in this interview, first published in May 2009 by the *AFA Newsletter*. Anne also offers insights into the upcoming Jupiter-Uranus conjunctions in Pisces and Aries.

AFA: How often does a Jupiter-Uranus conjunction occur?
AW: Every 14 years. There were eight during the 20th century, with two in Aquarius – one on 4 March 1914 at 9°32' of Aquarius, and the other at 5°55' of Aquarius on 16 February 1997.

AFA: What is its essential meaning?
AW: In brief, it is a combination of energies regarded as dynamic, unusual, disruptive, expansive, unpredictable – breaking down the old order, stimulating breakthroughs to new levels of expression and understanding, individually and collectively. The Aquarian conjunction is the one most powerfully connected to radical and disruptive social, political and technological shifts, for reasons which are explored in the book.

AFA: Few astrologers are doing research, and you may be the first, at least in many years, to undertake such a massive project linking both mundane and personal astrology. Why did you decide to do this research project?
AW: It feels as if it decided to do me! Seriously though – I have long been fascinated by the link between micro and macro levels of existence. I began to practise as an astrologer under the Jupiter-Uranus conjunction in Sagittarius of 1983, around that time hearing my first ever lecture on mundane astrology given by the late Charles Harvey. He inspired an interest in exploring the links between individual and collective life via astrology. By 1996, I was excited by the prospect of doing some original exploration of a planetary combination which had been present at the birth of my own astrological career.

AFA: Describe the project.
AW: It is a research study of the Jupiter-Uranus conjunction, set in its mythological and historical context, including a very broad tracking of the pulse beat of the conjunction through the four elements from 500 BC to 2500 AD which identifies some interesting correlations with broad historical changes. It then narrows down to an exploration of mundane

and personal life during the Aquarian conjunction of 1997-98, extending to 1999-2001 when Neptune transited the 5° Aquarius 55 Hot Spot where Jupiter and Uranus met on 16 February 1997.

AFA: What mundane events occurred?
AW: Lots! The major event – just 10 days after the conjunction occurred – was the announcement to the world of the existence of Dolly the Sheep, the first ever cloned animal, created by scientists based in Scotland. Over the weekend of the conjunction, 15-16 February, the crew of the USA's shuttle Discovery effected repairs to the Hubble Space Telescope, completing five space walks to do so. Chapter five in my book tells of many more happenings.

AFA: What are some examples of recorded monumental events that have occurred during previous Jupiter-Uranus conjunctions?
AW: Let's take the theme of exploration. Explorer Ponce de León stepped ashore near Cape Canaveral (thus named by the Spanish some years later) on the morning of 3 April 1513, when there was an exact Jupiter-Uranus conjunction in Aries, to claim the New World, later to become the United States of America. Precisely 33 Jupiter-Uranus conjunctions later, on 20 July 1969, there was an exact Jupiter-Uranus conjunction in Libra when Neil Armstrong stepped onto the Moon's surface, the first human to do so. The spacecraft on which the astronauts travelled was launched from Cape Canaveral.

AFA: How many people did you track during the project? Who are they? How did you find them?
AW: Seventeen individuals took part in the first phase of the research from February 1997 to January 1998. I had a sudden inspiration, while being interviewed for a magazine in late 1995, to ask readers whose birthdays fell between 24 and 26 January of any year (when the Sun would be transiting 5-6 degrees of Aquarius) to contact me before February 1997 so that I could follow developments in their lives that year. Out of the

response came three serious volunteers to whom I added three clients and 11 of my astrology students. Six participants knew no astrology. All 17 had extraordinary years.

AFA: Was the participant feedback surprising or was it what you expected?
AW: I set out with as open a mind as I could muster, bearing in mind Liz Greene's wry comment in one of her seminars: 'If you can predict it, it isn't Uranus!' A big surprise was the male client, 'Frank' (see chapter six in my book). He depressed me by answering all the questionnaires with monosyllabic negatives, then in his summing-up provided a vivid picture of his 'amazing year'. The biggest surprise was the Jupiter-Uranus effect showing up so clearly in all their lives. I hadn't expected that.

AFA: Were you able to validate any astrological precepts such as the influence of hard and soft aspects or orbs?
AW: Yes. All participants reported disruptive, unpredictable, expansive life changes. But those with a strong natal Jupiter-Uranus signature went through more radical disruptions and breakthroughs to new levels than those whose natal Jupiter-Uranus signature was absent – or weak, i.e., minor or soft aspects, wide orbs.

AFA: What differences did you observe between contacts from retrograde and direct planets? Were the stations outstanding in any way?
AW: Yes. Just one example. Questionnaire 2: Summer/Autumn 1997 asked if the period of 13-15 October was significant; Uranus turned direct on 5° Aquarius then. Almost everyone reported left-field Uranian happenings. The most markedly Jupiter-Uranus person in the study, Lucia, led a deprived group of inner-city youngsters through a powerfully life-changing artistic event involving the spontaneous use of her astrological knowledge, 13-15 October 1997. The book also details striking collective effects involving retrograde and direct planetary motion.

AFA: Why did you continue the research beyond 1997-1998, the year that the Jupiter-Uranus conjunction was operational?
AW: From April 1999 until the end of 2001, the planet Neptune transited the observational band of 4-7° Aquarius which I had set as the boundary for observing the Jupiter-Uranus conjunction's impact. I was curious to discover whether Neptune's crossing would reactivate the Jupiter-Uranus effect that I had demonstrated in collective and personal life in the 1997-1998 part of the research. To my great surprise, given the diffuse nature of Neptune, it did. This was an affirmation of the astrological precept that powerful planetary meetings on particular degrees of the zodiac 'charge-up' those degrees thereafter with the flavour of their meeting.

AFA: Were there any striking observations regarding house rulerships?
AW: Yes. It was clear, for example, that the houses or angles ruled by Neptune, as it traversed the observational band mentioned above, were the areas of life most up for disruptive, expansive, unpredictable changes for individuals during the stated time period.

AFA: Do you see Jupiter-Uranus as positive or negative change, or does it represent something else?
AW: Without the unimaginably destructive act of creation, the Big Bang, which as far as we can surmise began our universe, we would not be here to observe our world's wonders as well as its terrors. Positive and negative energies are two sides of the same coin, wherever we look. I hope I have conveyed that unity adequately in *Jupiter Meets Uranus*.

AFA: What can we expect in general terms from the upcoming 2010 Jupiter-Uranus conjunctions in Aries and Pisces?
AW: In essence, the unexpected! And this question needs a whole article, not a few brief paragraphs. The Jupiter-Uranus conjunction in Pisces-Aries-Pisces comes into orb (10°) at the end of March 2010, and separates (10° orb) in mid-March 2011. Fasten your seat belts! The human community and probably the natural world are in for a bumpy ride.

This Jupiter-Uranus conjunction will arrive at a turbulent point: joining the last Saturn-Pluto square since its conjunction of the early 1980s and amplifying the first Uranus-Pluto square from its conjunction which dominated the 1960s: that decade of the Vietnam War and its protesters, political assassinations, women's liberation, musical revolution and the beginning of the micro-technology metamorphosis which has utterly changed our world in only a few decades.

In common with the 1997 conjunction that linked in an astonishing bowl shape with Mars, Saturn and Pluto (Jupiter Meets Uranus, p. 40), this will be no 'ordinary' Jupiter-Uranus event: Jupiter conjunct Uranus at 0° Aries will form a t-cross with Saturn at 28° Virgo and Pluto at 4° Capricorn. Mars at 1° Virgo will trine Pluto, oppose Neptune and link back to quincunx the Aries Jupiter-Uranus conjunction. The Jupiter-Uranus predilection for seeing no limits, leaping before it looks and challenging the established order expressed through the filter of the rash, angry impetuousness of Aries and locked with the harsh, power-driven determination not to budge of the Saturn-Pluto square, offers a difficult and dangerous picture in the realm of international politics, for instance. Misuse of technology by angry, militant fanatics convinced they have God on their side and that the old order must be overturned, is a picture which arises from this.

We can also await more disruption and turbulence on the economic front, but I leave further speculation on this issue to those much better qualified to comment than I! Religion is not going to diminish in impact; the Piscean backdrop to much of the conjunction will see to that. We may well see an inspirational 'messiah'-type figure emerge with challenging and disruptive effect socially and politically in the Aries phase.

[NOTE BY AW: *19 September 2010: little did I think (it being Uranus of whom we speak) that we would have an 'anti-messiah', namely that self-styled High Priest of the Militant Atheism persuasion, Richard Dawkins and his plan to arrest the Pope during 2010. And in autumn/winter of 2010: Julian Assange, anyone? The 'messiah' of uncensored openness?]*

Also suggested is fiery eruption disrupting the very fabric of Earth itself. On a more positive note, the urgency of the accelerating environmental crisis may give birth to great leaps forward in the pioneering of new technologies, e.g., for harnessing solar power and reducing environmental damage.

The challenging pattern I have described, set against the cardinal backdrop of the natural zodiac (which I used for most of the Jupiter-Uranus conjunction charts in the book) also links in with the Super Galactic Centre, currently at around 0° degrees Libra.

A picture arises from this of major scientific breakthroughs in our understanding of the universe or multiverse of which our tiny solar system is a mere blip of ephemeral matter. Perhaps the CERN Large Hadron Collider will work this time, and we shall find the Higgs Boson particle at last. Or maybe it really will blow us all to bits! There is a most interesting article bringing the CERN particle accelerator and the Super Galactic Centre together in a news story titled 'Galaxy centre may harbour super accelerator' on *CERN Courier* for 27 March 2007. Check it out!

AFA: Do you have a particular area of interest where you expect the 2010 conjunction to deliver, as it were?
AW: One of my own special interests is in genetics and cloning. The 1969 conjunction in Libra saw a Harvard medical school team identify the first gene (see p. 93 of *Jupiter Meets Uranus*). The year after the 1983 conjunction in Sagittarius, a British scientist developed genetic fingerprinting (p. 93). In 1997 with tthe Aquarian conjunction, we had the announcement of the first cloned animal, Dolly (p. 43). The conjunction in Aries in 2010 suggests the next stage which could well be human cloning, currently illegal where the creation of a complete human is concerned. Maybe a defiant, pioneering male doctor/scientist is prepared to pit himself against the established order and rule of law to do so? There are 'maverick doctor' rumblings in the press about this already.

AFA: Do you have a special wish for the human community for something uniquely helpful which could emerge from this powerful and disruptive energy field?
AW: Yes. I would love to see science fiction fantasies over many decades become fact with the arrival on planet Earth of small but fabulously evolved purple people from Planet Zog to teach us how to mend our ways. Now THAT would be unexpected!

AFA: As an astrologer, what did you learn from the project?
AW: I began to study astrology more than 25 years ago as part of my quest to try and prove to myself that we do not live in a random, meaningless universe. Time and again, on the large and small scale, astrology has offered that proof, enriching my life and I hope in some measure, the lives of my clients and students along the way. This research has affirmed very powerfully that the personal and collective lives of humankind respond in the same core way to the great music of the spheres, played throughout space and time by the planets in their cycles.

AFA: Finally, a question on YOUR horoscope. Is Jupiter-Uranus prominent?
AW: Well, how did you guess?! My chart is an Eastern bowl shape, with Uranus leading from the 10th house, biquintile Jupiter which closes the bowl from the 3rd house. My Ascendant, on the Jupiter-Uranus midpoint, was squared by transiting Pluto during the whole research period.

[PS: this research is still available at my website anne-whitaker.com, re-published as an ebook in 2014 and updated to include further research – on the 2010/11 conjunction – titled 'Tales from the Wild Ride'. No doubt, if I'm still around, I'll become re-obsessed with the next conjunction at 22° Taurus (exactly conjunct the May 2000 Jupiter-Saturn 22° Taurus conjunction power point) in 2024 – the year that Pluto moves into Aquarius. Start fastening your seat belts now … .]

Anne and Victor's astro-spar

In the spring of 2015, thanks to Facebook, I had the pleasure of 'meeting' astrologer Victor Olliver, then newly appointed Editor of *The Astrological Journal* and star sign columnist for *The Lady* magazine. As well as sharing a love of astrology (and a very black sense of humour), we have collaborated since that time on many writing projects, most notably my 'Not the Astrology Column' which Victor offered me as a challenge. On hearing that there was to be an astrology column in *Journal*, I tartly observed that, in the interests of balance, there should be a 'Not The' astrology column too. Victor being Victor, replied 'Go on, then. YOU write it!'

One of the things I like about Victor is his love of a good argument. So, I decided he was just the person with whom to raise various doubts about the merits of popular astrology. Our written debate took place over three posts on my blog (https://astrologyquestionsandanswers.com), in the first half of March 2015. It begins with my open letter to him.

4 March 2015

Dear Victor

I have always refused invitations to write popular astrology columns, feeling that to do this would be to throw my lot in with the 'entertainment wing' of astrology. Those of us who are trained and experienced astrologers know that there is a profound, ancient and some would say sacred art hidden behind this popular mask. Some of us who know this – like yourself – still manage to combine in-depth astrology practice with writing astrology for the popular press, apparently without feeling any particular discomfort at straddling both worlds.

I suppose my big problem is that the astro-dismissers are almost invariably people who have never gone into astrology in any depth, because they never get past the shallow waters of popular astrology where they find plenty of ammunition for their scorn, much of it valid when you have a look around at a lot of the astro-stuff published in the world's media.

Personally, I see off any astro-dismissers by fixing them with a keen gaze, enquiring very politely whether they have ever studied the subject in depth, and responding to their evasions (very few direct admissions of ignorance are forthcoming) by suggesting they go away to study the subject properly for a couple of years then come back to resume our conversation. As a 'serious' astrologer, I have to admit to feeling defensive when asked what I do, invariably saying that I do in-depth stuff which has very little to do with the astrology to be found in the popular press.

Is there any way round this problem? Should we all just accept that astrology of whatever shallowness or depth will simply never be taken seriously within our current materialist culture, and cheerfully get on with it, whatever kind of astrology we do? Would it be helpful if 'serious' astrologers who also do popular astrology were to admit that for many of us, the gap between the public face and the private reality of astrology and its practice is a very hard one to bridge?

What are your views on this, Victor? How do you justify occupying both worlds to yourself and others – and what do you suggest those of us do (apart from go boil our heads) who feel uncomfortable at having our commitment to serious, in-depth work ridiculed by people who have taken their stance from perusing the shallow material available in much of the popular press?

True to form, Victor responded thus: 'This feels like a bull fight and you've just flicked the red cape … .'

5 March 2015

Dear Anne

Thanks for inviting me to contribute to your wonderful site. Though I'm the editor of *The Astrological Journal*, and *The Lady* magazine's resident stargazer, I am still relatively new to professional astrology and only recently have become a lot more aware of the huge psychological gulf between serious and popular astrology. This surprises me because in all worlds there's a spectrum of expression, from public face to purist core and in between. Why not in astrology, too?

Take the fashion world, for instance. Expensive haute couture and pret-a-porter are showcased at the international collections and these in turn inspire high street looks for ordinary budgets. The cheaply produced mass market is as much a part of fashion as Anna Wintour's *Vogue*. But we don't say that the clothes in shop windows are not fashion or that these looks are embarrassing. Indeed, without the retail outlets there would be no fashion except for the super-rich.

Likewise, in another sense, in astrology. Many practitioners of serious or scholarly star-gazing disdain the popular expression, namely in media Sun sign horoscope columns; and some even doubt the validity or credibility of the solar chart. Others are shamed by the apparent crassness and simplicity of these media columns and try to ignore them.

This really is self-defeating in my view.

The actual 'enemy' of astrology is prejudice. It comes in a number of forms. Chiefly, the prejudice of many secularists and what I call science cultists can be dismissed quickly. We know who they are. They rubbish astrology yet know nothing about it. They laud science yet respond most unscientifically to something they've never studied or researched. Then there's prejudice in the world of astrology against popularisation. Some serious astrologers fear that the media Mystic Megs are letting the side down and making it easier for science debunkers to debunk.

But here's the truth: debunkers/doubters/science cultists are not interested in whether your astrology has been assayed by the laboratory's finest geeks or simply dreamt up by fake stargazers. No matter how learned the astrological study and compelling the results, nothing will sway the know-all who's certificated with a science professorship. They believe astrology is rubbish. So, in their case, media Sun sign horoscopes is a non-issue – it's just the thin end of the fraudulent wedge. We need not concern ourselves with determined nay-sayers. We waste our time trying to play up to them.

Nonetheless, I fully support those astrologers who bring academic rigour to the subject and seek to find mainstream respectability – not because I think a professional debunker can be turned, but for the sake of a better appreciation of astrology. Science itself will in time gradually move towards a greater understanding of the nature of the cosmos, possibly through quantum mechanics – you've written about this yourself – and the time will come when the intellectual climate for astrology will be a lot more receptive than it presently is.

Now, what about Sun sign astrology. Is it valid? That's the real question. Let me quote the brilliant late astrologer Dennis Elwell who was known to be highly critical of 'trivialising' media horoscopes. This is what he actually wrote in a 1975 essay titled 'Is There A Solar Chart?': 'I do believe in the basic validity of solar chart transits but that is not to say that they can be relied upon to produce readings every day, week or month, depending on how often a particular journal happens to be published, or that they are always interpreted correctly.'

Elwell was quite idealistic in his expectation of constant reliability and perhaps forgot McLuhan's well-known dictum: 'The medium is the message'. In other words, a mass market entertainment magazine is not likely to play host to a discursive, learned, nuanced forecast from the house astrologer. Newspapers and magazines usually seek snappy one-liners that can be digested at a glance. The 'house style' is what matters and the astrologer must seek to fill the allotted space as well as she or he can.

A great many media astrologers these days are actually trained astrologers, such as myself. The 'simplistic' solar chart, with the relevant Sun sign cusp, placed at what in a natal chart is the Ascendant point, is all about transit ingresses and aspects. To state the obvious: if we accept that a transits-to-birth chart speaks to us, then transits-to-transits have something to say also – an idea that's no problem to, say, electional astrologers. The challenge is less the solar astrology and more what is selected for the column and how it is written up.

My approach to the solar chart, interpretively, is more-or-less the same as to a natal chart. My professional media grail is to find a form of words that is both entertaining and true to the spirit of the moment for each sign. It was Elwell who wrote so beautifully (in his book *Cosmic Loom*) of how an aspect can find concurrent expression in a multiplicity of ways in life and events, from the ridiculous to the sublime. We'd be wise to keep our minds open to this feature of astrology which even now we do not properly comprehend.

Astrology is a flexible thing: it communicates its wisdom no matter the house system, national culture, computer program, dubious birth detail or oblivious opposition.

Anne, to answer your question: there's nothing to justify. If one's mindset is dead against popular expression, then avoid reading the Jonathan Cainers. Avert your gaze. If you fear that Sun sign astrology is polluted by the Shelley von Strunckels, then here's a comforting thought: in the minds of science cultists, astrology is already polluted. It's dead! And if certain persons judge astrology by their cursory reading of Mystic Meg, you can rest confident that they probably skate over a lot of life's other treasures of the spirit. Perhaps their preference of depth is cricket or crochet.

Contrary to what many scholar-astrologers think, media horoscopes are the main bridge to the public, just as a short chic affordable jacket in Marks & Sparks may resonate with fans of high-end Chanel. We should be grateful for the enduring need for 'irrational' advice from our nation's stargazers. As Nick Campion has averred, the Sun sign column – for a great many people – offers the only one moment in the day when time is taken to consider the general shape of the life (or

Life) or to question the point of doing something. In a materialistic world, this is a form of spiritual awareness, albeit rudimentary in many instances. But don't knock it.

And, Anne, next time you're offered a Sun sign column, take it. And aim to turn a sow's ear into a silk purse. The experience may prove both humbling (in the challenge to bring high minds down to earth) and rewarding (as in, er, bank balance).

16 March 2015

Anne's reply:

We live in a vast energy field of constant movement, most of which is totally invisible to mere humans with their limited perceptual apparatus. The rippling patterns of order and chaos, that fundamental dance, govern everything. I have come to see the art of astrology (helped by what I am able to grasp of what the quantum world has revealed to us) as one which enables us to map those patterns as they are viewed from Earth via the constant shifting energies of the planets in their orbits.

Then astrologers take the step which in our reductionist, materialist culture pulls down all sorts of opprobrium and scorn upon our heads. We attribute meaning to those patterns. From ancient times, right up until the scientific revolution of the 17th century, which caused a major split between form described by astronomy and content described by astrology, the maxim 'As above, so below' governed people's worldview. We lived then in a cosmos charged with meaning, where form and content reflected and informed each other.

Some of us still live in that cosmos. Others do not. Where there is such a powerful clash of world views, the result is polarisation and prejudice. I think that you are right, Victor, in your eloquent and well-argued response to my doubts and questions about popular astrology, to point out that the real enemy of astrology is indeed prejudice.

Prejudice from without the astrological community, from those who believe that our lives are the product of cosmic chance, thereby devoid of meaning. Prejudice from those within the community who consider themselves to be 'serious' practitioners, towards the populist, mass-market astrology which millions avidly consume across a vast range of media on a daily basis, looking for some glimmer of meaning in life.

What do we do about this? In reflecting on how I might 'wrap up' our debate, which has generated a very great deal of interest (traffic to this site quadrupled in the few days that our posts were most active!) across the Web, the word 'occult' came strongly to mind. So, I pondered on it for a few days. According to the *Shorter Oxford English Dictionary*, the original meaning of the word is from the Latin 'occulere' i.e., 'to hide, conceal'. It also (in a more physical sense) means 'to cut off from view by interposing some other body', as in, for example, the occultation of one planet or heavenly body by another.

The word 'occult' in recent times has taken on a more sinister connotation, referring more to magical or supernatural practices. But I became more and more interested, on reflection, in the original meaning of the word. It has led me to a conclusion about the status of astrology, especially in our modern world.

This is it: the true depth of what astrology can reveal about human affairs, both in the collective and the personal sense, will always be inaccessible to the large majority of people. Astrology is an occult subject. As such, its influence and its great value is likely to remain masked, hidden from view, operating powerfully but behind the scenes of everyday life.

For example, in very ancient times its practice was held in high esteem e.g., by Babylonian or Egyptian rulers whose astrologer-priests scanned the stars and advised the kings (and sometimes, even, the queens!) of the fate of their nations. There were no personal horoscopes then. The general public were in no way consulted or informed regarding decisions made which affected all their lives. Astrological knowledge, deemed sacred, was deliberately kept hidden from 'ordinary' view.

In our time, mass-market popular astrology – paradoxically – could be seen as fulfilling the function of concealing the real power of astrology pretty effectively. Most of the public remain unaware of the depth which exists behind the mask of the Sun sign columns – although I do agree with you that there is a very big difference between the glimmer of truth which a quality Sun sign column can reveal and the kind of trashy stuff which any old tea lady could dash off. (I have been a tea lady in my day, so please, no offence given or to be taken!)

Sun sign columns are also rather effective in raising the ire and spleen of reductionists who thereby are permanently deflected from benefiting from astrology's true depth, which at times could have been life-saving, as evinced in a powerful example of astrologer Dennis Elwell's prescient warning in the 1980s. Elwell, the late well-known and respected UK astrologer mentioned in your reply, was revealed as having written in 1987 to the main shipping lines to warn them that a pattern, very similar to that under which the Titanic had sunk, was coming up in the heavens very soon. He strongly suggested that they review the seaworthiness and safety procedures of all their passenger ships. His warning was duly dismissed. Not long afterwards, the Herald of Free Enterprise ferry boat went down, with the loss of 188 lives.

It is true, as you point out, that mass market astrology is the stepping-stone which enables people who seek deeper meaning than Sun-sign columns can provide, from relative triviality to much greater depth. If someone wants to understand the profound link which exists between their small personal existence and the larger, meaningful cosmos which their unique chip of energy has entered in order to make its contribution, then they need actively to seek out a good astrologer to offer a sensitive and revealing portrait of their moment of birth via an accurate horoscope reading. Those of us who are in-depth practitioners know that a quality astrology reading with the right astrologer at the right time can be truly life-changing.

However, only a small percentage of people who read Sun sign columns take that step into deeper territory. Most do not. Either they are quite happy – or put off – by the superficiality they find there, or they spin off into active, enraged prejudice and sometimes very public condemnation of our great art.

My pondering on the word 'occult' therefore, has led me to quite a peaceful place, Victor – I am sure you will be very pleased for me! I can now stop being annoyed with my colleagues who are Sun sign astrologers: they are offering a valuable service in providing a smoke screen. This helps greatly to maintain astrology in its true place as an 'occult' activity, leavening the lumpen ignorance and crassness of our materialist, consumer age – from behind the scenes.

Astrodienst

2020

The Astrological Journal

November/December 2019

Lunar Stuff:
'do not swear by the moon, for she changes constantly'

There is already the Cycles section in this book as well as a separate section featuring the new 33/38-year Saturn-Pluto cycle which began in January 2020 and is in its opening stages as I write. However, since the familiar 29-day Sun-Moon cycle is a template for all cycles, I thought it should have at the very least its own section. Here, I reflect on the Virgo-Pisces, Leo-Aquarius and Cancer-Capricorn 18/19-year nodal cycles with their accompanying solar and lunar eclipses, illustrating them with some vivid and poignant personal and collective tales from my own and my family's history. And, of course, I had to include a piece on Moondark – that most mysterious, least understood final stage of the soli/lunar cycle.

The power of eclipses – and a personal tale

The Virgo-Pisces eclipse season began in mid-September 2015 with a partial solar eclipse at 20° Virgo. It concludes at the end of February 2017, including four attendant lunar eclipses, with the last of four solar eclipses taking place at 8° Pisces. The second solar eclipse of this season, a total solar eclipse at 19° Pisces, takes place next week on 9 March 2016.

Excitement is already mounting since eclipses tend to produce 'power surges', and crises of various kinds in our collective life. For example, in the preceding week we had two major threats building up: North Korea threatening a pre-emptive nuclear strike in response to provocation of an unspecified nature; and the threat in the USA of Donald Trump sweeping his way to success in the battle to be the Republican Party's nominee to fight the USA Presidential Election in November 2016.

And what of their impact on our personal lives? How does that work? What should we expect from the September 2015-February 2017 season of eclipses?

Research revelations

My major objective in conducting research for my book *The Moon's Nodes in Action* was to put actual flesh on the bones of all the theoretical stuff I had been reading about the Moon's nodes and eclipses over a period of many years. I wanted to find out whether the theory stood up in practice, arriving at my research conclusions via detailed study of six people's lives.

Three of the participants were 'ordinary' citizens: Marc, Andrew and Anna; and three were famous: Mary Shelley in relation to her authorship of *Frankenstein* on her first nodal return; Princess Diana of the UK and her untimely death on her second nodal return; and astronaut John Glenn's return to space, in his seventies, two whole nodal returns after his first space trip. Honouring the Sun-Moon link I chose three women and three men. Viewed from planet Earth at solar eclipse times, the Sun and Moon are of equal size and complementary symbolic significance.

Drawing together all the research threads by way of conclusion, I had this to say about eclipses in my book:

> 'I'm quite clear now, as the nodal axis regresses through the chart, identifying via the highlighted houses the overall territory up for change, that the transiting eclipses function as 'battery chargers', gradually building up the energies of the person's life in preparation to receive major change. An image comes to mind here from the female menstrual cycle, of the egg gradually being primed and prepared until it is at its maximum point of readiness to receive the male sperm, conceive and begin new life. I think the eclipses begin their work of charging-up as soon as the relevant eclipse season begins, which may be as long as eighteen months before the turning point in the person's life appears.'

THE METONIC CYCLE AND A PERSONAL TALE

One of the many fascinations of the study of eclipses is the fact of their return cycle every 19 years. The so-called Metonic cycle of 19-year intervals consists of an eclipse in approximately the same degree of the zodiac on the same date 19 years later. Interestingly, I am writing this article during the Virgo-Pisces eclipse season 19 years after events described in the following account!

This personal tale took place during the Virgo-Pisces eclipse season of spring 1997-autumn 1998, during the second and third years of my commuting by plane from Glasgow to London from 1995-8 to complete studies with Liz Greene and the late Charles Harvey at the Centre for Psychological Astrology (CPA). Hence my nickname 'the flying Scot'.

In spring 1997 I decided to hire an office away from home to create peace and space, mainly to write my CPA diploma thesis. I had decided by then that my research topic was to be the Moon's nodes in action. Having the North Node exactly conjunct my MC had led to fascination with this striking link early on in my astrological studies. In my natal horoscope, the Ascendant-Descendant axis is 9° Virgo-Pisces. Urania, the asteroid of astrology, is at 19° Virgo in the 1st house.

The Virgo-Pisces eclipse season started on 9 March 1997 with a total solar eclipse at 18°.5 Pisces, opposite Urania, closely linking in Mary Shelley's and Marc's North Nodes at 19° and 21° Gemini, respectively. It was at this time that I chose Marc as a main case study subject along with Mary Shelley.

On Friday, 7 March 1997, I saw an office which I decided on 10 March to rent, paying for it for a year from an insurance policy I had taken out 18 years previously. At that time, I had a feeling I might need money for a future adventure of some kind – long before I knew anything about either astrology or the 18.6 year nodal cycle. My bank manager, of course, thought that I was mad.

The middle period of that eclipse season saw me well settled into the thesis writing as the 9° Virgo eclipse fell exactly on my Ascendant in the autumn of 1997. The following year, the day before the total solar eclipse (7°55' Pisces) of 26 February 1998 fell on the 6th-house side of my Descendant, I had a call from my landlords saying that they needed to know by the next day whether I was going to renew my lease which ran out on 9 May 1998 – since the building was being sold. I decided to renew for six months and sent my rent cheque off just before the lunar eclipse on 13 March 1998 at 22° Virgo.

The lease ran out on 7 November 1998: the day I graduated with my diploma from the Centre for Psychological Astrology!

General points to observe

So – although individual eclipses are important, my research and subsequent astrology practice as well as personal observation has demonstrated to me that one should take note of the whole eclipse season of 18 months. Applying this principle to whichever pair of houses the Moon's nodes and eclipses (solar and lunar) are moving through by retrograde motion, one should also take careful note of those planets/angles/asteroids (if used) which are being triggered.

It is also very valuable, in gaining perspective, to go back to the previous eclipse season 18/19 years previously to reflect on the changes brought then and how they may connect to what is coming up this time around.

The more planets, especially Saturn, Uranus, Neptune and Pluto – and very especially Pluto, I have found – are involved in the eclipse dance, the more life-changing are the outcomes likely to be. As Alexander Ruperti wisely observed in his wonderful *Cycles of Becoming*:

> *'Eclipses simply measure intense confrontations with all those things in human nature which hinder spiritual progress by keeping one in a rut, albeit a comfortable and happy rut. They are opportunities to use the past and the present – all that one has previously acquired, as well as where he stands at a given moment – in order to build a more creative future. Since they always challenge an individual to discard all limiting influences and to start something new, they may be stressful times.'*

anne-whitaker.com

Solar eclipse in Cancer: the old order changes

The only certainty in life is change. Jupiter this week in the year 2018 turned direct in Scorpio and is soon to surface from those murky depths, entering his fiery, adventurous home sign of Sagittarius early in November 2018, just two days after the North Node enters Cancer, thereby ending the nodes' 18 months sojourn in Leo-Aquarius.

Therefore, this first eclipse of the Cancer-Capricorn polarity is an early herald of changing planetary weather as this especially turbulent year begins to wind down from the midsummer peak. The Internet is full of opinion and prediction regarding this Cancer solar eclipse.

However, in my usual contrarian style, I feel it's time to look back a little at the Leo-Aquarius nodal journey and an interesting personal tale – told earlier this year – which illustrates its core meaning very vividly:

Unless you live in a cave far, far away – with no WiFi – you will have noticed that Jupiter is still in Scorpio with the Moon's nodes travelling retrograde through Leo (North Node) and Aquarius (South Node). It's time for a story weaving all those symbolic energies together. Are you sitting comfortably? Then I'll begin …

A recent fascinating conversation with a friend about individuality, lineage and tribe – apt for Leo-Aquarius – evoked a long-buried memory. Many years ago, I took my good friend Emma (not her real name), then recovering from a serious illness, for a restful holiday to the Hebridean island of my birth. Transport links were poor, we were young and adventurous; hitchhiking to the remote places and beautiful beaches that I wanted to show her seemed the best option.

'What you need to remember,' I said to her solemnly as we set out for one of the wild outlying areas on the Atlantic coast where my Macleod ancestors had lived, 'is that I have been away for such a long time that I don't really know anyone in those parts anymore.'

We were soon offered a lift from a man aged around 60 – a total stranger. As we drove through increasingly wild, starkly beautiful countryside towards our destination, after chatting amicably about this and that, he looked quizzically at me and said, head to one side: 'You wouldn't be any relation of Calum Curlach (Calum of the curly hair) I suppose?'

Startled, I replied: 'Yes. He was my grandfather.'

Later that day, with rain pouring down and us getting soaked, whilst trudging past some houses on a hillside overlooking a stunning beach wreathed in sea mist, I said to Emma: 'I'm fed up of this – a cup of tea would be a good idea. Come on, I'm going to knock on the first door to ask if we can come in for shelter till the rain goes off.'

'You can't do that to complete strangers!' she said.

'Watch me,' was my reply. She had never experienced the tradition of Celtic hospitality in which I had been raised.

Five minutes later, we were warming ourselves by a peat fire whilst the lady of the house fussed around, making tea and sandwiches. After a few pleasantries had been exchanged, she asked me what I recalled as a very traditional Hebridean question: 'Who are your people?'

On finding out that I was Calum Curlach's granddaughter, she added scones and cream to the sandwiches. We spent the next hour eating, drinking tea and hearing stories about my distant relatives which I had never heard before. Emma sat there listening in open-mouthed amazement.

Heading back to town some hours later, on one of the very infrequent local buses, she remarked with a grin: 'You lied to me! I thought you didn't know anyone here anymore?'

'Well, I don't, in any personal sense,' was my reply. 'I was known today by lineage and by tribe, not for who it is I actually am.'

I added that I did not know whether to be comforted or disconcerted by what had occurred.

Many years later, as an astrologer reflecting on the above events – whose memory was evoked by that recent conversation with the friend who had been recognised in a similar way herself – a realisation dawned. In that strange engagement between my individualistic urban self and the Celtic community into which I had been born and raised, I had encountered the Leo-Aquarius polarity in a very striking form.

Leos – I have the Sun and several planets in Leo, in the 12th house – need above all things to be recognised and affirmed for their unique individuality. Aquarians, on the other hand, are quite comfortable with an identity shared with whatever tribe they consider they belong to.

I find it quite fascinating that our conversation should have occurred during the present Leo-Aquarius nodal/eclipse season; also, I am writing this column just after the much-hyped Super Moon lunar eclipse on 31 January – which triggered natal Pluto in Leo, ruler of my 29° Scorpio IC/South Node.

Furthermore, checking back in the ephemeris, I found that in the summer in which the experience described had occurred, the North Node was transiting my Scorpio/South Node IC. As a further thread in the weave of lineage, I had discovered some years ago that Grandfather Calum Curlach's progressed IC was at 29° Scorpio in the year I was born.

Natal Jupiter is in my 3rd house in Scorpio right now. I am currently at the end of one 12-year Jupiter cycle, awaiting the challenging new possibilities for learning and development which the new one will bring, as it will to all of us Jupiter in Scorpio folk.

In keeping with this, I had been thinking a great deal before that conversation about my grandfathers, wonderful old men, who both died during my first Jupiter return. I was then approaching twelve years of age. Their passing opened me out to an understanding of some deep truths: all human life is finite; love and loss are but two sides of the same coin.

There is a story, too, about my other grandfather. This involves his Victorian rose gold watch chain, and my choice to have it melted down and made into golden crescent earrings and a ring – which I collected just two weeks ago, several Jupiter returns after he died, during this Leo-Aquarius Nodal season.

But that tale is for another day.

The Astrological Journal
July/August 2017

Stopping smoking/solar eclipses

The writer Ernest Hemingway once memorably observed that all writers need a built-in, shockproof crap detector. Those of us who inhabit the Otherworlds of palmistry, I Ching, tarot, astrology, politics (!) etc., also need one of these in my opinion. An opening gambit of mine during the years of teaching astrology to beginners in classes was usually this: 'Don't necessarily believe a word I say, exciting, interesting and persuasive though it might sound. Always test it out in your own experience.'

This has always been, and remains my attitude, probably explaining why I have done so much astrological research. I've never taken the word of authority of any kind on trust. Now – what on earth is the relevance of the above to this week's topic?

Scroll back thirty years with me. It is 29 March 1987, London, UK, just before lunch: the final day of a weekend workshop on esoteric astrology led by astrologer Alan Oken. I am feeling tired, suffering from information overload, not very receptive to anymore new input, much less a new experience. Unbeknownst to me, however, I am poised to have one.

Alan informs us that there is about to be a solar eclipse at 8°18' Aries. I've not paid much attention to eclipses yet (that was certainly to change as the years went on!) and am not hugely interested. Nevertheless, it dimly registers that the eclipse opposes my 8°53' Libra natal 2nd-house Neptune which is closely sextile natal Mercury at 9°03' Leo in the 12th.

He then invites us, having briefly outlined the significance of eclipses, to focus on something in our lives we wish to leave behind – as he leads us through a meditation at the exact time of the eclipse. I have never been keen on guided meditations and am not at all visually oriented where imagining things is concerned. However, it seems churlish not to join in. I duly adopt an appropriate posture: closing my eyes, beginning to breathe slowly and deeply as instructed.

What did I want to leave behind? Smoking, that's what. I'd been trying and failing on that one for about ten years. As Alan talked us through, I focused on dropping my last fag packet into a bin – forever. The ethereal sceptic permanently resident on my left shoulder – my pet crap detector – was taking the view that I'd tried everything else, so why not?

To my amazement, as I participated with the group, waves of colour began to appear – a wash of sea greens and purples, almost like the Northern Lights – behind my closed eyes. The waves peaked with Alan's voice, then died away as he gently led us out of the meditation.

I was astounded by this experience, awed – and chastened. Something powerful had clearly occurred, despite my scepticism. As we all filed out for lunch, I had a strong urge to take my cigarettes and drop them in the nearest bin. So, I did. 'Goodbye, smoking' was my thought. 'I'm done with you!'

Half-past two the following morning saw me, sleepless, twitchy and angry, slipping out of my in-laws' flat into rainy North London. Heading for an all-night grocers, I bought 20 cigarettes, smoking the first one on my way back. My only company for that weekend was Tadzio, my brother-in-law's ferociously unwelcoming old cat. 'Well, Tadzio,' I remarked bitterly to him as he hissed at me on my return. 'Don't ever bother meditating on an eclipse.'

However, dissatisfaction at my inability to break that smoking habit continued to gnaw at me, especially since my husband, an even more dedicated smoker than I, had managed to stop that February, aided by a severe bout of mumps which (fortunately) only affected his throat. He could barely eat or speak for several days – and could not bear to smoke. (Chiron just happened to be sitting on his MC at the time … inconvenient benefic, indeed!)

On my return from London, I could see that he was struggling. Suddenly I had a bright idea. 'How about this,' I said. 'If you can stay off the fags until the Easter weekend, I'll stop then too.'

'Right,' he said through gritted teeth.

Two weeks after that 'failed' meditation, three days before the Easter weekend, I had a lightbulb moment (lunar eclipse, anyone?). A Leo one, shot with my usual leonine melodrama: 'I'm going to die as a smoker on Good Friday.' I announced to my rather sceptical Aquarian husband. 'And be reborn as a non-smoker by Easter Monday.'

And so, Reader, it duly came to pass. I have not smoked since.

The Astrological Journal
July/August 2017

Do you do Moondark? Maybe you should

That fine, poetic astrological writer Dana Gerhardt has this to say: 'As the final phase in the lunation cycle, the Balsamic Moon is the monthly 'sleep time'. During the three to four days of this phase, vitality and spirit are replenished, fueling your start at the next New Moon ... *if you could observe just one Moon phase per cycle, this should be the one*' (my emphasis).

Our increasingly frenetic 24/7 culture, revved up in recent years as it has been by the arrival and increasing dominance of social media, does not encourage us to build a few days of rest and recovery into each month. Can you imagine the average boss's reaction to the statement, 'I'm having retreat time now. It's Moondark. Bye!' And yet: we all know what happens if we run ourselves too hard without adequate rest, for too long. For some of us – and I speak from hard personal experience here, folks – the price can be very high.

So – what is this Balsamic lunar phase, and what is Moondark? Why should we pay it attention? There are eight key phases in the monthly lunar cycle flowing from the New to the Balsamic Moon.

The Balsamic lunar phase begins with the waning Sun-Moon semi-square. The Moon is a slim Crescent, forty-five degrees behind the Sun – that beautiful, fragile, slender Waning Crescent Moon which we may see each month if the skies are clear. Then it disappears. We are in Moondark now, the latter part of the Balsamic phase, the last couple of days of the dying energy of the previous month's Cancer New Moon.

My aim in this short post is to give you a flavour of three key facets pertaining to the Balsamic phase and Moondark in particular. Hopefully that will stimulate you enough to do your own reflection/ research. Those facets are: the Balsamic phase of each monthly lunar cycle throughout the year; those people born on the Balsamic Moon; and the 30-year progressed Sun-Moon cycle where the final, Balsamic phase lasts 3-4 years.

THE MONTHLY CYCLE – BALSAMIC PHASE

Having been born in the Balsamic phase, in Moondark just before a Leo New Moon, I have long been aware of the few days before any New Moon as a special time, a contemplative time: a time to take stock both collectively and personally. Those of us who wish and need to retreat regularly to preserve our balance and well-being tend to be regarded as odd by mainstream society, where 'time out' is increasingly hard to find and is not supported by the culture as a whole.

But humans have always benefited from times of quiet contemplation, in whatever way suits them best: listening to music, doing yoga/meditation, praying to whatever Higher Power sustains them, making or contemplating art, walking in nature – especially by the sea, that great universal symbol of dissolution and emergence.

Even half an hour a day of retreat time on a regular basis is nourishing for the spirit. In ancient times, women used to retreat together monthly during menstruation time which was seen as a period of potency and hidden power – a liminal time to link through dreams and ritual to worlds unseen.

It would be good if individually we could get into the habit of using the Balsamic moon time to find some retreat space in whatever way suited us. I certainly find myself feeling more 'scratchy' and irritable than usual during Balsamic times, if life demands that I put myself under more pressure than my spirit wants or needs. It would be interesting to know if other folk feel like this too, at the end of the lunar cycle, before New Moon energy comes in and takes form.

BORN ON THE BALSAMIC MOON

I have found both from my own life and the lives of clients and students with whom I have worked over the years that being born in the Balsamic Moon phase, and especially during Moondark – the very end of the old cycle – brings with it a contemplative nature, an 'inner' orientation, a need to give oneself more space and retreat than most people seem to need. Whilst doing some reading around this topic today, I found this quote which certainly spoke to me, and which may speak to some of you who were born in the Balsamic phase:

> 'This time is essentially one of transition, a chance to contemplate what has passed, tie up loose ends, journey inwards, and prepare for new beginnings ahead. You have inherited the meditative and introspective characteristics of this phase and yours is a dreamy, contemplative personality. Intuitive and far-sighted, you have innate wisdom and a mystical understanding of the workings of Mother Nature and of the human condition. For you, activity is spiritual and intellectual rather than physical. Your experiences involve endings and passings, so you are likely to live through many changes. Later life, rather than the earlier years, holds the key to your happiness and success.'
>
> – My thanks to TransAngeles.blogspot.co.uk for this sensitive and perceptive comment!

THE 30-YEAR PROGRESSED SUN-MOON CYCLE

I use this cycle as a very helpful guide to the stage of clients' life phases at the time of consultation. When a cycle is coming to an end, when the 3- or 4-year Balsamic period of life is upon us, then the wisest course to take is that of stepping back, turning inwards, taking stock and waiting – until the progressed New Moon arrives and with it the gradual taking shape of a new life phase. Just as farmers do not plant new crops in winter, so we are wise not to begin a new project during the Balsamic Moon phase or its end phase, Moondark. Here is Dana Gerhardt again with her words of wisdom:

> '"When will it end?" is everybody's first question on learning they've entered a progressed Balsamic phase. No matter how colourfully I paint its virtues, they peer beyond to a bleaker landscape, to a three-to-four-year sentence of all loss and no

gain. I can see it in their eyes ... I tell them this is the richest spiritual time. I tell them when my own progressed Balsamic phase was over, I had nostalgia for it. I cheer: "You will too!" But it's a tough sell.'

I would certainly endorse this from my own experience of beginning a new journey when I was approaching the end of a whole 30-year cycle. The result was a long period of enforced retreat until the progressed New Moon told me it was time to emerge and begin again. It was an enriching and deepening time. But very tough whilst it was happening. I should have taken astrology's advice, not that of my own ego!

There is a great deal more to be said about this fascinating and important life phase which lies behind the New Moon. I do hope this short post piques your interest sufficiently to devote more attention to it in future.

anne-whitaker.com

Sea tragedy at Moondark: the Iolaire disaster of 1919

It was Moondark, just before a Capricorn New Moon on New Year's morning 1919. HMY Iolaire, an overcrowded naval yacht, under-equipped with lifesaving equipment, had set sail from the Scottish West Highland seaport of Kyle of Lochalsh on 31 December 1918, carrying 283 war-weary sailors.

As they approached the town of Stornoway on Lewis – where their families were waiting on the pier – the Iolaire struck the rocks known as the Beasts of Holm. Stormy weather made it almost impossible to reach the shore only fifty yards away. Two-hundred and one of those on board died: literally within sight of home. There were 82 survivors. Around one-third of the bodies of those who perished were never recovered. Apart from the loss of the Titanic in 1912, this disaster represents the second greatest loss of life at sea in the UK during peacetime.

So devastating was the impact of this tragedy that once the dead had been buried, a great silence of profound grief descended on Lewis. It was too hard to talk about. It took forty years for the public silence to be broken and for a memorial to be erected.

Having grown up on the island of Lewis, I was aware of this terrible tragedy from a very young age. The most telling detail I can recall, from my mother's accounts of what she had heard from her parents' generation, was this: the local undertaker at the time was my late grandfather's best friend. Following the harrowing circumstances with which he had to deal in January 1919, he had a nervous breakdown.

I had known for some time that there would be many moving ways in which those terrible events of New Year's Day 1919 would be commemorated at the centenary. If any form of redemption was possible, then the generations arising – and especially those relatives whose lives had been marked directly or indirectly down the subsequent years – would enable it through their public events, their poetry, their music, their art. I became very conscious of the momentum towards commemoration building during a recent visit to Lewis in September 2018 and was moved by what I saw.

However, I was unprepared for how deeply folk memory would affect me personally as 2018 drew to a close. By New Year's Eve, I was feeling very emotional, almost tearful, despite our family's festive season having been relaxing and peaceful. My spirits were invaded by a darkness and melancholy that I simply could not shake off.

With five 12th-house planets, I have always been mediumistic, although it has taken me a very long time to face and make peace with this facet of my makeup. I recognised that what I was feeling was only partly personal. Then on New Year's Day, reading some online material about the Iolaire disaster, I came across the precise time at which the ship had struck the rocks: 1:55 a.m.: I put up the chart [overleaf]: stunning details struck me immediately.

The Midheaven (MC) of this event – namely, its direction – is in the sign of Cancer, described in another of my posts as 'centring on the relationship with home and family, the pursuit of emotional security and a sense of belonging.' With poignant aptness, Vesta, the asteroid of home and hearth, is exactly conjunct the Cancer MC. However, both MC and Vesta are in the very last minutes of Cancer. It is nearly the end of the matter. The IC (point of home, roots, origins) is in the opposite sign of Capricorn, a facet of which is 'facing the pain of inevitable times of separation and loss.'

These men perished within sight of home. As the chart so tellingly points out, they never quite got there. As the minutes ticked by on that devastating night, Neptune, god of the sea, reached the MC of this horoscope, gradually claiming most of the lives of those on board by drowning. The next planet to come to the MC was Saturn, ruler of the IC. Grim Reaper Saturn's message at its bleakest.

(There are other significant pointers to what happened appearing in this horoscope's symbolism. I have presented only those which struck me most forcefully.)

In view of the nodal axis' having shifted into Cancer-Capricorn in

Iolaire Disaster chart

1 Jan 1919, Wed
01:55 GMT +0:00
Stornoway
58°N12' 006°W23'
Geocentric
Tropical
Placidus
True Node

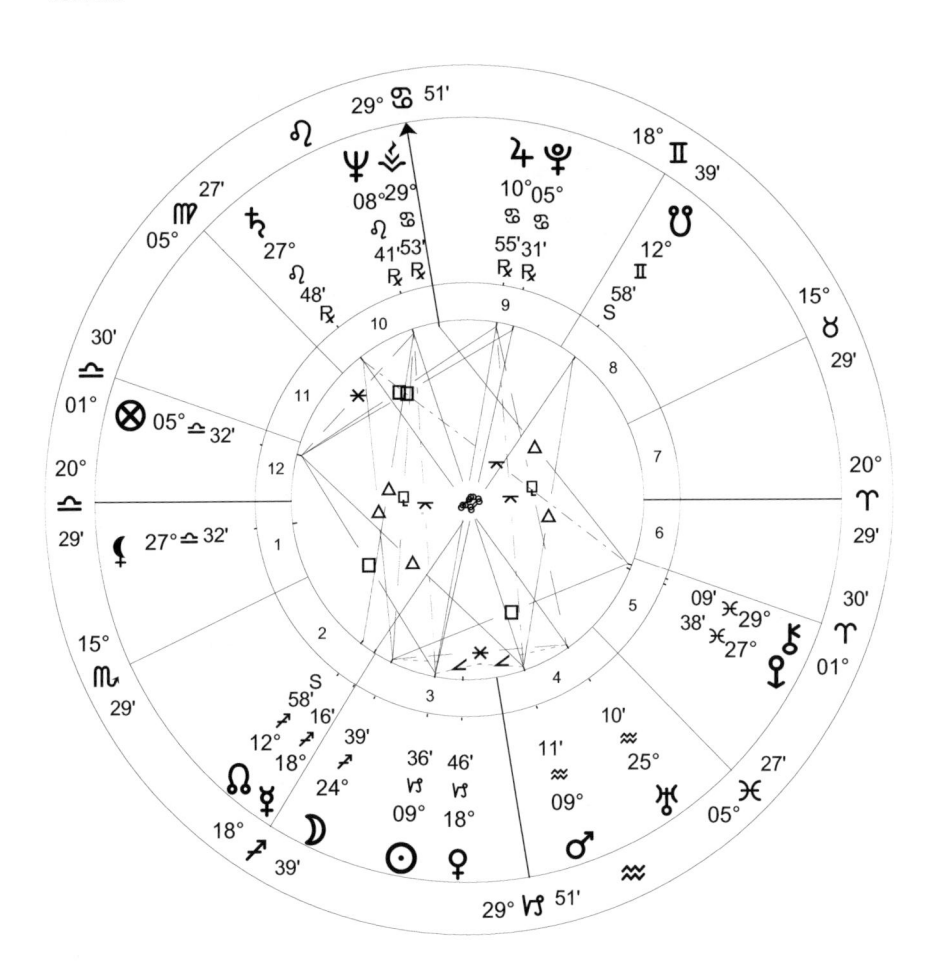

November 2018, it's most apt that the commemorations have been taking place with the transiting nodes crossing the MC/IC axis of the Iolaire disaster's horoscope.

Two weeks before the tragedy occurred on 1 January 1919, there was a 9th-house lunar eclipse at 25° Gemini, opposite the horoscope's 3rd-house Moon at 25° Sagittarius, emphasising the theme of travelling both far and near. The Ascendant of the Iolaire disaster's horoscope, progressed to New Year's Day 2019, is exactly conjunct the chart's natal Moon (MC ruler) and opposite that fateful eclipse degree.

The 2019 commemorations took place just before the eclipsed New Moon in Capricorn, approaching Moondark, with transiting Saturn conjunct the Sun of the disaster's horoscope, emphasising the solemnity and also the respectful nature of those events.

Chiron in the chart is at 29° Pisces closely conjunct Eris, goddess of strife, at 27° Pisces. The commemorations are occurring exactly two 50-year Chiron returns from the tragedy, Chiron currently being at 28° Pisces. Perhaps that indicates the healing which will hopefully arise in time from the creativity, dignity and eloquence with which the people of the Western Isles, and Lewis especially, have marked the most devastating tragedy ever to strike their shores. One can but hope so.

The Astrological Journal
January/February 2019

My Mary Shelley obsession:
it has never gone away

I seem to have been mildly but persistently obsessed by Mary Shelley – especially in relation to her authorship of Frankenstein *– ever since first setting eyes on her horoscope in the early 1990s. She and* Frankenstein *featured in both my original qualitative research studies,* The Moon's Nodes in Action *and* Jupiter Meets Uranus: from Erotic Bathing to Star Gazing, *which I wrote and completed between 1997 and 2001. Both these studies have been published in print (*Jupiter Meets Uranus, *AFA, 2009) and as e-books and are still available as e-books from my website anne-whitaker.com where they have continued to be purchased and read.*

Mary, Dolly and Andi – O Brave New World? *was published by* The Mountain Astrologer *magazine in 2001 at the time of the waxing Saturn-Uranus square in Taurus-Aquarius. By an interesting 'coincidence' it is surfacing again in this volume under the waning Saturn-Uranus square, this time in Aquarius-Taurus. It has the unique distinction of containing the first ever synastry between a human (Mary) and a dead sheep (Dolly).*

Dreaming Frankenstein: the Creation of a Modern Myth *was published by* The Mountain Astrologer *magazine in 2016 to commemorate the 200th anniversary of the conception of* Frankenstein; or, The Modern Prometheus *(published 1 January 1818) and features my analysis of Mary Shelley's totally fascinating horoscope.*

And yet again: my most recent piece in The Mountain Astrologer *(December 2020/January 2021 issue),* Waning and Waxing Crescents: Windows to the Future/The Jupiter-Saturn Cycles, *features a fascinating comparison between Mary Shelley's horoscope and that of Greta Thunberg. Because it addresses the future, I have put this essay at the back of this book in 'PS'.*

And last but not least – I had fun in the winter of 2020 introducing my The Astrological Journal *column readers to the excellent Scots word 'stooshie' – and to my take on the controversial 'tiny silver nude atop large silver blob' statue which appeared in a London park in November, commemorating Mary's fiercely feminist mother, Mary Wollstonecraft. Yes, you've guessed: Mary Shelley's chart is in there too!*

I should here record my thanks for the patience and tolerance of my students between 1997 and 2001 where barely a class went by without my going on about Mary and Dolly – and Jupiter-Uranus conjunctions. It got so bad that we almost got to the stage of students crossing the street to avoid me. Instead, though, they took to buying me clicky pens with pictures of woolly sheep on them. Bless!

Mary, Dolly and Andi – O brave new world?

In a mere four years, humanity has taken unique, irrevocable steps into a brave new world. In February 1997, Dolly – the first cloned animal – was announced. On 11 January 2001, we were introduced to Andi, a delightful baby rhesus macaque monkey who is the world's first genetically modified primate. 'Andi' is a reverse acronym for inserted DNA. In his case, a glow-in-the dark green dye gene from a jellyfish was inserted via a virus into a monkey egg which was then fertilised in vitro. Out of 126 embryos thus created, just three monkeys were born alive – only Andi carries the extra gene in his body.

There is a very mixed reaction to Andi's birth. Optimism over medical breakthroughs which might follow is set against great alarm that we are moving ever deeper into dangerously questionable physical, ethical and moral territory. It seems an appropriate time to look at what's going on astrologically as technological advances turn science fiction into reality with bewildering speed.

Saturn square Uranus – the old order versus the new

A major pattern dominating the heavens right now is the square between Saturn in Taurus and Uranus in Aquarius. This pattern began to build in summer 1998, peaked in summer and late autumn 1999/early summer 2000, and after its current period of potency, will be on the wane by summer 2001. Saturn in Taurus respects tradition and is resistant to change in the fabric of things; if it moves at all, it does so slowly. Uranus in Aquarius is anarchic, arrogant, disruptive, innovative, fast – loving change for its own sake, bringing stunning breakthroughs in science and technology. Saturn in Taurus holds firm to the past; Uranus in Aquarius heralds the future.

As we advance into exciting times, full of unique possibilities and threats, the area causing most disquiet is that of genetic manipulation of the natural world. Andi is a primate, shares 98% of our DNA and looks like us. Will genetic modification of human beings come next?

As I write this article, the answer to that question looks like yes. It was announced in the week ending 24 February 2001 that the first attempt to clone a human baby 'will begin next month in a secret location in the US.'[14] An American couple have apparently paid an organisation called Clonaid £300,000 to attempt to 'recreate' their dead baby son.

Enter Dr Frankenstein

In mid-February 1997 Saturn and Uranus were reasonably amicable partners in a unique pattern: a five-planet crucible formed in the heavens around the 'discovery duo' Jupiter and Uranus who met in the sky at 5°55' Aquarius – Saturn at that point was in a sextile aspect to both. Out of this crucible came Dolly the sheep. *Time* magazine's '1997 Annual' described thus the Scottish scientist who had created Dolly:

> *'Dr Frankenstein wore a wool sweater and a baggy parka ... Dr Ian Wilmut, the first man to conceive fully formed life from adult body parts since Mary Shelley's mad scientist. Wilmut may not look the part of Frankenstein, or God the Father – but he played it.'*

Mary Shelley – a seer in our midst?

It is a remarkable fact that Mary Shelley, born in 1797, wrote her masterpiece *Frankenstein* when she was only aged 19. Her horoscope [shown in 'Dreaming Frankenstein' which follows this essay] is fascinating. Saturn (limits, separation) rises in Cancer (home, family, mother) square Venus conjunct Chiron in Libra (wounds through relationship). This poignantly signifies her own inner loneliness and brutal losses of loved ones, and the sensitive, alienated Monster in *Frankenstein* who longed for nothing more than the solace of human companionship but was doomed by his creator's rejection of him to terrible loneliness.

---

14   UK's *The Week*, issue 24 February 2001.

Pluto conjoins an Aquarian MC, its ruler and Pluto's dispositor Uranus conjunct Mary's 4th-house Virgo Sun. This squares a 12th-house North Node in Gemini opposite a 6th-house Sagittarian Moon. These significators evoke the unconventional, restless masculine spirit in Mary whose personal life and writing defied the mores of her time.

From them we can also visualise the questing, brilliant, hubristic Dr Frankenstein. Unfettered either by moral concerns or self-doubt, he took on the role of creator in his ruthless pursuit of scientific progress – paying a terrible price. His rejected monster took revenge by slaughtering Frankenstein's loved ones. The story is a myth which speaks powerfully to us now of what may befall us, if we are foolish enough to disrupt too much the subtle and delicate balance of nature.

Ripples to the far future

One of the great fascinations of astrology lies in its ability to show meaningful links between people and events connected to them. Mary Shelley has been dead since 1851. But her contemporary relevance as the author of *Frankenstein* means that key parts of her horoscope continue to link in a significant way with the unfolding pattern of events since 1997 concerning cloning and genetic engineering.

Dolly's world debut in mid-February 1997 reminded us all of Mary's warning in *Frankenstein* – and the synastry between Mary and Dolly is stunning. Dolly's name was initially to be Mary, after Frankenstein's creator.[15] Dolly's 1st-house Pluto at 0° Sagittarius falls in Mary's 6th house, in last quarter waning square to Mary's Pluto-MC. This indicates arrival at a major stage in the outworking of what Mary wrote about with such relevance nearly 200 years ago, concerning the impact of science on the fabric of life.

Dolly has a Grand Cross in cardinal signs, mirroring Mary's angular cardinal t-square. Those mutual patterns occur in almost the same

---

15   From Peter Clarke's Diary, *The Sunday Times* (UK), 30 November 1997.

degrees of the zodiac. Saturn in Cancer square Venus conjunct Chiron in Libra (Mary), and Sun in Cancer t-squaring Saturn opposite Chiron in Libra (Dolly), poignantly call forth what they both have in common: motherlessness. Mary's mother died ten days after her birth. Dolly is an artificial creation, born not from a womb but cloned from cells taken from a sheep's udder.

Dolly's Venus conjunct Mars in Gemini, square her Pisces Moon, falls on Mary's 12th-house Gemini North Node with her Moon in Mary's 10th house. Dolly's square provides a vivid image of the artificial separation of the incarnation and growth process shown by the Moon, life's container, from the sexual meeting of male and female shown by the Venus-Mars conjunction.

Its links with Mary's 12th-house node in the writer's sign of Gemini square Uranus and Mercury in Virgo are intriguing. This suggests that Mary's destiny was to cast upon the waters of the collective unconscious, via her writing, a warning about the disruptive impact of science on the rhythms of nature in the far future. Such prescience has long been recognised as the gift of creative artists of genius, be they painters, musicians or writers. This warning surfaced in a major way in the form of Dolly the Sheep. To reinforce the point, Dolly's Virgo MC links with Mary's Mars-Sun-Uranus conjunction.

Life after Dolly ... more boldly going!

The 9th house and Jupiter, its associated planet, are highly relevant to authorship. The 9th is the house of 'meaning-making' – conceptualising, sending opinions and beliefs out into the world, offering education. Mary's 9th house has Aquarius on its cusp. This indicates that what she formulated and sent out is futuristic and scientific: indeed, she is regarded as the founder of the science fiction genre.

The degree of this cusp (Placidus) is 5°43' Aquarius – a highly sensitive point in the zodiac, therefore, in relation to the future of scientific discovery from Mary Shelley's vision of how it might be. This sensitivity was reinforced in February 1997 with the meeting of Jupiter and Uranus at 5°55′ Aquarius, coinciding with Dolly's appearance.

By July 1998, Saturn and Uranus were moving from their relatively benign 1997 locations in Aries (pioneering spirit) and Aquarius (innovation) into the position of tension and conflict in which they now find themselves. Excitement, which had been palpable throughout the many scientific breakthroughs of 1997, began to give way to a strong sense that humanity is perhaps being rushed too fast along the road to the future.

From the birth of Dolly onwards, the planet Uranus has been travelling through Mary Shelley's 9th house. Almost every month since then has brought news of further advances in the fast-moving world of genetic manipulation. It is approaching a conjunction with her Aquarian MC as a bemused world digests the news of Andi's birth.

This conjunction is exact for the first time next spring 2002, also conjoining Mary's Pluto, the planet of power, death and rebirth in the scientific sign of Aquarius. Watch the papers! Uranus does not complete its traverse of Mary Shelley's MC conjunct Pluto until the start of 2004. Mary's vision of a far future in which the unchanging structure of our bodies and the physical world (Saturn in Taurus) is radically altered by the manipulation of science (Uranus in Aquarius) may herald particularly potent and disruptive new shocks and surprises during that period, taking us even further into a brave new world.

THE LAST WORD FROM NEPTUNE

The planet Neptune (dreams, fantasies, the universal sea, longing for divine connection, for perfection) has been in the sign of Aquarius (human brother/sisterhood, innovation, scientific discovery) since 1998. Neptune amongst many things speaks of the way fashions, ideas, beliefs and discoveries ripple out like sea currents, touching everyone, everywhere. On 11 January 2001, the day Andi[16] was announced to the world, the planet

---

16   It is most intriguing in this context to realise that the gene which was used to modify Andi's make-up was a glow-in-the-dark green dye gene from a jellyfish. How very Neptunian!

Neptune was at 5°43' Aquarius, exactly to the minute on Mary Shelley's 9th-house cusp. This is a stunning piece of synchronicity. How do we interpret it? The long traverse of Neptune through Mary's Aquarian 9th house, which has now begun, could be seen as a metaphor for the slow, inexorable consequences of what she foresaw seeping into every facet of human life, radically altering it forever.

An image arises of Mary Shelley, standing alone on the shoreline of her imagination and her dreams, calling out a message to the far future like the Oracle in ancient times. Dolly's and Andi's births are like echoes of that message returning. Are we projecting the divine onto science now? Will it bring us the perfection and the immortality we long for?

DATA
Mary Shelley: see chart caption on page 233. Source: father, William Godwin's journal: he was present at her birth.
Dolly the Sheep: 5 July 1996, Roslyn Institute nr. Edinburgh, 5:00 p.m. L.T. Source: Gina Kolata, Clone (Allen Lane, The Penguin Press, London, 1997).

The Mountain Astrologer
2001

Dreaming Frankenstein: the creation of a modern myth

Mary Shelley's horoscope is on p. 233.

Two hundred years ago this year, in the early hours of 22 June 1816, two months before her 19th birthday, a young English writer called Mary Shelley went to bed. According to her account, in that liminal time between waking and sleep:

> 'I saw the pale student of unhallowed arts kneeling beside the thing he had put together. I saw the hideous phantasm of a man stretched out, and then, on the working of some powerful engine, show signs of life ... Frightful must it be; for supremely frightful would be the effect of any human endeavour to mock the stupendous mechanism of the Creator of the world ... '
>
> – Mary Shelley, *Frankenstein, or The Modern Prometheus*,
> from the Author's Introduction
> to the Standard Novel's Edition, 1831, p. 50.

Less than two years later, in January 1818, that waking nightmare had taken shape, leading to the publication of one of the world's most famous novels, *Frankenstein, or The Modern Prometheus*, in which Mary Shelley offered us a warning of what might be the consequences of humankind's stepping over moral limits in the pursuit of scientific discovery. This warning has resonated down the centuries; it is more relevant now than ever, as we engage with a new millennium and as the pace of technology-led progress leads us fast into dangerously uncharted physical, emotional, ethical and spiritual territory.

The modern myth which Mary Shelley created centred on the scientist

Victor Frankenstein who created a human out of reassembled body parts and then, repelled by his creation, rejected it with devastating results. The following quote, commenting on the announcement in February 1997 of the world's first cloned sheep, Dolly, in the 200th anniversary year of Mary's birth, beautifully evokes her book's continuing significance:

> *'[This] Dr. Frankenstein wore a wool sweater and a baggy parka ... Dr. Ian Wilmut, the first man to conceive fully formed life from adult body parts since Mary Shelley's mad scientist. Wilmut may not look the part of Frankenstein, or God the Father – but he played it.'*
>
> – From the Science (Biology) section of *Time* magazine's *Time Annual 1997: The Year in Review,* Time Books, 1998, p. 116.

BACKGROUND

Mary Shelley was born in London, England, on 30 August 1797. Aberrant storms and wild weather were sweeping Europe, the tides of political passion generated by the French and American revolutions still ran high, and the Romantic movement in literature was at its peak. Her life profoundly, dazzlingly and poignantly reflected her times.

Her mother was the progressive feminist writer Mary Wollstonecraft, author of the famous book, *A Vindication of the Rights of Woman* (1792), probably the first feminist social manifesto. Her father was the equally progressive philosopher and novelist William Godwin: his stature approached that of French philosopher Jean-Jacques Rousseau whose revolutionary ideas had provided much of the fire for the French Revolution of 1789.

Mary Shelley's mother, then in her late thirties, died ten days after her daughter's birth, leaving a painful emotional void in Mary. Her father remarried in 1801 when Mary was four, bringing her a stepmother whom she always hated and two stepsiblings, Charles and Jane. Mary grew up in a highly intellectual household with distinguished literary visitors, such as writers Samuel Taylor Coleridge and Leigh Hunt. Her precocious intellectual development was nurtured by her father; her feminism, by her mother's legacy.

Mary first glimpsed the famous and notorious English poet Lord Byron in 1811, and briefly met the poet Percy Bysshe Shelley on 11 November 1812. In the spring of 1814, she met Shelley again. On Sunday, 26 June 1814, at her mother's graveside, they declared their love – an evening that decided her destiny. Percy Shelley was still married to his first wife at the time, and Mary was only 16 years old. Their elopement to France in July of that year, followed by their open cohabitation after they returned several weeks later, scandalised their contemporaries.

From then on, until Percy Shelley's untimely death by drowning in 1822, when he was only 29, the two young radicals' life together was dogged by scandal, debt, frequent moves of residence, the constant drain on their resources caused by literary hangers-on of various levels of talent, Percy's ex-wife Harriet's suicide, and the premature deaths of three of their four children. However, despite all the turmoil of their life, they never ceased their daily studies of literature or their writing. Percy was a great supporter of Mary's writing in general and her authorship of *Frankenstein* in particular. [17]

From the moment I first set eyes on Mary Shelley's horoscope [see page 233], it has compelled and fascinated me. As an astrology teacher, I have used it in many of my interpretation classes since the late 1980s. Some years ago, I realised that Mary had conceived the plot of *Frankenstein* during the summer before her 19th birthday, and finished writing it before she was 20, thus highlighting the 18.6-year lunar nodal cycle – the time it takes for the nodes to return to their natal position.

---

17   All dates and biographical details taken from Emily W. Sunstein, *Mary Shelley: Romance and Reality,* Johns Hopkins University Press, 1989.

Foreground: Moon's nodes

The Moon's North and South Nodes 'are not planets but are the two points at which the Moon's monthly path crosses the Sun's annual path (ecliptic) around the Earth. These are abstract points, but astrology accords them the power and effective status of planets.'[18] The North Node returns to its natal starting point every 18.6 years, highlighting the significance of the whole nodal axis and its connections with a person's unfolding life.

My favourite metaphor of the meaning of the Moon's nodes is very succinct: it comes from astrologer and writer Michael Lutin who set it in the context of taking on a drinking problem, with the South Node being the bottle and the North Node the (Alcoholics Anonymous) meeting. This made me laugh out loud, but its pungent wisdom has stayed with me as an apt summary.[19]

There are many definitions of the nodes' significance in a natal horoscope. Most boil down to the South Node's denoting the place of comfort, ease, familiarity, holding gifts which one can easily access (from former lives or one's genetic inheritance, depending on what you believe). The North Node, on the other hand, points to the direction towards which you should strive in order to develop and use those gifts to their fullest potential in the unfolding of your personal destiny. This axis speaks of a life pattern rather than personality traits.

As is often the case when one is inspired by a new idea or concept, my attraction to the nodes as a particular focus for study had personal links. In my chart, the North Node is exactly conjunct my Midheaven (MC) at 29° Taurus, square a 12th-house Sun-Moon conjunction. I came to realise that my first and second nodal returns had coincided with life-changing endings and new beginnings which pushed me out of my comfort zones at the time and into difficult but developmental territory.

---

[18] Nicholas Campion, *The Practical Astrologer.*

[19] Michael Lutin, *SunShines: The Astrology of Being Happy*, Fireside Press, Simon & Schuster, Inc., 2007.

I found this core dynamic to be true of clients and students whose lives I subsequently began to observe through the lens of the nodal axis, with particular reference to the nodal returns. It also became evident that the more prominently the nodal axis was highlighted in an individual's horoscope – e.g., if Uranus-Pluto opposite the Moon squared the nodal axis – the more critical were the developmental challenges confronted and (hopefully) taken on during the nodal return at ages 18/19, 36/38, 55/57, and so on. Eventually, my fascination led to a whole research study, *The Moon's Nodes in Action*, in which I explored Mary Shelley's authorship of *Frankenstein* as one of the case studies.

Mary's horoscope through the nodal lens

Looking more closely at the 12th-house placement of the North Node in Mary Shelley's chart and how it connects with Jupiter, Uranus, Mercury and Pluto–MC (see chart on page 233), sent me on an examination of her horoscope from the perspective of the nodal axis and its links. Astrology certainly offers good symbolic pointers to suggest why she, as such a young woman, had been chosen to deliver a foreshadowing via *Frankenstein*, her masterpiece, of the grim results which might well follow scientific endeavour being pursued without compassion or due regard for ethics or morality.

Mary's North Node falls in Gemini, so the South Node is in Sagittarius. This denotes a life path centred around the conceptualising and disseminating of information and ideas. The Sagittarius South Node shows a background in philosophy, education and the developing of an ethical base for life, as well as a desire to proselytise from that base, as foundational to her life. A love of learning, along with a restless, questing, travel-oriented spirit and an appreciation of the perspective which comes from exposure to different languages, cultures, and broad knowledge, all characterised her inherited gifts – and the cultural context from which her life journey began.

The South Node also suggests (and its wide conjunction with the

Moon backs this up[20]) a need from the beginning for a 'grand', adventurous life – a life infused with vision and possessing a big canvas upon which to paint a vivid picture. Mary Shelley's political and artistic context was the aftermath of the American and French revolutions of the late 18th century and the impact they had on the fabric of her time, plus the Romantic movement in art and literature into which her nature fitted so well. Also indicated in this linking of the South Node and Moon is a distaste for the restrictions of the ordinary and mundane and the potential for arrogance through conviction of one's own rightness.

The North Node in Gemini conjures up the image of Mary's taking the gifts she was given and putting the inspiration they provided into words – getting her ideas out into the world. It also denotes frequent changes of environment whilst attending to this core task, with sibling issues playing an important part in the whole scenario. Indeed, they did: her stepsister Jane/Clare/Claire Clairmont (who liked changing her name!) dogged Mary's footsteps for most of her life. Restless movement and frequent change were very much part of Mary's and her poet husband Percy Shelley's existence; perhaps the North Node in Gemini demanded this as a way for Mary to shake free her ideas and keep them flowing.

When contemplating the location of the North Node – in the 12th house in one of the Gauquelin Plus Zones[21] – the notion of the Big Picture comes in again, from a different perspective. Here is someone whose life path requires an offering of her ideas in such a way as to reflect the hidden, unconscious currents running beneath the surface of her time – perhaps a transmitting of images which would be borne on those currents to provide insights to generations as yet unborn.

---

20   I have always been comfortable with using the same orbs for the Moon's nodes (i.e., up to 10°) as are generally used for both the Sun and Moon, the intersection of whose orbits the lunar nodes depict. I have found this orb allowance to work well in horoscope analysis.

21   For more about Gauquelin Plus Zones (the 12th house), see Michel Gauquelin, *Written in the Stars*, Aquarian Press, 1988, p. 120.

The location of the South Node and Moon in Sagittarius in the 6th house opposite the North Node in Gemini in the 12th evokes a picture of the visionary writer, in touch with the collective unconscious of her time through the 12th-house North Node, having to struggle to extract her vision from the mire of the mundane which was forever besetting her. The nuts and bolts of ordinariness – of the body, of routines, of maintenance tasks which keep the main thrust of life running smoothly – strike me as a major provenance of the 6th house. Mary had trouble with ordinariness all her days. She regularly moved her goods and chattels, relatives, friends and children around. Her health was always delicate, childbirth drained her, and the deaths of three of her children made it sometimes impossible for her to dredge up any inspiration to offer through the 12th-house North Node. Until Percy Shelley died, he protected her from the sharpest edges of their constant financial troubles.

Mary had a strong masculine side which her horoscope clearly portrays. For example, Mars, the Sun and Uranus in the angular 4th house are vividly indicative of the reckless defiance with which she disregarded the conventions of the times dictating how women ought to conduct themselves. Although Virgo, being a feminine/yin sign, is often seen as submissive, the word 'submissive' was probably largely absent from Mary's vocabulary, driven out by the sheer wilful force of that lineup of Mars, Uranus, and the Sun at her horoscope's very core.

Powerful contacts to the lunar nodes

Looking at the planets aspecting the nodal axis offers further sharp images of the nature of Mary Shelley's life path and her struggle to follow it. Jupiter is retrograde in Aries in the 11th house, partile trine the South Node and sextile the North Node. A quote from Mary's biographer, Emily Sunstein, sums this up well: 'Aspiration, enthusiasm, challenge, active mind and spirit, and optimism were among her cardinal qualities ... it was her incapacity for resignation to cold reality that eventually wore her down.'

Jupiter, dispositor of the Sagittarius Moon and South Node, placed in Aries in the 11th house shows how group associations, frequently involving famous men and usually encountered at home, shaped her life. Jupiter's falling on the southern side of the nodal axis, trine the South Node and sextile the North Node, indicates gifts from the past which could be used productively by Mary in actualising her full potential – as indeed they were.

There was her father, the renowned social philosopher Godwin, and his salon, that brought young Mary in contact with the famous English symbolist poet Samuel Taylor Coleridge. Hearing him reading from *The Rime of the Ancient Mariner* had a profound impact on her, and this came out much later in some of the imagery in *Frankenstein*. She met her husband Percy Shelley through Godwin when Shelley was his young acolyte, but their relationship did not begin to develop fully until the early summer of 1814, following Shelley's visits to her home to arrange to lend Godwin money. Subsequently, through Shelley, she met Byron whom she had seen only very briefly some years before. She was in the company of Byron, Percy Shelley and others at the atmospheric Villa Diodati, overlooking Lake Geneva in Italy, during a violent storm in the summer of 1816 when Byron challenged all present to write a ghost story. Mary's waking dream that night turned into the horror tale that became *Frankenstein,* the most famous and notorious novel of her era.

Perhaps retrograde Jupiter in Aries indicates an early leap to fame (with transiting Jupiter conjunct her Moon when *Frankenstein* was published in January 1818). Such fame was never to be replicated, although Mary remained in the public eye as a writer, editor and critic. I think Jupiter also shows the arrogant and unrealistic side of her optimism. For example, by eloping with the still-married Shelley while she was in her teens in the early 19th century, and having an illegitimate child, she flouted the conventions of that time to such a shocking degree that she was never accepted back into the mainstream of society, despite her expectation that this would eventually happen. This social ostracism caused her great pain all her life, although she learned to live with it.

Uranus (which rules the MC and disposits Pluto) in the 4th house in Virgo, square the nodal axis, is the most vivid significator for her unorthodox inheritance, her own defiance of convention, her connection with Percy Shelley and her authorship of *Frankenstein* which assured her place in literary history. This significator is strengthened if we extend it to include the Uranus-Mercury midpoint, the Sun-Venus midpoint and the Mercury-Sun midpoint at 18-20° Virgo – all square the nodes. This major t-square is powerfully linked with the horoscopes of key individuals in her life, such as her parents, Byron and Shelley. It also links with events critical to the unfolding of her destiny.[22]

Frankenstein, or The Modern Prometheus is the full title of Mary Shelley's first and most famous book. In the myth of Prometheus lie core images of Mary's own origins; the times in which she lived; the essential nature of Percy Bysshe Shelley, born like her with the Sun conjunct Uranus; how she defied convention; the price she paid for this; and, most of all, the central theme of her masterpiece.

In essence, Prometheus in Greek mythology was a Titan who stole some of the fire of knowledge from the gods and gave it to humanity to help them in their development. For this hubristic act, the gods punished Prometheus savagely. He was chained to a rock, and during the day an eagle came and pecked out his liver, which grew again during the night so that he could be subjected to the same pain the next day, *ad infinitum*.

The myth of Prometheus speaks most vividly, dynamically and poignantly of the human condition. Following the example of this Titan, we seem driven by an unceasing restless quest to push back the frontiers of knowledge, thereby defying our limits as mortal human beings chained to the programmed lifespan of the body and the inexorable cycle of birth, growth, flowering, decline and death which governs everything in existence.

---

22   Further detail on those connections can be found in my work, *The Moon's Nodes in Action*, Chapter 2, Case Study 1: Mary Shelley, *Frankenstein* and a Sheep called Dolly, p. 23.

Conclusion

Viewing Mary Shelley's authorship of *Frankenstein* through the lens of astrological symbolism, with special focus on the Moon's nodes, certainly helps to explain why she wrote it.

Frankenstein's geophysical backdrop was the famous 'year without a summer' of 1816, with major climate disruption caused by the massive volcanic eruption of Mount Tambora in Indonesia in 1815. The novel's sociopolitical backdrop was the disruptive fallout from the American and French Revolutions. Its immediate context was the community of socially and politically radical writers in which Mary Shelley grew up. Its author was the very young, motherless and troubled but highly literate and gifted Mary. These interwoven conditions were galvanised by the highly charged presence of the charismatic Byron and the challenge he delivered on that stormy night of 22 June 1816.

Perhaps we could view Mary Shelley's nodal axis, in the year of its first return, as the symbolic lightning rod conducting the creative charge which ran through her mind, mirroring the lightning over Lake Geneva that famous night, bringing to life the unforgettable monster of her darkest imaginings.

It remains extraordinary that, at such a young age, Mary Shelley should have become, through her writing, the vehicle for a modern reframing of the myth of Prometheus which endures to this very day. I'd like to give the last words to Emily Sunstein, whose wonderfully readable, scholarly book *Mary Shelley* I'd recommend to anyone who is interested in Mary Shelley's remarkable life:

> 'Mary Shelley ... *will be best remembered for her perception in* Frankenstein ... *that the Promethean drive is at the heart of human progress and yet a bringer of new ills if not focused on ethical means and ends.*'

The Mountain Astrologer
2016

AUTHOR'S NOTE: The much longer case study from which this article is adapted was published in *Considerations* magazine, XIX: 3 (August-October 2004) as 'Mary Shelley: Frankenstein's Creator'. A short extract appears on my blog, Writing from the Twelfth House, as 'Mary Shelley: Modern Mythmaker', posted in March 2011. The study also appears in full in *The Moon's Nodes in Action,* which can be purchased from my site Writing from the Twelfth House – www.anne-whitaker.com.

Of silver blobs and famous feminists

It's time I introduced my readers here to that excellent Scots word: 'stooshie' (etymology obsessives, feel free to research). People tend to create a stooshie about something that irritates them, no matter how serious or trivial. You could reasonably argue that the internet is the most potent stooshie-enabler on the planet. Anyway, a considerable stooshie erupted in the UK early in November 2020, following the unveiling of a statue titled 'A Sculpture for Mary Wollstonecraft' which one journalist explained is "for' not 'of' her. It was never meant to be a straightforward depiction of Wollstonecraft herself ... ' but ' ... a piece of abstract art inspired by her life and work.' (Ellen Peirson Hagger in the *New Statesman*, 12 November 2020).

The work of artist Maggi Hambling, the statue ' ... does not depict the women's rights advocate dressed in a bonnet and skirts, perhaps reading or writing. Instead, it shows a small, silver, naked female figure emerging from an abstract mass ... ' (Ibid.). Memorably, *The Telegraph* called the statue 'a flimsy, Barbie-like embarrassment.'

Any students of mine from 1997/8 reading this column may remember my Mary Shelley obsession of that period: I got very excited about the links between Mary Shelley and Dolly the Sheep (Professor Ian Wilmut, the cloned creature's creator, was called 'Frankenstein in a woolly jumper' by *Time* magazine [23]). Having patiently endured my going on about this all year, they presented me with a clicky pen with a woolly sheep on it and matching woolly sheep brooch at the end of term.

So, not having astro-obsessed about Mary for some while – apart from in my recent article in *The Mountain Astrologer*, that is – I was delighted to have an opportunity to do so, albeit indirectly, via the

---

23   From the Science (Biology) Section of *Time* magazine's *Time Annual: The Year in Review* (Time Books 1998), p116).

Mary Shelley's chart, with asteroids

30 Aug 1797 NS, Wed
23:20 LMT +0:00:40
London, United Kingdom
51°N30' 000°W10'
Geocentric
Tropical
Placidus
True Node

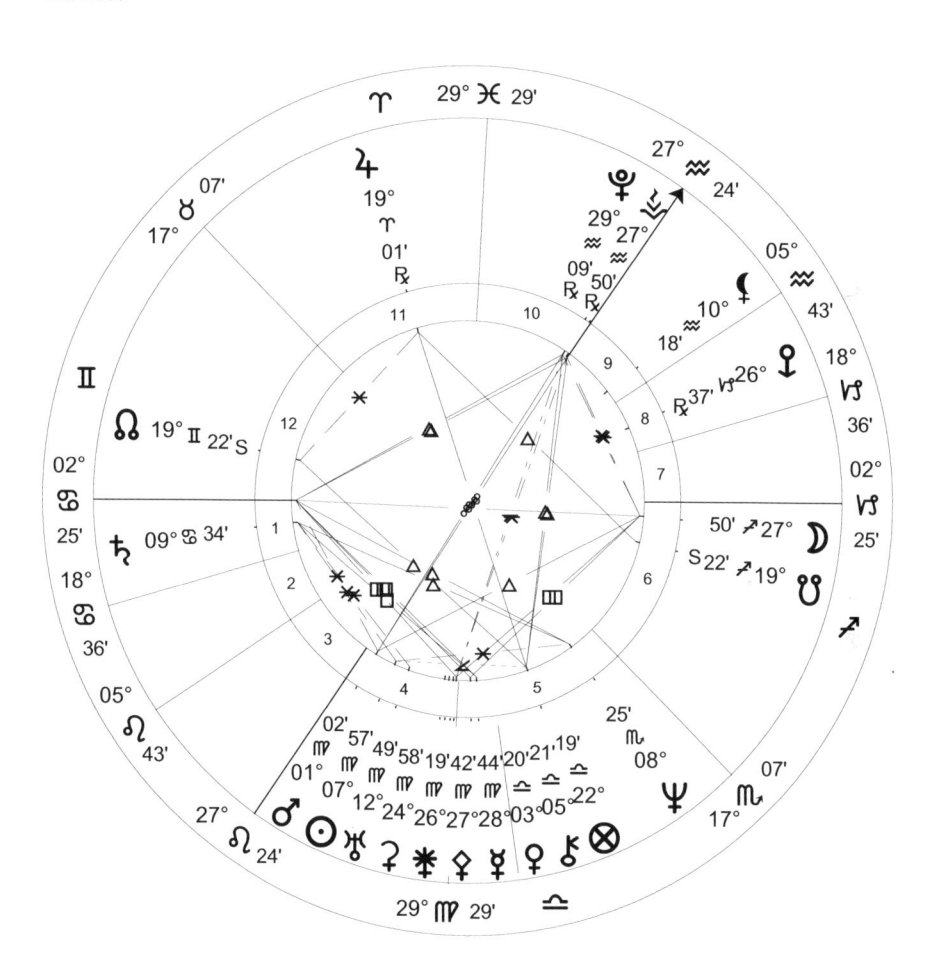

233

stooshie surrounding her mother Mary Wollstonecraft and that statue. In essence, it was roundly criticised, and in some quarters, raged over. Womankind was generally speaking not happy. We failed to see why the eminent, feisty, early feminist author of *A Vindication of the Rights of Woman* (1792) should be associated with a tiny female nude on top of a large untidy-looking silver blob.

Having put up sunrise charts for both Mary W and for 10 November 2020 (the statue's a.m. launch day) I was knocked out by the correspondences. Here, I've picked out briefly only the key ones which struck me. No doubt readers will find more.

The prominent presence of the four major asteroid goddesses Pallas, Juno, Vesta and Ceres in both charts is striking – as is Eris, the goddess of strife. The last forms a turbulent t-square in Mary's chart, linking with the waxing Uranus-Pluto square which was to come to its opposition at the time of the French Revolution. At this point Mary – a vibrant, argumentative, notorious public intellectual and unmarried single parent – tucked her baby daughter Fanny under her arm and set off to check out the Revolution for herself.

At the time of the statue's launch, Mary was experiencing an exact Jupiter return. This involved a close conjunction with Pallas, Jupiter, Pluto and Saturn in the launch chart, squaring Mary's close Mars-Pallas conjunction which itself is closely conjunct launch chart Eris and widely conjunct Mars (which turned direct on 14 November 2020). Mary was born with Eris conjunct Pluto at 22/25° Sagittarius.

Given the very long return cycles of Pluto and Eris, 248 and 556 years respectively, it's an amazing piece of synchronicity that this launch statue has waited to appear in the collective for Pluto and Eris once again to form a major aspect – this time, a waning square.

Adding to the radical turbulence and challenge to the status quo indicated in the charts, we also have Uranus at 8° Taurus currently transiting Mary's 6° Taurus Sun – probably her Sun-Moon conjunction too. This indicates, amongst other things, passionate political rejection of the physical form in which this controversial statue is offered. (Sculpture as

Mary Wollstonecraft's chart

27 Apr 1759 NS, Fri
04:45:58 LMT +0:00:40
London, United Kingdom
51°N30' 000°W10'
Geocentric
Tropical
Placidus
True Node

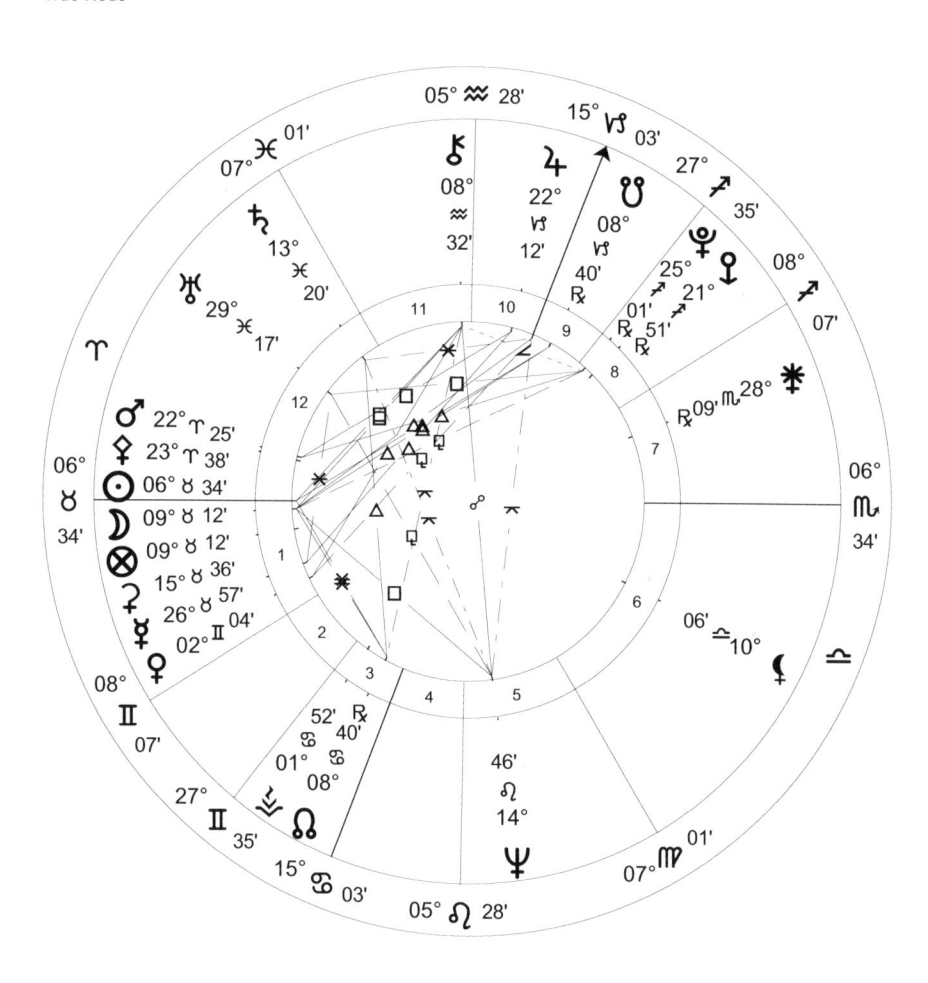

235

Mary Wollstonecraft's statue launch chart

10 Nov 2020, Tue
07:16:04 GMT +0:00
London, United Kingdom
51°N30' 000°W10'
Geocentric
Tropical
Placidus
True Node

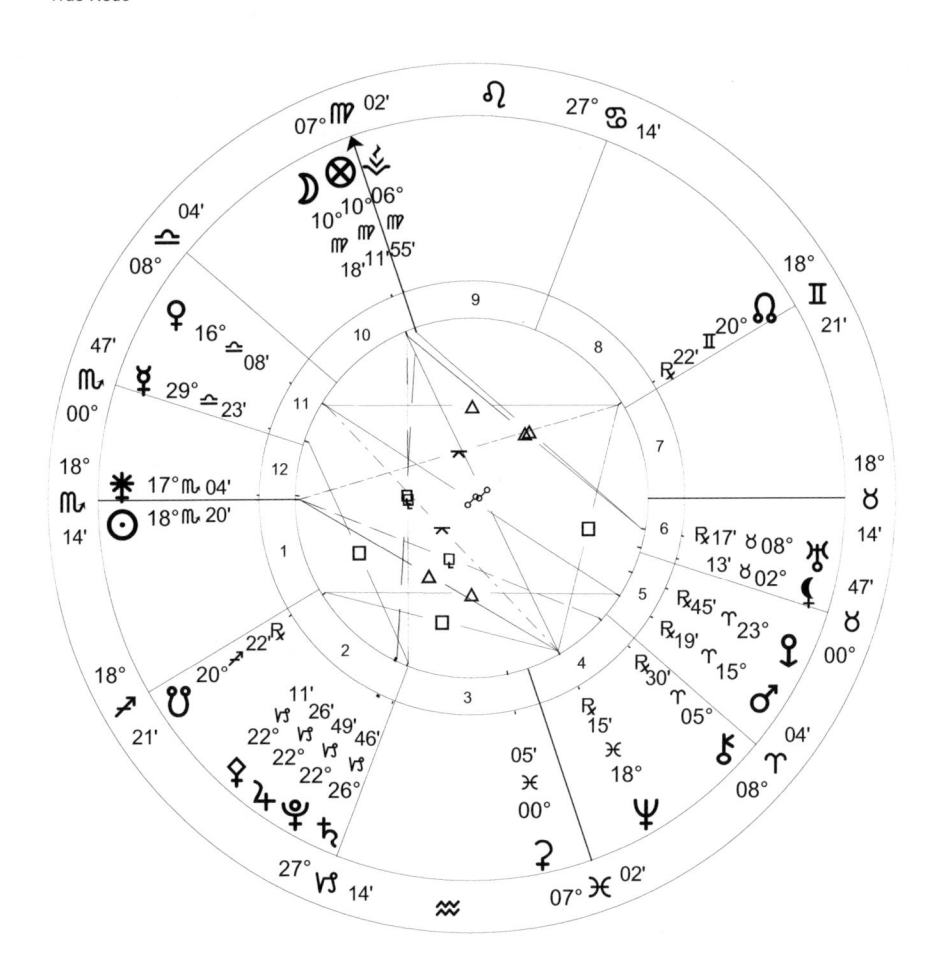

an art form very much resonates with Taurus.) Its idealised version of the female nude is precisely the kind of objectification of womankind against which feminism has struggled ever since Mary's pioneering lead over two centuries ago.

In essence, the stunning combination of those two charts speaks eloquently of Mary's continuing impact on the world – the rise of the #MeToo movement being a recent offshoot – as well as the hugely strong feelings the appearance of this statue has provoked. This will ensure Mary Wollstonecraft and her significance reaches a whole new upcoming Millennial audience, as Mars' direct motion slowly triggers off the major challenging planetary links between the two charts over this coming winter of general worldwide turbulence.

The 11.6 years Jupiter return cycle at ages 11/12, 23/4, 35/6, 47/8, 59/60, 71/2, 83/4 when people are living (continuing as all cycles do, even when we have shuffled off this mortal coil) always opens up new horizons, new learning and teaching opportunities. This November 2020 Jupiter return of Mary Wollstonecraft's is especially powerful, given the collective planets and goddess asteroids with which it combines.

To me, this suggests wider significance than a small, albeit provocative event playing out in a London park from 10 November 2020 might suggest.

Who knew, for example, that the publication of *Frankenstein* by a 20-year-old Mary Shelley on New Year's Day 1818 would prove to be such a prescient warning of the consequences of science being allowed to run unchecked by either ethics or compassion for our planet and all its creatures? Or that another very young woman, Greta Thunberg, by embarking on 20 August 2018 on a solo school strike in Sweden at the age of 15, would instigate the worldwide Extinction Rebellion movement which seeks to challenge substantial worldwide political inertia and denial in the face of an acute climate crisis?

Shelley's and Thunberg's horoscopes have stunning links, as I have pointed out in my recent *TMA* article. [See last essay of this book.]

One of the many fascinations of astrology lies in how one can look at the horoscope of a 'small' event in the present time and get a flavour of the future on the larger scale. Albert Einstein pointed out that past, present and future are all part of one continuum, the distinction being part of a 'stubbornly persistent illusion'.[24] In my opinion, the sunrise chart of 10 November 2020 of the unveiling of a controversial statue to an 18th century woman (whose influence has had a long reach to the present moment) offers a strong flavour of increasingly female challenges to the status quo of the passing 200 years (element) earth era, as we move into the new air era described so vividly by the Jupiter-Saturn meeting at 0° Aquarius on 21 December 2020.

This sunrise chart has a close Vesta-Moon line-up right up there on a 7° Virgo MC (conjunct Mary Shelley's Mars-Sun-Uranus conjunction, incidentally!) trine Uranus in Taurus. The major asteroids are strongly linked in with dynamic planetary patterns already mentioned. There is a very strong emphasis on powerful, mould-breaking female energy in this chart which links so closely with both Wollstonecraft's chart and her daughter's. In the very same week as the statue launch, we heard that Kamala Harris, a woman of Jamaican/Indian origins, had been elected the first ever woman of colour to be Vice-President of the USA. Who knows: when Pluto moves into Aquarius in 2024, the year of the next USA presidential election, she may end up being elected 47th US President.

Isn't it interesting? That 'stooshie' in a London park, its fallout currently ongoing, may prove to be a major early harbinger of a very different future for us all.

The Astrological Journal
January/February 2021

---

24   From Einstein's letter of condolence dated 9 June 1937 to the family of his late friend Michele Bess.

PLANETARY INGRESSES, TRANSITS, PROGRESSIONS:
surveying possible futures

INGRESSES

I've always been fascinated to observe how the 'tone' of personal and collective life changes as Jupiter through to Pluto shift from one sign to the next. The longer the cycle, the more dramatic the shift. My favourite example concerns Pluto's entry into Sagittarius in January 1995. On the day, two major world events stood out. One, the Kobe earthquake which was dramatically spread over newspaper front pages as the Japanese city went up in flames. And two, the then Pope John Paul II preaching in Manila to a vast religious gathering of over a million people.

I am very fond of the Jupiter 11/12-year cycle, being strongly plugged in to Jupiter myself. And I love doing qualitative astro-research. Enjoy those two studies into Jupiter's ingresses, firstly into Libra and then Scorpio. Next comes Saturn's recent entry into Aquarius [2020] to which we are all still adjusting as a world pandemic upends our careless and wasteful way of living on planet Earth. The fourth, somewhat of an outlier, takes a bold speculative leap into some of what might lie ahead for us – when Pluto enters Aquarius in 2024. Such contrasting celestial moods.

Transits through signs
Firstly, a small but telling local tale which demonstrates some striking Mars effects as he moves through the sign of Cancer, grumpily in this case. Next, a meditation upon Saturn's transit through Sagittarius – honouring both Jupiter and Saturn. And most recently, the wonderfully inspiring tale of how one determined community activist, inspired and galvanised by Uranus' seven-year transit through Aries, led a whole local area in saving a treasured piece of local wild land from the clutches of developers and their bulldozers.

Progressions
From the time I discovered Secondary Progressions as a Faculty of Astrological Studies student in the 1980s, their accuracy in tracking the unfolding pattern of people's lives – my clients', students' and my own – has continued to fascinate me. Join me here in celebrating their mysterious significance.

Ingresses
Jupiter into Libra: putting flesh on symbolic bones

Preceding Jupiter's shift into Libra on 9 September 2016, the media were alive with astrologers delineating the meaning of that planetary combination and its possible impact on both collective and personal life. Given my abiding interest in investigating such matters, I thought up a mini project likely to be of interest to me, to clients who would agree to have their lives researched, and hopefully to the readers of *The Mountain Astrologer*.

The mini research project
The project's objective was to illustrate Jupiter's 2016 entry into Libra through the lives of four of my astrology clients. I was also keen to demonstrate the workings of the 11.6-year Jupiter return cycle in relation to Libra. Former US President Bill Clinton's life, from the 1990s to the present day, enabled me to do this. His generous allocation of Ascendant and three planets, including Jupiter, in Libra seemed too good to miss from a study point of view.

No one planet works on its own. There is always a complex dynamic involving the interplay of them all. The third and final exact square between Saturn (conjunct Mars this time) and Neptune occurring on the same day as Jupiter's entry into Libra is a striking example. Bearing this fully in mind, I hoped nevertheless to tease out and demonstrate the specific symbolic action of one bright thread in the current planetary weave – Jupiter in Libra.

To achieve this, I kept the focus of the study quite narrow and the questions simple and minimal, asking the participants only to note any inner or outer events in their lives which seemed to them to be unusual: from just before Jupiter's shift on Friday, 9 September, to over that whole weekend. Secondly, I requested them to take notes if they wished until the end of September by which time Jupiter would have reached

5° Libra and be settling into his transit of that sign. I also asked them to let me know if nothing of significance occurred during that critical weekend and the rest of September.

The four clients – Nora, Eliza, Philippa and Louise (all names are pseudonyms) – were chosen because they have planets located in the very early degrees of Libra and, in one case, the progressed Midheaven (MC). Louise's horoscope has a particularly dynamic line-up of planets triggered by Jupiter's entry into Libra. Therefore, I chose her for a longer case study. Of the four clients, only Louise knows anything much about astrology. She began her formal astrological studies in September 2016.

Jupiter in Libra

By the time this article appears (I am writing during September-October 2016), the above combination of energies will have been exhaustively examined. Nevertheless, it seems appropriate to give a brief summary for those who are new to astrology, and a refresher for the rest of us, before presenting the vividly illustrative feedback provided by my research subjects.

English visionary poet William Blake's marvellous line, 'The road of excess leads to the palace of wisdom' ('Proverbs of Hell' from *The Marriage of Heaven and Hell*), tells us a great deal about Jupiter's symbolic role. Blake had many planets in Sagittarius, the mutable fire sign ruled by Jupiter. He knew a thing or two about excess. As the quotation indicates, Blake believed that challenges arising from an excess of exuberant experimentation in life teach one more than being overcautious ever does. Jupiter brings undoubted blessings: robust faith in life's essential value and goodness, the longing to know and to grow in wisdom, the ability to have fun and inspire other people. However, all forms of overconfidence can also arise from a strong dose of Jupiter in one's horoscope.

The restless drive to grow, to expand, to live a life rich in meaning, to push the boundaries of knowledge and experience as far as possible, lies at the core of astrological Jupiter. He is the archetypal *puer aeternus* – the 'divine child' who does not willingly accept the limits set by age and time, Saturn's domain. As we will see from Louise's horoscope and her feedback, Jupiter crossing her 9th-house Pluto in Libra also triggered a square to 7th-house Saturn, pulling transiting Jupiter's expansiveness down to earth.

Libra is a cardinal air sign and, as such, represents in essence a communicative, initiatory spirit. It is also the first of the social signs – Aries through Virgo being more personally oriented. Using the charm and grace bestowed by its ruling planet, Venus, Libra's drive is to reach out in relationship to others in bringing harmony, justice, fairness and balance to bear. The grace and beauty gifted by Venus also remind us of Libra's strong links with all the arts.

However, it is always important to remember that signs work in polarity: Libra sits in the Scales opposite Aries. Someone once described Libra as 'a polite Aries'. You can push Libra quite far – but don't push your luck! Apart from revealing an aggressive streak if pushed, Libra's Scales indicate a real gift for strategy and tactics, balancing one option with another to arrive at the most diplomatic, least offensive way forward. The shadow side of this points to a Libran's biggest downsides: being indecisive in the face of many choices and being too nice in order to avoid giving offence, thereby undermining one's own position.

Fire and air make a lively, curious, creative, inspirational mix of energies: Jupiter (ruling a fire sign) generally works well in the air sign of Libra, bringing an expansive Big Picture perspective to the drive for fairness, harmony, justice and aesthetic expression. The capacity to be in the right place at the right time, to take advantage of opportunities offered to widen one's horizons, seems to be a striking feature of Jupiter in Libra periods for many people, but especially those who are experiencing their Jupiter returns. We will see notable examples of this in Bill Clinton's life.

On a more negative note, becoming carried away with new ideas, and investing more hope in a new relationship than subsequent developments merit, are two distinct possibilities with the Jupiter in Libra combination. When Jupiter traverses this sign, there is a propensity for being carried away by unjustified optimism regarding what relationships can deliver, and this is a downside worth guarding against.

THE CLIENTS' STORIES

Let's now take a look at what my intrepid band of research participants had to say about September 2016.

Nora, a musician, came for a reading on 28 September 2016. She has Neptune at 0° Libra in the 4th house, Neptune being her 9th-house ruler. I casually asked her if anything out of the ordinary had occurred around 9 September. 'Why, yes!' she replied. 'The week after that date, I set up a new photographic society in my home village, returned to ballet classes, and started learning Qigong – so that I can teach it myself.'

Eliza, whose progressed MC at 3° Libra (in the 11th house) is sextile Uranus conjunct the natal MC, reported 9 September to be very significant: 'Although apparently mundane. Our new cleaner came, the first since moving house nearly four years ago. I felt this was a major step forward as I had been completely blocked for these years and unable to give myself this privilege – too expensive, too difficult to arrange, etc. I had been feeling increasingly overwhelmed by housework, so this represents a real liberation.' [She has a busy career as a therapist.]

Eliza also went to a well-known Buddhist centre in the Scottish Highlands on 16 September for a week to teach yoga on retreat; there, she met many new people, including an interesting new yoga teacher. At an astrology update reading on 5 October, she reported that the retreat had been wonderfully affirming of her teaching with one student planning to come over from Scandinavia to study with her.

Philippa's 6th-house Sun at 1° Libra is part of a dynamic Grand Trine with her Ascendant at 1° Gemini and the South Node at 0° Aquarius conjunct her MC at 28° Capricorn. As you might expect, her father features prominently in her feedback which was very detailed and striking. She said that on 7 September 2016 she got to see her father who lives in the Philippines and whom she has not seen for two years.

I was actually dreading it as we have a very fractured relationship, or at least we did have. Both he and his wife came up to Glasgow to visit me and my daughter. Dinner went well, lots to catch up on. By the end of the evening, I was in awe of my father – for his ferocious appetite for life. He turns 70 this year. He and his wife run an organic farm on one of the islands and have been working incredibly hard to get the place up and running properly. He is also completing his dissertation for his PhD.

I love my father, but he and I fell out and have had a difficult relationship since my teens. This time, it was like all of the past hurt had been washed away. I had got my father back again. He really wants to help me to grow my business [Philippa teaches yoga and meditation] and gave me a large sum of money (something he has never done!) in order to help me build something profitable.

That evening I went to bed and woke up at 1:11 a.m. exactly on 8 September. I could feel this tremendous energy coming from my heart and pulsing incredibly strong. I sat up to do some yoga breathing. It was incredible, and I have no idea what it was. My father and I spent three days together, and I feel like a wound has healed. He has continued to help me strategically sort out my business, helping me to set goals for what I would like to achieve for my life and business within the next year. It's been incredible. I have been asking the universe for a mentor and she has given me back my dad.

LOUISE: A LONGER CASE STUDY

Louise is a single parent in her early 40s who has carved out a positive life for herself and her daughter from a very troubled and painful family past. Her daughter, Jess, started college in the autumn of 2016, thereby freeing Louise to plan her departure from one of the traditional professions in which she has worked with increasing reluctance for the last 20 years.

She has found recent Reiki therapeutic work and training to be transformative, helping her gain the confidence to take a business development course over the summer. In this course, she even won a competition by presenting one of her many ideas: a plan to set up an I Ching reading business on the web, doing videos and making I Ching cards. She has also signed up to take an online introductory astrology course. She has diverse talents and an unconventional streak regarding her occupational life, needing to find ways to accommodate all this.

Jupiter's ingress into Libra triggered major patterns: the very striking line-up of early-degree planets Saturn, Neptune and Pluto; the harsh square between 9th-house Pluto in Libra conjunct the MC and 7th-house Saturn in Cancer; and the powerful minor grand trine (favouring creativity) bringing natal Jupiter, Neptune conjunct the Ascendant, and Pluto all together.

Her feedback for the period of Jupiter's early September ingress into Libra, triggering the above lineup, is vivid and powerful – as indeed it is for the rest of September. In keeping with Jupiter's fondness for excess, she also sent lots of it. This is a brief summary of a most distinctive, expansive, turbulent period of Louise's life, mostly in her own words.

Feedback: September 14, 2016: *It's been quite a tumultuous weekend, and the general themes are: how I earn a living (as usual!), how I express my emotions (I usually don't but have been recently), and the support network I have around me just now (which is fantastic!).*

On Friday (9 September) I made the decision that I was going to distance myself from my business coach. Although an amazing opportunity, working with him has been a big challenge and has triggered a lot of stuff for me. I am constantly waiting for his advice, opinion and approval (daddy issues!!!). I'll have to take responsibility for myself and my future business/career rather than just do what he tells me.

I also have an admirer who has been messaging me all week, but I decided today that he's not for me and I'm going to distance myself.

On Saturday (10 September), after several wonderful weeks off, I went back to work as a locum to pay the bills until my new venture takes off. I woke up feeling sick to the pit of my stomach and despite working for only two hours and seeing only one client, I spent the rest of the day crying my eyes out and feeling as if I'm never going to escape it.

Her daughter Jess and her former work colleagues were a great support in what proved to be a miserable weekend for Louise, continuing through Monday (12 September) when I was still in a very low mood at the business development group.

She became tearful with her coach who 'promised he would help and support me in getting out of my current career.' Once again, colleagues were kind. A supportive call from the business coach caused her opinion of him to swing 'for the millionth time from negative back to positive'. By Tuesday (13 September), her 'emotional meltdown' had cleared.

Feedback: 30 September 2016: *After my meltdown about work, it finally dawned on me that it's me who is choosing it. I made a very definite decision to stop choosing it and start putting my energy into all the new options that are opening up before me.*

This was followed by resignation from her professional association, the clearing out of old university notes and a decision not to renew her professional licence in March 2017.

The following Saturday (17 September) I had to work again but felt a lot calmer and more detached. On Sunday (the 18th) I had to go to a work conference. This would be the last she would ever attend, but positive encounters with people from her past professional life made it a good day: *Still very appreciative of the support networks I have and the new people I'm meeting, and I feel as if I've found 'my tribe.'*

The relationship with the coach is still causing a great deal of aggravation. I'm grateful that he's set me on a new path, but he's not the right coach for me. I'll continue to attend group classes and learn what I can, but I'm having no more one-to-one meetings or phone calls and am not following his modus operandi of 'rustle up any old thing to make a fast buck'.

He's not the only authority figure I seem to be having problems with this month (not that this is unusual for me!). I seem to be questioning:

are certain people really who they say they are, and do they really know what they claim to know? Do they really know better than my own inner wisdom? Starting to feel I should have more confidence in myself and less unquestioning reliance on others.

Finally, I did distance myself from my admirer but quite enjoyed the attention at the time and am going to make a more concerted effort to find a new partner. Lock up your sons, everybody!

Feedback: 3 October 2016: *I collected my Level 2 Reiki certificate last night, so I can now work as a practitioner and intend to start building a client base straightaway. I've started my astrology course ... it feels good to have begun on that path.*

I'm about to start a blog about food addiction and weight loss. I also intend to work as an affiliate with an American lady who has brought out a commercial program about weight loss for food addicts. The lady in question does not know this yet!

Lastly, people in the business development group keep telling me I should be in marketing, and they would be willing to pay me, so I'm going to look into that option.

The business coach – who told me two months ago, when he chose me as the competition winner, that I was a natural at marketing and should be a consultant – has been telling me ever since that there's no money in that. However, by amazing coincidence, he has this week announced that he's setting up a marketing business! It seems he's been deliberately leading me down the wrong path for months to protect his own interests rather than mine. Lots of lessons learned!

AND NOW, BILL CLINTON

Clinton's horoscope — with its Libra Ascendant and 1st-house stellium of Mars, Neptune, Venus, Chiron and Jupiter all in Libra — is instantly recognisable and has been widely written about. (His chart can be found on many sites including Astro-Databank at astro.com.) All the Libran strengths and weaknesses are there, writ large and amplified by Jupiter's presence: good looks, stellar charm, and the ability to relate to people and bring them together; considerable gifts as a lawyer, negotiator, and persuader; musicianship. Even his birthplace, Hope, Arkansas, bears that optimistic Jupiterian stamp.

Venus in Libra has been described by astrologer Kelly Surtees as 'cosmic honey'. This combination with Mars and Neptune gives us Clinton, the legendary charmer and seducer of women, with Chiron in the mix showing the wounding downside for others and himself of such excesses. It also gives us 'slick Willie', the ducker, weaver and manipulator par excellence who possesses a whole deck of metaphorical 'get out of jail-free' cards. Rumour and scandal have dogged his career since his earliest days in politics; he is the only US president to have been impeached who continued to hold onto his job and serve out his full term of office. All the Libran strengths and weaknesses are there.

However, it is Clinton's Jupiter returns with which I am mainly concerned here. All the planets have a return cycle, varying in length from the tiny 27.5-day lunar return to the epoch-defining 248-year return cycle of Pluto. Jupiter returns, in essence, bring us the chance to open up to new levels of experience and understanding, through new opportunities appearing which offer us the potential to grow and develop.

Here are the Jupiter in Libra periods during Clinton's lifetime: August 1945-September 1946, December 1956-March 1958, November 1968-April 1970, October 1980-November 1981, October 1992-November 1993, September 2004-October 2005, and the current period of September 2016-October 2017. Readers will have to do their own research for Clinton's first three Jupiter in Libra returns (1956-81). There is only space for this article to look briefly at the more recent ones – and to speculate what this current Jupiter return may bring.

Given that his Ascendant and four planets plus Chiron occupy almost the whole of Libra, I am treating the entire year of Jupiter's transit through Libra as his Jupiter return.

The period of October 1992-November 1993 saw Clinton elected as president of the United States in November 1992, taking office in

January 1993. September 2004-October 2005 produced another high point for Clinton: his autobiography *My Life* – a gargantuan 1,008 pages long, much to the mirth of some commentators – was published in June 2004: it was a runaway success, selling some 2.25 million copies and netting Clinton the world's largest book advance of $15 million. The audiobook, read by Clinton himself, also won a Grammy Award in 2005 for Best Spoken Word Album.

And what of the September 2016-October 2017 Jupiter return period for Bill Clinton? Although there was a range of achievements during the entire periods in the previous two examples, I chose to feature one particular high point from each. As I write this article in October 2016, it is obvious that one would have to be hiding in a remote cave somewhere without Wi-Fi not to know that Clinton's wife Hillary is running for president. Her campaign was damaged at an early stage by her very public collapse whilst trying to work through a bout of pneumonia.

However, sexual scandal erupting around Donald Trump during the time of their three debates, combined with Hillary's generally assured performances, have placed her in the lead in the two weeks prior to the 8 November 2016 Presidential Election. By the time this article appears in February/March 2017, we will know the outcome. However, Bill Clinton's 6th Jupiter return – if the series runs true to form – should produce another high point of public achievement, success and recognition for him.

(Retrospective note: Jupiter is also known for promising more than he can deliver. Until the last day of the election campaign, Hillary Clinton – who 'won' the presidency by the popular vote – thought she would become president and Bill the first-ever First Man. But we all know how that turned out.)

Conclusion

I chose Nora, Eliza, Philippa and Louise because their planetary placements (and the progressed MC, in Eliza's case) were striking – right at the beginning of Libra. Surely, I thought, their experiences would clearly reveal the dynamic, expansive impact of Jupiter's entry into that sign, with its emphasis on education, arts, and relationships. As you can see from their feedback, this has indeed proved to be the case. Bill Clinton's life also proved to be a gift in illustrating how recurring life-pattern themes unfold in tune with the planetary cycles.

I love doing this kind of simple, direct research. And it fits the current spirit of Jupiter in Libra really well: a cooperative, fun, educational exercise that brings astrologer and clients together in an equal partnership, offering a small but meaningful example of how clearly our tiny personal lives respond to the vast, ever-changing energy field of space and time.

The Mountain Astrologer
February/March 2017

Ingresses
Jupiter in Scorpio: Lord of the Starry Heavens enters 'The Great Below'

'Something is always born of excess: great art was born of great terror, great loneliness, great inhibitions.' – Anaïs Nin

'It looks like freedom, but it feels like death.' – Leonard Cohen

One of the many seductions of being an astrologer is waiting for the heavens to speak when a significant planetary shift is imminent. As usual, the astro-world was buzzing with speculation regarding Jupiter's move from Libra to Scorpio on 10 October 2017. On cue, a few days before, a *New York Times* article rocked Hollywood with sexual harassment allegations against film mogul Harvey Weinstein who was sacked by the Weinstein Company on 8 October. When I began writing this article on 13 October, at least 30 women, including celebrities of the stature of Angelina Jolie, had come forward to claim that they had been sexually harassed or even raped by Weinstein – accusations he has denied.

This deeply unsavoury case, whose details and implications will doubtless unfold for months to come, is a textbook illustration of the shadow side of Jupiter in Scorpio: the abuse of power by larger-than-life characters, usually but not invariably male (think of the infamous Glenn Close 'bunny-boiler' female character in the movie *Fatal Attraction*). Outside the entertainment world, other realms such as politics, big business and religious institutions provide other well-known contexts for abusers – sexual and otherwise – on the prowl.

However, it's not all bad when Jupiter is resident in Scorpio. Planetary pictures always come in shades ranging from very bright to extremely dark. I should know, having been born with a 3rd-house Jupiter in

Scorpio square Mercury, Pluto, Saturn, Venus, Moon and Sun in the 11th and 12th houses. Thus, when *The Mountain Astrologer* invited me to follow up my research study of Jupiter's ingress into Libra in 2016-17 by tackling Jupiter's ingress into Scorpio, I accepted, although not without a degree of trepidation. Taking an investigative dive into Scorpio's deep, dark waters, hopeful of emerging with some pearls of perspective to share, is indeed daunting.

A THREE-PART APPROACH
In this article, I present three different takes on Jupiter in Scorpio, after providing a brief description of the combination itself. Firstly, an exploration of Jupiter's natal placement via pop legend David Bowie's horoscope, viewed through the lens of his 9th-house Jupiter in Scorpio. Secondly, an examination of the 11/12-year Jupiter return cycle and a progressed planet conjunct natal Jupiter, using my own horoscope with its heavily aspected Jupiter in Scorpio placement as an example of that cycle's unfolding over time. In part three, I was keen to use Jupiter's change of sign to pursue one of my abiding interests as an astrologer: that of small-scale qualitative research, investigating astrological theory's claim that certain planetary patterns produce clearly identifiable effects both in personal and worldly affairs, and asking the question: 'Well, do they or don't they?'

I kept the focus quite narrow, the questions simple and minimal, asking my five research participants (none of whom has natal Jupiter in Scorpio) to note any inner or outer events in their lives which seemed unusual. They were directed to look closely at the one-week period from Sunday, 8 October to Saturday, 14 October 2017, but to continue note-taking until Tuesday, 7 November 2017, by which time Jupiter would have reached 6° Scorpio and be settling into his transit of that sign.

No one planet operates on its own, always being part of a weave of symbolic textures. Nevertheless, I hoped that using this three-part approach would be able to demonstrate the symbolic action of Jupiter in Scorpio, natally, cyclically and as one stand-out thread in the current planetary pattern via the live experiences of five people at the time. Two of them are current students/mentees of mine. The other three have only a passing acquaintance with astrology beyond the Sun signs.

Jupiter in Scorpio

Ah, Jupiter – that expansive energy, dear friend and close companion of excess, that fountain from which the ambrosia of optimism flows, inveterate seeker of even bigger pictures and greater truths. Without his powerful, fiery promptings, we humans would never have reached past our mortal limits to the stars and way beyond. We would never have created great culture, art, music or words that changed the world. Nor would we have allowed human greed, arrogance and callous disregard for our mother planet and its indigenous cultures to generate huge swathes of destruction which threaten to engulf us all.

Jupiter, the all-knowing king of crafts of palmistry, tarot, the I Ching, astrology – to name but a few. Either famous or not, people with this combination do not walk the road of moderation in those dimensions of life which carry a dark, powerful 'charge'. In my astrology classes, I have often described Jupiter in Scorpio as the sex, death and rock 'n' roll placement – think of Elvis Presley here, for example, who has this placement and David Bowie whom we will meet shortly. A quick Internet search for famous people with Jupiter in Scorpio came up with an interesting list, showing the combination in its spectrum from very bright at one end – his holiness the Dalai Lama – to extremely, notoriously dark at the other: mass murderer Charles Manson.

Another exemplar: 'Poet, magician and occultist, Aleister Crowley was a true explorer of all that is considered mysterious or forbidden.'

The above quotation from Linda Goodman pretty much sums up the essence of Jupiter in Scorpio. Those of us both blessed and challenged by this most potent of planetary combinations should, first of all, be honest with ourselves about its pluses and minuses. Without self-honesty and self-acceptance, we are going to have difficulty accessing and channelling its powerful preoccupations in constructive directions, especially in youth. However, to offer one of my favourite quotes from the poet William Blake (*The Marriage of Heaven and Hell*) who was born with Jupiter and Pluto in Sagittarius and no stranger to excess: 'The road of excess leads to the palace of wisdom.'

With a bit of luck and effort, we Jupiter in Scorpio folk can get there, too, given time and maturity! Mining wisdom from the depths of life, then offering that wisdom to widen life's horizons for self and others, is Jupiter in Scorpio put to its best use.

Take 1: David Bowie

Let's take a look at David Bowie's extraordinary life through the lens of Jupiter in Scorpio. Upon reading through Bowie's long, detailed and well-referenced biography on Wikipedia, with one eye on his horoscope [which can be viewed at Astro-Databank at astro.com and at other sites], I felt sufficiently overwhelmed to walk away and revive myself with a cup of strong coffee. Even limiting ourselves to exploring Bowie's Jupiter in Scorpio in the 9th house gives us a strong flavour of the unique person he was and the depth of his influence on several facets of popular culture.

Money, power and fame

The 9th-house Jupiter rulership of Bowie's Sagittarius Midheaven (MC) amplifies that planet's significance. In keeping with Jupiter in Scorpio's connection with fame and power, biographer David Buckley called Bowie 'both star and icon. The vast body of work he has produced ... has created perhaps the biggest cult in popular culture. His influence has been unique ... he has permeated and altered more lives than any comparable figure.' Jupiter also sextiles Bowie's Sun-Mars in Capricorn – he was an extremely wealthy man who knew how to make the power of money work to his advantage.

Performance

Bowie brought great showmanship, depth, intensity and sexuality to his performances, both in music and acting. An early film role as Major

Celliers in *Merry Christmas, Mr. Lawrence* (1983) ended in a deeply Scorpio fashion with Bowie's character buried up to his neck in sand, left to die by his Japanese captors. In one of his final roles, Bowie portrayed physicist Nikola Tesla in Christopher Nolan's film *The Prestige* (2006), about the bitter rivalry between two magicians in the late 19th century, illustrating Scorpio's long-popular association with magic and the occult in which Bowie had more than a passing interest.

Rock 'n' roll excess
A television documentary, *Cracked Actor*, was filmed in 1974 when Bowie was struggling with cocaine addiction. It has become notorious for showing his fragile mental state during this period. Bowie said: 'I'm amazed I came out of that period, honest. When I see that now, I cannot believe I survived it.' His sexual excesses were also well documented. David Buckley wrote that Bowie 'mined sexual intrigue for its ability to shock,' and was probably 'never gay nor even consistently actively bisexual,' instead experimenting 'out of a sense of curiosity and a genuine allegiance with the 'transgressional'.' How much more Jupiter in Scorpio can you get?

Religion
I loved this comment on Bowie's younger life as an emerging musical talent: 'Upon listening to Little Richard's song 'Tutti Frutti', Bowie would later say that he had 'heard God'.' Over the years, Bowie made numerous references to religions and to his evolving spirituality, with Buddhism perhaps appealing to him the most profoundly. He was to ask in his will that his body be cremated, and his ashes scattered in Bali, in accordance with the Buddhist rituals.

Death and beyond
In 2015, Bowie was diagnosed with terminal liver cancer. His cause of death is eerily appropriate, given Jupiter's rulership of the liver and Scorpio's association with death. Bowie made his last public appearance

in New York on 7 December 2015 at the opening night of his musical *Lazarus*. His final album, *Blackstar*, was released on 8 January 2016, on his 69th birthday – he died two days later. Both titles are most apt for a man with Jupiter's starry placement in the dark sign of Scorpio.

Reading through accounts of David Bowie's death and the huge public interest it aroused, I came across this fascinating detail which fits beautifully with the symbolism of Jupiter in Scorpio, a sign whose traditional ruler is Mars: 'On 13 January 2016, Belgian amateur astronomers at MIRA Public Observatory created a "Bowie asterism" of seven stars which had been in the vicinity of Mars at the time of Bowie's death; the "constellation" forms the lightning bolt on Bowie's face from the cover of his Aladdin Sane album.'

No doubt David Bowie would have loved this posthumous heavenly link with the all-powerful, lightning-hurling king of the immortal gods.

TAKE 2: JUPITER RETURN CYCLES, SCORPIO STYLE

Jupiter returns to his natal position every 11.6 years. Everyone can track this unfolding throughout their lives: at 11-12 years of age, then at 23-24, 35-36, 47-48, 59-60, 71-72, 83-84, and so on. In essence, the start of each cycle represents the opening out of a whole new learning period whose archetypal purpose is to expose us to new experiences – all kinds of symbolic and actual travelling, both light and dark, within our inner and outer life.

The Jupiter cycle: unfolding in my lifetime

My birth chart, which I explore here, is published near the beginning of this book – on page 14. Natal Jupiter in Scorpio is in my 3rd house and strongly linked to most of the planets in my horoscope. I was preoccupied from childhood with topics and questions that many people prefer to avoid. Why are we here? Is there any existence after death? Is there life on other planets? What do cosmology, science, religion and myth have to teach one another? No wonder I ended up as an astrologer! My whole life journey has been driven by an intense preoccupation with gathering and sharing all kinds of information, to place it in contexts which expand my own and others' understanding of life's deeper meanings. This journey continues as I grow older.

Two major events, which were powerfully influential in triggering my obsessions, took place when I was between eleven and twelve years old. My beloved grandfathers – wise old men both – died within five months of each other. Grandpa Calum was the only person I was able to talk to in childhood about what really mattered to me. He was extraordinarily open-minded for a man of his generation.

A few months later, when my other grandfather died, I was traumatised by my father's (unsuccessful) attempts to drag me at night into a dark room to look at Grandpa Fred's body laid out in an open coffin – classic male abuse of power whilst under the influence of alcohol. This, I think, triggered a fear of the dark which I eventually conquered in my twenties by choosing to live alone for long periods of time.

Also, at age 11/12, I entered secondary education in the top class, feeling very sad that my grandfathers had not lived to see my success. At 23/24 I completed a post-graduate Diploma in Education, having already been an adult education teacher for two years. At 35/36, I was awarded the Certificate of the Faculty of Astrological Studies (UK), prior to beginning an astrological career.

In 2018, I will have my next Jupiter return, this time with a twist which both intrigues and somewhat alarms me. I had been looking forward to progressed Mercury, my ruling planet, departing intense, watery Scorpio (my horoscope is highly Plutonian: enough, already!) and entering fiery Sagittarius in my later years. To my dismay, a few years ago, I noted that progressed Mercury, currently at 21°30' Scorpio, would in fact be going retrograde by progression in early 2018. Returning to greet natal Jupiter at 19° Scorpio, he will then retrace his journey through Scorpio for the rest of my life.

On the one hand, this natal and progressed Jupiter-Mercury partnership in the 3rd house in recent years has been great for writing, teaching and consulting. On the other, I have had all kinds of extravagantly dark imaginings about what retrograde progressed Mercury will bring, especially when it's soon to be temporarily turbo-charged by the Jupiter return. Will I turn into some kind of recluse, given that I'm bad enough on that score already? Will I get Alzheimer's? Will I lose the power of speech? Will I quit writing altogether? And so on. Fortunately, I have learned over the years not to take my morbid drama-queen side (thanks, Jupiter in Scorpio!) too seriously.

It is interesting to see how my reading has become deeper and more concentrated in recent months. For example, I am currently reading *Die Wise* by Stephen Jenkinson. This long-term practitioner of the 'death trade' (as he calls it) takes an in-depth look at how our culture has lost touch with the sense that death is a vital part of the cycle of life, instead perceiving it as some kind of failure to be forestalled at any cost by medical science.

And it appears that my next writing venture may involve taking up suggestions made by a few colleagues that I should revisit my writings from the last few years, bring them together in an essay/article/mini-research study collection and publish them. That project should be enough to keep me out of too much Scorpio mischief for a while. Of course, all reasonable suggestions on how to channel that retrograde progressed Mercury would be most welcome!

TAKE 3: RESEARCH STUDY. WHAT HAPPENED BETWEEN 10 OCTOBER TO 7 NOVEMBER 2017?

It has been fascinating to hear so many intense personal stories over recent weeks, all of which have the same Jupiter in Scorpio core signatures threaded through them. 'What on earth is going on with the planets just now?' is a question I've been answering a lot in recent weeks, as no doubt have my astrological colleagues. Space limitations preclude me from sharing many casual anecdotal tales which would make up a whole article in themselves.

Of my five research participants, the most powerful feedback came from a young woman with several planets in Scorpio, a client with no formal knowledge of astrology. She has given me permission to write a whole case study around her experiences, so she is not included here – except to tell you that she boarded a plane and departed Scotland for North America the very day Jupiter went into Scorpio.

Here are some vivid snapshots from the other four participants with my gratitude for their contributions. (My clarifying comments are italicised.) I have had to make cuts for reasons of space; however, as you will see, each snapshot carries the same Jupiter in Scorpio core signature, but with different branches of manifestation depending on the planets involved. For economy and focus, I have (mainly) referred to transiting Jupiter only in conjunction, square or opposition to natal planets and angles. I should add that I have altered the names of all four and certain biographical detail. All four approved their write-up here.

Anna (age 39)
Jupiter in Scorpio is transiting Anna's 3rd house, opposing Chiron in Taurus in the 9th and squaring Mars in Leo in the 12th.

11 October 2017: *Power Struggle! Today, I was talking with one of our employees about a new project* [involving the community group with which Anna works as a volunteer coordinator]. *The employee said, in passing, 'Make sure you speak to Joe.' This comment made me cross because I believe Joe* [the sole member of another group in the same community] *doesn't consult on things, but demands we consult with him ... My perception is that the past behaviour of this person has been passive-aggressive, and I know part of it is because I am in a position that is causing a power struggle between us ... I thought Joe had left the country and so (selfishly) I was disappointed when he was back in town causing me stress.*

14 October 2017: *Love! I have been noticing my feelings in my relationship with my husband. Things are particularly lighthearted and fun for us at the moment. I feel deeply connected and in love with* *him both physically and spiritually, and I feel that it will always be this way (although my rational head reminds me that it will not and relationships always wax and wane; however, my heart doesn't feel that right now). It's not that I don't always feel strongly about my husband, but somehow it has been more noticeable, surprising, and different recently.* [Anna and her husband married ten years ago and have been together now for nearly twelve years – a complete Jupiter cycle. This may explain her recent feelings of especially deep connection and happiness in the relationship.]

17 October 2017: *Feeling Content! I feel things are going well in life, and that I have a clarity of mind that I have not felt in a long time or ever? I feel organised, calm, content, sociable and that I can cope with anything life throws at me. I can see the bigger picture of what I want to do and how I will do it, and it's a surprising and nice feeling. This feeling of contentment and calm is not something I am used to and it's great.* [Given this overall feeling of well-being, it's noteworthy that Jupiter's shift into Scorpio trined Anna's natal Jupiter, powerfully placed at 0° Cancer.]

26 October 2017: *Feeling threatened! Today in the space of about ten minutes I felt threatened by someone in the street and had a strong feeling of paranoia when getting into my car. I then travelled on, only to have the exact same feelings with a different man when I stopped at the traffic lights. It was so unusual for me to feel like this that it surprised me.*

JAMES (AGE 60)
Transiting Jupiter in Scorpio is conjunct James's Neptune at 0° Scorpio and his Ascendant at 2° Scorpio and squares his Uranus in Leo in the 9th house.

10-12 October 2017: *On the morning of the 10th I had a quite unusual thing happen. For a month or so I had been experiencing a very heavy feeling of both mental and physical lack of wellbeing, to the point where I was wondering about ill-health being the root cause. That morning I was aware of both a mental and a physical sense of the 'poison' draining out of me – that was the phrase/thought that went through my mind at the time. It was a very peculiar feeling and lasted through this period and beyond. I had an odd discussion – almost a violent argument with a close friend around feminism – basically about whether men should call themselves feminist. It became a bit of a thing over the next few weeks and even the pre-current media debate (regarding largely male abuse of power, especially in a sexual context) cropped up a number of times. Seemed to start with this discussion and did lead to a fair bit of reflection by me on issues of masculinity. I noted a few times over the period, particularly the first couple of weeks, that I experienced vivid dreams on about four nights (not sequential) which involved my father (who is dead) and who I don't normally dream about.*

Karen (age 51)

Jupiter in Scorpio is transiting Karen's 2nd house. It is not triggering any fixed planets, but natal Jupiter is in the 9th in Gemini, conjunct her MC, and is a very dominant influence symbolically. Here is her summary of the entire research period.

Big time of transition and change. Lots of thoughts and ideas and wondering what my direction is – what path is my path? Not clear where I fit in, who my tribe are, what I believe anymore. Like emerging from a shell/form that I've outgrown but no idea what the new landscape looks like. [In the couple of days before Jupiter's shift, Karen reported 'money concerns and whether I need to let out the house'].

10 October 2017: *Bumped into ex-husband at 1:10 p.m. Hugely significant. We split and sold house 12 years ago this month'* [in October 2005, at the end of which Jupiter last entered Scorpio].

Kate (age 51)

Jupiter in Scorpio is transiting Kate's 6th house but is not triggering any fixed planets or angles. However, Kate has a close Sun-Jupiter conjunction in Cancer in the 2nd thereby amplifying Jupiter's overall influence.

Just before 10 October, a catalyst helped me decide to formalise my astrology studies by investigating some courses to do while I am away in India for a month in December. The catalyst was my teacher deciding to cancel her latest block of astrology classes, due to start on 10 October. It made me realise how much I love the subject and wish to continue studying it.

Round about 16 October, I decided to face up to my ex-husband about the way he communicates with me and the way our joint finances are organised to help pay for clothes and other things for the children. This was unpleasant.

I haven't noticed anything significant for 24 to 27 October, except that it has been really interesting watching the unfolding picture emerge of all the abuse claims highlighted on social media and news. It has made me reflect on an incident that happened to me around the age of 15. Thankfully, nothing sinister happened but it left me feeling very shaky. Most women have a story to tell. Overall, I have had a very optimistic month. I am enjoying my relationship with David [her new partner] *and my children.*

Conclusion

I am writing this final section on 11 November 2017. What a month! It has been an exceptionally intense, vivid period, both for the collective and for individuals living out their personal strands of this potent Jupiter in Scorpio thread in the current planetary weave.

It has been a real privilege to collect and share the intimate snapshots provided by Anna, James, Karen, and Kate. Jupiter in Scorpio has shone through their power struggles, their confrontations over shared finances, their deepest feelings of love and satisfaction, their encounters with partners once loved and long absent, their dreams of fathers long dead, their emergence from old lifestyles that no longer serve them, their commitment to in-depth study, their feelings of inner strength in the face of whatever life throws their way. I have had my own profound engagement with childhood pain triggered by some recent family events, gaining deeper insight into how the past, present and future all flow between and influence one another, for both good and ill.

Scorpio's ruler, Pluto, purging his way through Capricorn (2007-8 to 2024) is intensifying Jupiter in Scorpio's mining and exposing of institutional corruption centring around personal abuses of power by those who thought they could get away with it (think mythical Jupiter!). The tsunami of personal stories from women – and men – concerning their experiences of various kinds of sexual and other abuse has been extraordinary.

The Paradise Papers tax avoidance scandal [25] currently raging worldwide has also dredged to the surface another murky level of Scorpio abuse of power. In the end, there may not be much change in the way that the world's elite arrange our collective tax affairs largely to protect their own interests. However, there seems little doubt, even at this early stage, that a cultural shift of considerable proportions has taken place in recent weeks.

Abusers, beware! We are standing up, calling you out. And from now on, we will not stop. Many thanks, Jupiter in Scorpio!

The Mountain Astrologer
April/May 2018

---

25   The Paradise Papers is a special investigation by the UK's *Guardian* newspaper and 95 media partners worldwide into a leak of 13.4 million files from two offshore service providers and 19 tax havens' company registries. It reveals the vast scale of tax avoidance throughout the world.

INGRESSES
Saturn enters Aquarius: prequel to a New World Order

Saturn entered Aquarius on Sunday, 22 March 2020, at 3:59 a.m. UT (UK). On Mothering Sunday. That symbolic 'coincidence' really struck home. The planet is our mother and we humans have been abusing her for a very long time. To me, the symbolism (and the coronavirus [COVID-19] with its attendant worldwide consequences) is saying clearly to our human community (Aquarius) that it is time to take responsibility, accept widespread restrictions (Saturn) for the sake of our communities and our planet.

The very next day, the UK Prime Minister Boris Johnston told the nation in no uncertain terms that we are now in lockdown (another vivid manifestation of Saturn's entry into Aquarius), following the actions of other countries from China onwards in attempting to limit the spread of the pandemic.

SATURN IN CAPRICORN

Saturn entered Capricorn on 20 December 2017, beginning his long march towards a grim summit with Pluto, coming within close orb of their conjunction during the spring and early summer, then the winter of 2019. Since that entry, intensified hugely by the conjunction, all our organisational systems from nationhood, to politics, to health, to education, to formal religious institutions, to finance and business, have been tested to their very limits, and been found seriously wanting one way or another.

At the conjunction's closest point in April 2019, their symbolic *danse macabre* with the South Node in Capricorn gave rise to Greta Thunberg, the youthful feminine voice of the Great Mother? Certainly, of the Extinction Rebellion movement. To an astrologer's symbolic eye, the North Node in Cancer was now forcing us to pay attention to the crisis point which our planet has reached and pointing us in the direction that we needed to go in actually dealing with it, instead of our politicians worldwide indulging largely in ineffectual posturing or downright denial. 'Crisis – what crisis?'.

That much-feared Saturn-Pluto conjunction took place exactly on 12 January 2020: we are now at the outset of a drastic but hopefully positive if painful cycle of restructuring, culminating in the next Saturn-Pluto conjunction at 13/14° Pisces in 2053/4. I am not alone in thinking that a major instrument of that reconstruction arrived in the shape of the coronavirus, now shaping up as a global pandemic.

As a consequence, all our complacent ways of living are now being upended. Everyone is feeling the pain, one way or another. Anyone could die of this virus, even Trump or Bolsonaro.

We have found out in recent days that Boris Johnson and several members of his team spearheading management of the pandemic in the UK are now self-isolating, having tested positive for the virus. Prince Charles, UK head of state-in-waiting, has also contracted it – more manifestations of Saturn in Aquarius, as male leaders fall prey to an affliction crashing like a malevolent wave through the worldwide human community.

Capricorn and Aquarius

Both Capricorn and Aquarius are ruled by Saturn, Aquarius' 'old' ruler. I take some comfort from this as I watch events unfold, stunned and awed as usual by the symbolic accuracy of the planets' unfolding patterns. Saturn is at its potentially most constructive as it moves through those collective signs.

The transit through Capricorn has been saying, in essence: 'I have checked out all your systems. They are not what our mother planet or its creatures need – although much of it may be what some humans want: e.g., no minority on the face of Earth needs to accumulate billions whilst many of the majority go hungry – so I have given these systems, and the illusions and denials that go with them, a good kicking. I have joined forces with Pluto and the Nodes – since a good kicking is apparently not enough – and sent you the highly unpleasant gift of coronavirus. Great for the planet, but awful for humanity. Let's see if that's enough to make you pay attention to what needs to change.'

Saturn in Aquarius

And now we have Saturn in Aquarius: he dips in for a while, then returns to Capricorn from July until the end of 2020. Saturn has just told us that the old order represented by Capricorn is no longer viable – it's long past its sell-by date, so to speak. Aquarius is a forward-looking, collective sign, more concerned with the hidden potentials hovering in the future than with the past. Uranus, its 'new' ruler, amplifies that with its brilliance in developing new technologies in service of the human project. So – we can look forward to new, as yet undreamt solutions to the problems threatening us all with possible extinction in the present time.

A much bigger context, though, is this: there is a vast epochal process of turbulence and change happening which reaches a major developmental stage when Jupiter meets Saturn at 0° Aquarius on the Winter Solstice of 2020. What does this portend? Baigent, Campion and Harvey in *Mundane Astrology* describe this powerful 20-year re-curring cycle as 'the ground base of human development which marks the interaction between perception of ideas, potentialities (Jupiter) and their manifestation in the concrete world (Saturn).'

There is more. The symbolically world-shaping duo of Jupiter and Saturn take over 800 years to go through the four elements, reflecting changing epochs as they go. I've written about this in some detail in 'Some Notes on Cycles in a Time of Crisis', published last year on Astrodienst if you'd like to take a look.

The materialist era

For now, let's just look back to 1802. That was the year of the Jupiter-Saturn conjunction's early entry into the earth element where it remained for over 200 years. Its last meeting in earth took place at 23° Taurus in May 2000. That 1802 date coincided with the Industrial Revolution's gathering pace and impact at the beginning of the 19th century as the materialist age of exploitation of Earth's natural resources for profit began. Let's not get too holier than thou, here, though. Political philosopher Thomas Hobbes in the mid-17th century posited that in the state of nature, people's lives are 'solitary, poor, nasty, brutish, and short,'[26] and there is no doubt that the lives of a massive number of humans – especially in developed Western countries – have gained hugely improved health, longevity, quality of life and opportunities for personal fulfilment as a result of our astonishing progress in harnessing the forces and resources of nature.

However, the point would appear to be that, at the very end of Jupiter-Saturn's sojourn in earth, we have been brutally made aware (especially in the last couple of years) that the costs of the march of progress now heavily outweigh the benefits, to the extent that the very survival of our lives on Earth is under threat.

THE AIRY FUTURE

I find it fascinating that the years since 2000 (if you like the 12th-house phase of the long Jupiter-Saturn traverse through earth) have offered us more than a glimpse of what the impending shift of the conjunction into air may look like. The appearance of the first iPhone in June 2007 and its spread (like a virus!), so much so that smartphones have become a ubiquitous technology across the globe in less than ten years, has revolutionised the way we live. The generation known as the Millennials are the first in human history never to have known what a life without airy inter-connection was like.

Astrologers have known for a long time that the year 2020 was to be one like no other: it is the first year for over 200 years of 'the transition

---

26 From *Leviathan or The Matter, Forme and Power of a Common-Wealth Ecclesiasticall and Civil*, commonly referred to as *Leviathan*, by Thomas Hobbes (1588-1679). Published in 1651.

of the (Jupiter-Saturn) conjunction from one element to another. The "mutation conjunction" has always been considered to be of particular importance, marking a major shift in emphasis and orientation in the world' – from *Mundane Astrology*.

Thus far, as we live through stormy turbulence at the beginning of 2020, we can see the 'emphasis and orientation' of the approaching air era becoming clear. One major consequence of the coronavirus pandemic sweeping through our world as Saturn shifts into Aquarius, inviting us to live differently and more responsibly as humans, is already very obvious. In the last couple of weeks, there has been an explosion of collective Zooming, Skyping, WhatsApping, etc., as we set about working from home and transferring our individual and group lives to the airwaves.

Still to come after the mutation conjunction into 0° Aquarius on the Winter Solstice of 2020 – Pluto's shift into Aquarius in 2024. Fasten those seatbelts, folks. We've been selected to be present at the dawn of a new epoch.

anne-whitaker.com
March 2020

Ingresses
Pluto enters Aquarius in 2024: a major step in 'Boldly Going'

There I was two days ago, lying in a heap in bed, listening to the early morning news, slowly coming round, hand clutching a cup of tea. Situation normal in our house, of a morning. Then my ears pricked up. According to BBC Radio 4, the first stone of the Extremely Large Telescope (ELT) had been ceremoniously laid only the previous day – on 26 May 2017. The ELT is an astronomical observatory and the world's largest optical/near-infrared telescope now under construction. Part of the European Southern Observatory (ESO), it is located on top of Cerro Armazones in the Atacama Desert of northern Chile.

Along with – probably – countless others like me (and not a few fellow astrologers, I bet) not having a scientific background but nonetheless a lifelong interest in science, I had been following the progress of this project with great interest.

> '*The ELT will tackle* (to quote from eso.org) *the biggest scientific challenges of our time, and aim for a number of notable firsts, including tracking down Earth-like planets around other stars in the "habitable zones" where life could exist – one of the Holy Grails of modern observational astronomy.*
>
> *It will also perform stellar archaeology in nearby galaxies as well as make fundamental contributions to cosmology by measuring the properties of the first stars and galaxies and probing the nature of dark matter and dark energy. On top of this, astronomers are also planning for the unexpected – new and unforeseeable questions will surely arise from the new discoveries made with the ELT. The ELT may, eventually,*

revolutionise our perception of the universe, much as Galileo's telescope did 400 years ago.'

Approval for this stunning project came through on 11 June 2012, with construction work on the site starting in June 2014. By December 2014, over 90% of the total funding had been secured. The first stone of the telescope was ceremoniously laid on 26 May 2017.

Now – here is the bit that made me sit bolt upright, almost spilling my tea: the start of ELT operations, according to Wikipedia, is currently planned for 2024. Yes, 2024, the year that Pluto fully enters Aquarius after dipping in and out of that sign during its slow exit from Capricorn in 2023/4. The two statements 'probing the nature of dark matter and dark energy' and 'planning for the unexpected – new and unforeseeable questions will surely arise' could hardly be more appropriate summaries of the essence of this momentous planetary shift of the most symbolically powerful, transformative planet Pluto into Aquarius: the most scientifically oriented, unpredictable, revolutionary sign of the zodiac.

This entry of Pluto into Aquarius represents a major stage in a lengthy process of radical change for our world which I summarised very briefly in a recent post on this blog [astrologyquestionsandanswers.com]:

'Next up, Pluto shifts from Capricorn into Aquarius in 2024, beginning a long trine aspect to the 1892 Neptune-Pluto conjunction in Gemini. More air. The next Uranus-Neptune conjunction, in 2165, will take place in early Aquarius, their first meeting in the air element for a thousand years.

Thus, since 1980, when the Jupiter-Saturn conjunction at 5-8 degrees Libra entered the air element for the first time since its last entry in the 12th century AD, we have been moving gradually into an air-dominated era, with the sign of Aquarius in high focus. We are moving from an emphasis on material development and planetary exploitation, which characterised the Industrial Revolution and the whole materialist culture arising, to one of global social development – that of ideas, information, communication and relationships – expedited by technology, for the coming 200 years or so.'

By now, I was fully awake, excited – and once again awestruck by the powerful symbolic links between major steps taken in the human project for good or ill and major planetary shifts. The first light of the Extremely Large Telescope in 2024 is just one bright strand in what will be a complex and intricate weave of all kinds of profound changes from 2024 onwards, which will usher in a radically different world from the one into which we Baby-Boomers were born. Let's hope the upcoming generations make a more constructive job of it than we have done.

Dell Horoscope
March/April 2018

Transits
'Seems you can't outsmart Mother Nature'
– Mark Hyman

Mars has just moved from watery Cancer into fiery Leo as I write this column early in July 2019 – a good time to entertain you with a small but telling local tale which spans one two-year Mars cycle from around the summer of 2017. Natal Mars in Cancer – *I know, I have one of those!* – doesn't get the best press. But boy, are we tenacious and persistent when we are deeply angered. So, this is an excellent Mars in Cancer story as far as I am concerned, although the managers of Glasgow Botanic Gardens and Kelvingrove Park would almost certainly disagree.

We have had the good fortune to live right beside the Botanic Gardens and Kelvingrove Park for many years. A long, wide, sloping path takes us down into the park, then levels out to follow the banks of the River Kelvin for a couple of meandering miles, eventually leading up onto Kelvin Way, Glasgow's world famous Kelvingrove Art Gallery and Museum, the Kelvin Hall and Glasgow University. I have lost count of how many times we've done that walk in all weathers – usually wet, this being Glasgow of which I speak.

The right-hand side of the path opposite the river is rich in vegetation – the usual untidy, seasonally varying greenery and self-planting tree seedlings so beloved of nature left to herself (clue here to what's coming). Locals of all ages frequent the path: couples, individual walkers, small children, parents, cyclists, runners, dogs. A favourite landmark of mine for all the years of walking this stretch has been two small, modest springs of iron-rich water, a few feet apart, arising from the soil close to the path. These springs have been leaving red deposits in the earth for as long as I've noticed them. I really like them – and have only just now realised that, perchance, having Mars in Cancer means like responding to like.

The springs only occasionally flowed slightly over the path; one needed merely to sidestep them. I don't think any of the locals walking there regularly would have described this as a nuisance. However, the Powers That Be took it into their heads to have other ideas: around a couple of years ago, very possibly when Mars was last in Cancer.

Thus began a concerted series of slowly escalating attempts to block the very modest occasional tricklings of iron spring overflow onto our riverside path. First of all, there was the digging of a long ditch along a thirty-foot stretch of the path, just below where the springs arose. This was slowly filled in with loose stone chippings by several workmen in between checking Facebook etc., on their mobile phones. For a while, this seemed to have been successful. No overflow.

However, having begun to take a somewhat displeased interest in this process – could the money in materials, wages and time not have been better spent funding rent for premises for a local youth club, for example? – we began to notice that the soil all along the length of the ditch was growing soggy. This didn't bode very well for the health of the local vegetation, up to their knees now (metaphorically speaking) in iron-infused spring water.

A few months later, we noticed that the iron springs had soaked their way along the stone chippings. The overflow was starting up again. Only there was more of it now. Cue more time, labour, Facebook-checking, expenditure. An exit pipe was duly installed below the path from beneath the offending springs' location, discharging by now an increased volume of spring water into the River Kelvin opposite. For some time, success. No overflow onto the path.

However, this temporary bureaucratic respite didn't work for long either. The soggy soil got soggier and longer in area, and we noticed that the red deposits at the outlets from the two springs had markedly grown. Hmm, we thought, becoming increasingly interested in this escalating war. 'I think those springs are getting angry!' I remarked. My Aquarian husband, like me not a great friend of formal hen-brained authority, agreed.

The next round consisted of even more labour, more Facebook checking, with maybe a smattering of Instagram this time, and the creation of a low wooden fence the whole length of the unsuccessful ditch and the equally unsuccessful stone chippings. That might well have funded a part-time park keeper to empty the bins more frequently. Just a thought.

After a few months of this, you can now see the results. To my delighted astrologer's eye, the iron springs got especially pissed off during Mars' recent transit through Cancer, liberally staining the offending wooden fence with a big splat of watery iron beside it and flowing liberally all the way across the path.

A few days ago, with Mars still transiting Cancer, I encountered two men, the younger wearing a red jumper (you couldn't make this stuff up!) gathering what turned out to be iron water bacterial samples for his PhD research. The other guy was his supervisor. I regaled them with the story of how those wonderful little iron springs had gradually risen up and stuck it to the Powers That Be. Then – as you would – I informed them that in symbolic terms the planet Mars rules iron, anger and the colour red. 'Wow, put that in your PhD!' quoth the supervisor to his student. And off I went on my way, punching the air in a victory salute on behalf of those wonderfully Martian springs.

In the very small and the very large scale – as we are currently finding out – nature will always win in the end. We would do well to remember this, now, right across the globe.

The Astrological Journal
September/October 2019

Transits
Saturn through Sagittarius: the Joyful Child grows up

Saturn, the great realist of the zodiac, has now settled into his journey through the exuberant, joyful sign of Sagittarius, remaining there until the end of 2017. A dominant Jupiter-Saturn square in my own horoscope has been causing me to reflect on the need for Jupiter's natural, spontaneous exuberance to be modified and curbed by Saturn's practicality and realism if we want to generate anything lasting in our lives. This reflection has made me think of the importance of retaining the capacity for simple Jupiterian joy, as life tosses its inevitable Saturnian challenges our way.

In honouring both Jupiter and Saturn, then, let us first celebrate the spontaneous, resilient, Joyful Child within all of us; explore how it fares as we mature. If we are lucky, this part manages to survive the batterings, brutalities and tragedies of existence, continuing to provide inspiration and faith that life is worth living.

The Joyful Child in essence

Who, exactly, is this Child? The basic stuff of which s/he is made is the element of fire, that which the gods prized so much they wanted to keep to themselves. But Prometheus stole some, hidden in a fennel stalk, to give to us. He was savagely punished for his misdemeanour – but ever since, we humans have had at least one chip of that magical, divine substance lodged in us. Everyone has some, some people have too little, others have too much.

What is it? It's the spark of divine light, that which tells us we are special and immortal, that we're here for a reason, that our lives have purpose, that we have a future worth seeking out. It fuels wonder, injects the passion of inquiry into mere curiosity, causes learning and exploration to be a joyful end in themselves. It gives the capacity to look out at the world with a fresh set of eyes, taking pleasure at what's there because it's new, exciting. It brings spontaneity and the gift of laughter. It fuels play which is at the core of a response to life which is fundamentally creative and imaginative.

It is highly protective and supportive of life, especially when the going is rough, giving the hope that things will get better. It enables tough times to be survived through the unquenchable belief that suffering may be awful and protracted – but it means something; it is not just the random brutality of quixotic gods or fate. It brings the capacity *in extremis* to laugh at the sheer absurdity of life and oneself – a capacity which can drag one out from under the worst of times for just long enough to reaffirm that life, despite everything, is worth living.

The precious creature formed from such magical substance never grows up in the sense of assuming worldly responsibilities, and never gives up on life's possibilities and delights. It cannot be ordered forth – it just appears, then disappears: will-o'-the-wisp. Readers will recognise the Gemini-Sagittarius polarity here!

Leaving the Otherworld

The advance through adulthood, as the Saturn seven-year cycle unfolds, alters one's perception of what it is to be young. Having been scarred by life as we all are, watching a pre-school child absorbed in play is delightful, but also poignant. Delightful because it demonstrates clearly that there is another world than the one that we usually inhabit which is full of Saturn's deadlines, duties and demands. This Otherworld is full of goblins and fire engines, magic bubbles and imaginary friends, bright green tigers who speak, and amenable adults happy to give you the keys to the scary castle where you can spend days of adventure without anyone telling you that it's impossible for giants to keep a special pocket full of ice cream that never melts, just waiting for you to come and eat it.

It's poignant because we wonder, looking at this absorbed child, how s/he will cope with an adult world whose entry tariff is extracted from the struggle between the fantasy world of childhood where anything is possible and the reality testing which takes place as we grow and confront the limits which life sets for us.

The seven-year stages of the Saturn cycle offer a helpful containing context within which to explore how the Joyful Child within us fares as life's journey unfolds. There is a case to be made for not starting children at school until the first square of the cycle. Five or six, the common age, seems too early to remove children from the Otherworld of play and unbounded imagination. Shakespeare vividly expressed the average child's response to being dragged from the Otherworld in *As You Like It*:

'And then the whining schoolboy, with his satchel,
And shining morning face, creeping like a snail
Unwillingly to school.'

If we did start children at school at the later age of seven or eight, socially disruptive though that would be in many ways, perhaps it would give more time for the Joyful Child's domain to become established. Thus, it might be easier for the growing person to retain contact with the Otherworld as a source of inspiration throughout life.

Essentially what happens from the time of starting school through to the first Saturn square, as we step across the boundary of family, is that the Joyful Child begins to hide, its energy becoming redirected as we become more aware of ourselves in relation to what the outer world expects. By and large, that outer world is more interested in us being able to tie our shoelaces, read, tell the time and be truthful than it is in knowing what a wonderful chat we had in Chinese last night with the bright green tiger who sleeps under our bed.

Early adulthood

The first Saturn opposition at age 14/15 is the point where we take bigger steps out of family, begin to challenge parental authority, move towards greater identification with the peer group. The need to play and daydream which is fundamental to the Joyful Child's world, and the creative energy fuelling these activities, gets sublimated further at this point. It channels into the pursuit of achievement of an academic or vocational nature, and exploration of the exciting, troubling world of relationship and emerging sexuality as bodily changes propel the young person towards physical adulthood.

The Joyful Child's impetus towards discovery and exploration of the new engages in a complex dance with the tough Saturnian realities also emerging. Too much time spent playing, not enough on taking responsibility, can have a high emotional cost, e.g., exam failure or unwanted pregnancy.

The waning square at age 21/22 brings with it the world's expectation that we should begin to assume adult responsibility, get a job if we've been studying for years, get serious. Many people marry or enter into long-term partnerships at this stage, perhaps out of unconscious fear of facing the adult world and its responsibilities alone. I have gained the impression from my varied professional work with people of differing ages over a long period of time that part of the vulnerability of this life stage comes from a realisation that childhood is, indeed, over.

Recently I came across a scrapbook of newspaper cuttings from my Personally Speaking column which I wrote in my early twenties for the *Stornoway Gazette*. In it was a piece called 'Thoughts on Childhood' published in September 1970 which supports the view just expressed:

> *'I am close enough to childhood for my memories still to be clear and reasonably untainted by the rosy hues of nostalgia, although I realise now that as soon as we have ceased to be children, the world of childhood becomes a closed world to us, one which we can never recapture except through flashes of memory and watching our own children grow up. As adults, no matter how hard we wish to recapture the feeling of childhood, we must always remain "watchers by the threshold".'*

This is a critical age in terms of the emerging individual's capacity to retain that spark of vital creative energy which ensures that engaging with the world as it is does not mean stifling the Joyful Child who has been curbed by now and knows that much of the time it's not safe to be too overt. But it is important that the re-channelled energy continues to flow.

It can express itself in passionate commitment to a career, as opposed to working purely to provide life's necessities. It can manifest through joy in good friends or absorbing hobbies and interests outwith work. For some people, early parenthood brings, along with responsibility, the opportunity to view the world again through the eyes of their growing children.

There is also a direct route for expression through the sheer animal vitality of youth which all by itself can make life feel worth living. I recall a middle-aged male friend of mine's recent comment on seeing a young man running effortlessly up several flights of stairs recently, not because he had to, just because he could. 'I can't do that anymore – my back's too bad!' remarked my friend. 'It made me feel wistful, reminded me of the youthful grace and energy which I once had.'

Point of entry

From the Saturn return at age 28/30 onwards, the major underlying task changes: from discovering the overall shape of who you are in relation to your own life, to beginning to use the platform you have built as support in offering your unique contribution to the wider world. By this stage, the balance achieved between necessary realism and the joyous, inspirational, creative aspects of life is crucial to how the next 14/15 years unfold. The poet Dylan Thomas senses and honours the presence of the child he was, in his marvellous 'Poem in October' written on his 30th birthday:

> *'And I saw in the turning so clearly a child's forgotten*
> *mornings...where a boy...whispered the truth of his joy*
> *To the trees and the stones and the fish in the tide.'*

In the poem's last verse, he writes:

> '*And the true*
> *Joy of the long dead child sang burning*
> *In the sun.*'

For Dylan Thomas, as for many poets and even more of us ordinary citizens, being in nature can powerfully evoke that within us which never ages, which rejoices in being alive and is powerfully connected to the endless cycle of birth, maturation, decline, death and return.

The thirties and forties are decades where a major challenge lies in the grinding process of reality testing our hopes, wishes, dreams and ambitions against the world as it is. Most of us eventually get to the Saturn opposition of the mid-forties: we are still here, we may still be functioning tolerably well, but we're not young anymore.

MIDLIFE

From the mid-forties on, we only have to look in the mirror – or realise that our idea of a good Friday night is increasingly of going to bed early, not with a hot lover, but with a good book – to be aware of the relentless advance of mortality. It becomes harder at this stage for most people to keep in touch with the Joyful Child, keep its energies flowing. For many people, brutalities of an environmental, political, social or personal nature have borne down so hard that the vital spark of life of the Joyful Child can now fuel only the dogged survival instinct.

I have found that one of the compensations of middle age is deeply paradoxical and was first alerted to it a number of years ago by a comment made by my late mother-in-law, then approaching eighty. The way she dealt with an old age full of physical infirmity was inspiring. She had a lively sense of fun and humour, maintained great interest in the wider world as well as that of her own family and friends, and kept up a prodigious correspondence right up to her passing. The

Joyful Child in her was alive right to the end, sustained in her case by a strong, ecumenical religious faith.

'You know,' she said, 'occasionally when I'm not thinking about anything in particular, I catch sight of my face in the mirror and get an awful shock. I see an old woman's face looking out at me – but inside I don't feel old at all – I feel just the same as I did when I was young.'

The paradox is this. The body ages to the point where you are faced with increasing physical evidence of the passage of time; but an opportunity can also slowly arise to perceive, with a clarity not possible in youth, that this ageing body has been carrying something else through life which is different, ageless, woven with the physical – that spark of immortality which comes in with life's quickening, flying free at physical death. Thus, as mortality's approach via Saturn becomes more and more difficult to ignore, a major compensation can be offered via Jupiter: that which is clearly immortal becomes more and more evident by contrast.

In this way, the great archetypes symbolised by astrological Jupiter and Saturn can achieve balance as ordinary human life reaches its conclusion.

Apollon: The Journal of Psychological Astrology
Issue 5, April 2000

TRANSITS:
Uranus through Aries: fire and fury

The world certainly feels like a more turbulent place in the wake of revolutionary, high-tech, unpredictable Uranus' fiery traverse of Aries, the first, Mars-ruled and most hot-headed of all the zodiacal signs. That turbulence has been greatly deepened and amplified by Uranus' long square to Pluto's purging presence in Capricorn which reached exactitude in 2012-13. At the core of the Uranus transit through Aries has been the call to challenge limiting circumstances, break free of constraint or restraint and take initiatives in engaging with possibilities hitherto unseen or unknown. 'Choose radical change – or have it forced upon you' was the essence of the Uranus in Aries message as that planet slashed and burned its intemperate way through the 2010-19 period.

We are certainly living through very unstable and frightening times. However, it is clear from the bigger planetary patterns shaping up over the next five-to-six years and beyond that a whole world order is coming to an end, as a new one slowly arises from its ashes. Throughout history, birth – whether of a new world order or a tiny new person – has never been accomplished without turmoil, upheaval and pain.

As Baby-Boomers, those of my generation are unlikely to live long enough to see the shape of this world order settle and become clear. But in the unprecedented changes of the last few years, we can certainly see its chaotic beginnings as the old order crumbles. I have faith that the Millennial generation, whose values are rooted much less in materialism than ours, will in the end be able to address the huge environmental and political problems currently facing our world. Perhaps Millennials can come up with ways of living which run more *with* the grain of our interconnected lives than those of us gradually leaving the stage have been able to accomplish.

From global to local

As I write this in May 2019, the Saturn-Pluto conjunction with the South Node in Capricorn, allied by sign element with Uranus' recent entry into Taurus, is forcing collective recognition that planet Earth is in crisis. Young Greta Thunberg's brave, solitary picket of Sweden's parliament led to the Extinction Rebellion movement which has mobilised the young (and the not so young!) across the world. Politicians will be left with no choice but to act – as we all will, if we are to avert the juggernaut of environmental catastrophe that appears to be heading our way.

However, I have an interesting and inspiring local story to tell, most appropriately now that Uranus is in Taurus. It concerns innovative and environmentally respectful land use by and for a whole community, a project which has captured the imagination of people far beyond Scotland where it takes place.

This story has had many stages, culminating in its most recent and successful seven-year Children's Wood development phase in Glasgow whilst Uranus stormed its way through Aries: I checked back in old local records to the 1930s to discover that the land was first listed as a public space the last time Uranus was in Aries. It subsequently became football pitches which were extensively used by local young folk for several decades and were still being used as such when my husband and I moved into the area in the mid-1980s.

A few years after that, the city council knocked down the goalposts, and the land was allowed to fall into disrepair. At this point, local residents, realising that the council's intention was to sell off the land, began to set up initiatives to save it for community use. The most notable were Compendium Trust and then the North Kelvin Meadow initiative which continues to this day. But the latter initiative's focus is more on land management than on community and child development through engagement with nature, for which purpose The Children's Wood charity gradually came into being.

Community fire and focus

Throughout this whole period, it has been my great privilege to play a very small part in a bold community initiative which demonstrated how that defiant, optimistic, fearless Uranus in Aries energy could be harnessed to take on the might of the Powers That Be: a classic David versus Goliath tale. In essence, during 2011-18, a local community here in Glasgow fought hard, against all kinds of opposition to keep the developers at bay and conserve a wild space for community use. We eventually won – a real testament to what faith grounded in determined collective action can achieve. The book which Emily Cutts wrote about this whole process, *The Dear Wild Place: Green Spaces, Community and Campaigning,* was published with perfect astrological timing in March 2019, just as Uranus shifted into Taurus for the long term. No (since you ask), astrological advice was *not* involved!

As an astrologer, I have been enthralled to see how this period of passionate, single-minded Uranus in Aries action unfolded, from its early beginnings in 2011 to its eventual success by the end of 2018. It has also been my good fortune to know and closely observe the pioneering work of the Children's Wood campaign initiator, Emily Cutts. Without her persistent, galvanising energy and, at times, seemingly crazy optimism, this campaign would never have gathered the momentum needed to succeed in the way it has done.

Emily knows she is a Sun in Aries person, but not much more than that. However, being very open-minded, she was happy for me to draw up her horoscope and have a look at it, as she had become intrigued by my description of what transiting Uranus in Aries meant in essence and how closely it appeared to describe her life and actions at that time. What I discovered was a symbolic picture of a radical community activist, which could have been designed as a textbook case! When Emily agreed to my writing about her and the campaign, I couldn't have been more delighted. Emily's story during 2011-18 is also the story of the Children's Wood campaign and its success.

Emily's natal horoscope

Let's begin with Emily's well-stocked 9th house, the place of perspectives, vision and faith (chart on page 289). It is home to her South Node, Eris conjunct Mercury retrograde, and the Sun, all in Aries and all opposing Pluto in Libra in the 3rd house. This powerful, fiery, combative combination speaks of someone who has come into this world with the capacity to use her personal drive, power, aggression, determination, communication skills and vision to make a real difference through espousing a cause close to her heart.

But *what* cause? Clues to this lie in her vocational significators: the Midheaven (MC), Chiron and Venus – ruler of the MC and dispositor of the Libra North Node – all in the fixed earth sign of Taurus. These placements show a deep love of nature and of Earth, and a great sensitivity to Earth's woundedness and need for nurturing and healing, suggested by that Chiron-MC conjunction. Venus is also trine Ceres, the dwarf planet signifying fertility and guardianship of Mother Earth, located in Capricorn in Emily's 5th house of creativity, of which a major expression is commitment to the care and nurturing of children and young people. This is reflected in the name, the Children's Wood, which became a registered charity in 2015.

Emily has the politically- and community-oriented, maverick, rebellious planet Uranus conjunct the Part of Fortune in her Scorpio 4th house of family, roots and the home base, opposite that solid, stable Venus in Taurus trine Ceres. This Uranus-Venus-Ceres pattern strongly allies with Emily's powerful Aries planets in the 9th house, indicating her being prepared to adopt whatever unorthodox collective methods worked in furthering innovative projects centred on land use.

However, Aries energy is best known for its fearless, sometimes reckless, pioneering spirit. Brilliant for setting things in motion, it needs grounding, determination, persistence and visionary zeal to sustain its initial impetus. In Emily's horoscope, the aspects of 1st-house Saturn in Leo trine the 9th-house Aries planets and trine Neptune and asteroids Vesta and Pallas in Sagittarius in the 5th house can provide just the combination required to develop not only a vision of how things could be, but also the strength over time to carry it through to completion.

TRIGGERS TO ACTION

In 2005, seven years before Uranus' shift into Aries supplied the symbolic impetus setting off the dynamic energies described above in her natal birth chart, Emily began working for Glasgow's innovative Centre for Confidence and Wellbeing. This Centre was set up by independent thinker and researcher Carol Craig, following the interest generated by her groundbreaking book, *The Scots' Crisis of Confidence,* originally published in February 2003. Subsequently, Carol wrote several other books analysing in depth how culture – including historical forces, common assumptions and shared values – shapes individuals' lives. Initially focusing on promoting Positive Psychology (in which Emily gained an MSc to add to her Psychology degree), Carol, the Centre and Emily soon became disillusioned with Positive Psychology's narrow focus on the merely psychological and individualistic aspects of human experience. Instead, they were 'more and more convinced that a large number of factors were important for human wellbeing – contact with nature, connection to others, exercise, diet, equality and non-materialistic values.' [27]

Emily then spent the next few years reporting on the above topics via her feature *Emily's News* on the Centre's website from the viewpoint of her immersion in considerable amounts of wellbeing research. She gradually developed a perspective and vision perfectly timed for Uranus' entry into her 9th house, triggering first her nodal axis, in the summer of 2011, then Eris, Mercury and the Sun for the next seven years. Here, in her own words, is how theory began to translate into direct action:

It was only in 2011 and 2012 that I could see a way to use what I was learning to make a practical difference to people's lives. I could

---

[27] This and all the following quotes are taken from Emily Cutts' *The Dear Wild Place: Green Spaces, Community and Campaigning,* first published by CCWB Press, 2019.

see how we could take a wild patch of land in our community, which was under threat from a housing development, and turn it into a community resource that could tackle some endemic contemporary problems. In fact, I believe what we have achieved with our wild place is part of the Centre's legacy. Ultimately this community project had the strength to save the land.

Progressions of Emily's natal chart show significant shifts which symbolically indicate an inner receptivity to the external Uranian challenges described. Her 9th-house Mercury in Aries turned direct when she was around 10 years old, and progressed into grounding Taurus in 2010, bringing a need to put all the ideas and theories she had been researching into practice (progressions not shown). This is supported when we look at the natal lunar nodes' placement in the 3rd and 9th houses at 5° degrees Libra-Aries, forming a cardinal t-square with caring Jupiter dynamically located at 0° Cancer in the 11th house of community groups.

Emily's learning began to translate itself into the need to bring people together in our local community in order to begin to 'tackle some endemic contemporary problems' just as her progressed Moon moved into Libra, activating the cardinal t-square and crossing her natal North Node-Pluto conjunction during 2011-12.

Planning a battle, waging a war

Using a 10° orb applying and separating, the violent and disruptive Uranus-Pluto square was in effect from 2010 to 2018, peaking with seven exact squares between 2012 and 2015. This 'chip' of the prevailing world energy was observable in the energy and turbulence of our local campaign.

As Emily puts it in her book, 'Folk have joked with me about how we've spent these years planning and leading a battle, or waging a war' (p. 14) – a war with local pessimists who thought at first that the campaign could never succeed, with the local authority who wanted the money, with the developers who wanted to buy the land and build

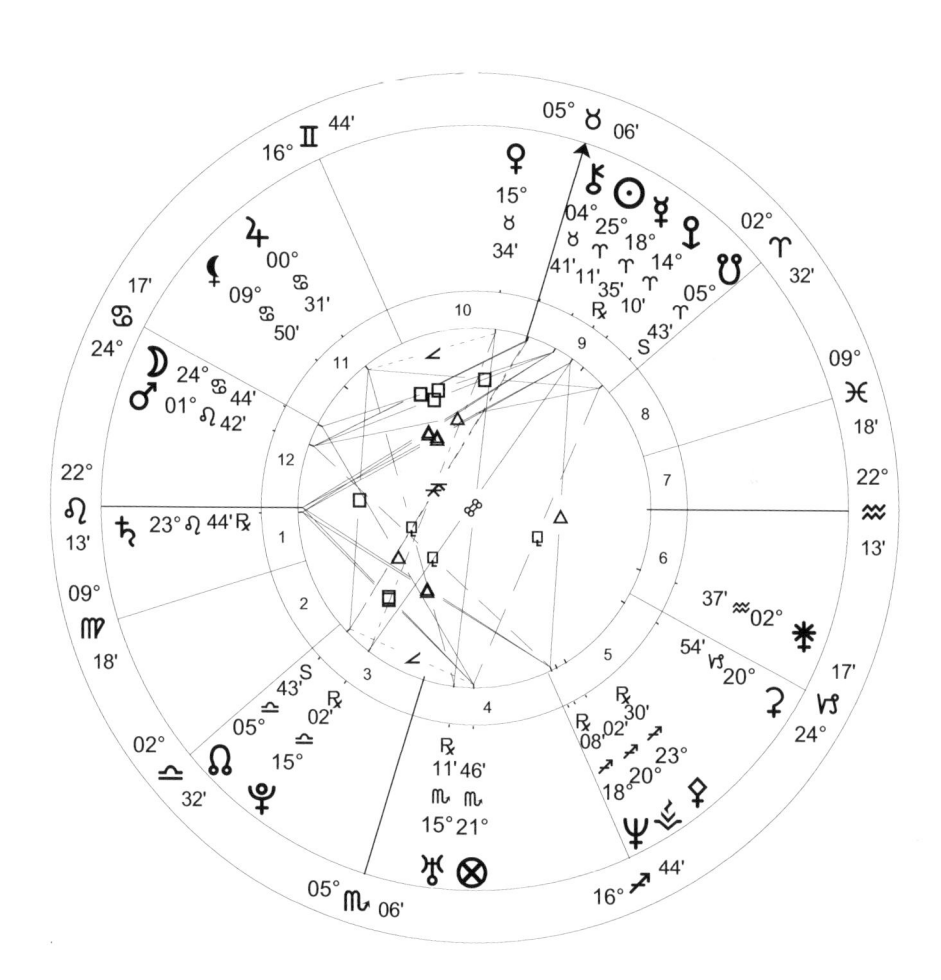

Emily's natal chart, data withheld

high-end housing unaffordable by local folk, with the city planning department and with the Scottish government. 'But in fact, this analogy works rather well. By encouraging local people to care about the land, my energy has been magnified many hundreds of times, and we have ended up winning the battle … That could only have happened by hundreds of people working together, making connections, friendships and forming a community based around shared values. All this was acted out on the shared stage of the land' (p. 14).

Uranus' shift from pioneering Aries to consolidating Taurus – first in May 2018, then settling in from March 2019 – very fittingly follows the gestation and writing of Emily's book about our campaign which was at last published in March 2019. Perfect astrological timing!

In conclusion

Several days each week, I walk through the local Children's Wood on my way home. Each time – rain, hail or shine – it makes me happy to do so. I see the well-developed community garden, including a sensory garden, run by a part-time paid worker and lots of local volunteers. There is a tree house and a fire pit which local people use for barbecues. There are lots of sawn-off logs arranged here and there as seating. There is a mud kitchen, much beloved of local children who enjoy it under the watchful eye of their parents. There are various play areas amongst the trees which have grown up in recent years. There is a labyrinth for meditative walking. And there is a wonderful 12-foot-high beehive called a Bee Dookit which now produces its own local honey.

The whole area is enclosed by fencing which makes it safe for youngsters to run about. There is a community shed for which planning permission has recently been granted to instal a toilet and running water. There is a brightly coloured mural painted by local children on the wall of this shed – as yet un-vandalised. No litter is lying about, and the many dog walkers mostly pick up after their animals. There are plenty of refuse bins, emptied every day by a local man who has lived in the area for several years.

I also know that more than 20 local schools use the area for curriculum-supported outdoor education. Children from those schools visit a nearby old folks' home to share experiences with the residents, often accompanied by a wonderfully energetic lady of 90 years who is a local volunteer. An outdoor nursery provides infant and toddler care three mornings a week. There are groups run by experienced youth workers who are beginning to win over local young people whose lives are already blighted by drugs, alcohol and adverse family circumstances.

The facility hosts all kinds of events, from Hallowe'en parades to bee festivals to fundraising sales to book launches. In fact, *The Dear Wild Place* was launched on the Meadow in the spring of 2019, with wine tastings. Every season of the year has its own special festivals. The most exciting recent development, as Uranus settles into Taurus, is the application the Children's Wood charity has submitted for asset transfer: if the application is approved, this will secure the lease of the land for community use for the next 50 years.

Since June 2010, the month that Jupiter's conjunction with Uranus at 0° Aries announced Uranus' spectacular seven-year bout of worldwide 'boldly going', some terrible events have played out across the globe. But we have also been treated to what humanity can do at its most visionary, most inventive, most unforeseen.

The story of Emily Cutts and Glasgow, Scotland's *Dear Wild Place* is proof of that!

Author's note: Emily read through and approved this article before it was submitted for publication.

The Mountain Astrologer
March/April 2020

Progressions
Secondary progressions: stepping into the mystery

'I would love to live like a river flows, carried by the surprise of its own unfolding.' – John O'Donohue

Consider this surprise. Astrology textbooks tell you that the planets from Jupiter outwards move so slowly by progression that their shifts are of no consequence. On the very day in June 2016 that my 3rd-house Jupiter moved by secondary progression from life-long occupancy of Scorpio into Sagittarius, I was offered a large library of astrology books from a university lecturer whose wife, a keen student of astrology, had recently died. Phoebe, a participant in the 1997/8 research I did on Jupiter-Uranus conjunctions, started piano lessons for the first time and became very interested in fashion/image in 1997, the year her natal Neptune in Libra went direct by secondary progression. No doubt readers could add their own examples of progressed planetary effects which supposedly are of no consequence!

Introduction

I am very well aware that there are several ways of progressing a horoscope which are no doubt valid. However, traditional Secondary Progressions, or SPs as I shall now call them for short, are the only type which have consistently spoken to me with great accuracy. These are calculated by moving the planetary positions in the ephemeris for the day of birth forward one day for every year of a person's life, offering a way of determining the timing and understanding the meaning of significant developmental points in that individual's unique unfolding journey.

In this article, I am not proposing to reinvent the astro-wheel by offering detailed tuition on what SPs are, how to calculate them, work with them and relate them to whatever transits may be in operation at any given time. There is plenty of information of that type available on the Internet, as a quick Google search will reveal. However, my USA colleague Dawn Bodrogi in my estimation has done the finest recent work on the topic. Although Dawn sadly died in November 2017, you can still find her writings at The Inner Wheel website at theinnerwheel.com.

Instead, my aim is to offer a personal reflection on SPs, continuing in the same spirit as the opening paragraph. I'd like to share my clients' experiences of those mysterious symbolic tools as well as my own. My observations are also offered to experienced practitioners in such a way that they can take a moment to step back from their astro-toolkit and be freshly awestruck by the essential mystery which SPs evoke. Most of all, I'd like to intrigue and inspire readers who are fairly new to astrology to begin their own journey into this misty, awesome territory.

From the time I discovered SPs as a Faculty of Astrological Studies student in the 1980s, they have fascinated me. This fascination was amplified as I slowly became an experienced astrology teacher, using my classes (as you do) for the brilliant qualitative research opportunities that they undoubtedly provide on the hoof. When you first go round a class of a dozen students, tracking their Suns changing signs by SP, discovering their corresponding life changes as well as your own, it does rather cause you to scratch your head – after you and your students have come down from the sheer buzz of it all – and ask, 'But *why* does astrology work? And *why* does a purely symbolic technique like SPs seem to work, too?'

HELP IS AT HAND FROM QUANTUM SCIENCE

Good questions, which astrologers have been asking for centuries, millennia probably, ever since those Chaldean priests on their chilly watchtowers scanned the night skies for helpful advance warning signs that their kings and kingdoms were under threat. I do not propose in this short article to add to the vast amounts of erudite speculation which has arisen from such questions.

However, very briefly, my conclusion is this: modern science has demonstrated that we live, move and have our being as part of a vast energy field which ripples and changes in a sinuous, shapeshifting dance between order and chaos, order arising out of apparent disorder, in invisible patterns which would appear to hold 4% matter, 23% dark matter and 73% dark energy together in a vast cosmic web.

I think that astrology works by tracking and mapping those energy patterns through planetary cycles against the backdrop of either the constellations via sidereal astrology or our more familiar tropical astrology which is pegged to the ecliptic. By a blend of astronomical calculation, mythic imagination, intuition and observation of correlations between life on Earth and planetary movements over millennia, humans arrived at a way of deriving meaning from the energies generating our tiny corner of that vast cosmic web, the solar system. It is no surprise that reductionist thinking cannot cope with the possibility that something of great value to the human project could have arisen from this eclectic weave.

There are several ways in which one can creatively reflect upon that 4%, 23% and 73% ratio. I like to think of it in terms of the worlds of consciousness, personal unconscious and collective unconscious, finding Jung's term 'psychoid' very useful in enabling me to make sense of energies which can and do manifest simultaneously, all the way from very obvious and tangible to being highly influential in a person's life although invisible to the wider world.

For example, consider the client I saw some years ago with a dominant Saturn square Neptune aspect in his horoscope. James' profession was highly tangible: he made musical instruments. But a significant factor in the unfolding pattern of his life, also linked to that Saturn-Neptune square, was his having had to survive growing up with a severely alcoholic father. Being very aware of an inherited tendency to indulge in addictive escapist behaviours, he was trying to address this when he came for a consultation – as his secondary progressed Sun triggered natal Saturn square Neptune.

I think that an important part of the creative value of being a practising astrologer lies in helping clients like James to understand, accept and work constructively with the shape-shifting potential inherent in the particular energies with which they came into the world.

From the above perspective very briefly outlined, it isn't too difficult to tie in the planetary patterns in the sky here-and-now to the static picture of the natal horoscope. You are working, at least in part, with what you can actually see. However, in working with SPs, you are stepping into the mysterious, intangible world of the purely symbolic. I find that my (metaphorical at least!) understanding of that 4%, 23% and 73% ratio is very helpful in feeling comfortable with such mysterious territory. That which cannot be seen, perceived or understood via our five senses within the 4%-world of matter still has energetic validity in the landscape of the unseen 96% – that which modern science tells us is there, although we can only perceive it by inference and don't yet know what it is.

SPs AND FAMILY INHERITANCE

The most striking example of the mysterious power of SPs that I have ever had occurred a number of years ago when I was playing around with the weave of interconnectedness which you find as soon as you begin to spend time looking at family horoscopes. Having acquired the birth certificates of all four of my grandparents, three with accurately recorded birth times, and having calculated their horoscopes, I took a notion to progress the birth charts of the two grandparents who had been most significant for me, and whose characteristics I most clearly recognised blended in myself, i.e., my maternal grandfather Calum and my paternal grandmother Isabella – both born in different years at different times. I progressed their charts, both with accurate birth times, to the day of my own birth.

The result stunned me. *Both* grandparents' progressed Ascendants were 9° Virgo, *both* progressed Midheavens were 28° Taurus. And my angles? Yes, you've guessed it. My natal Ascendant is 9° Virgo, and natal Midheaven is 28° Taurus. My North Node is also 28° Taurus – and my pre-natal solar eclipse is 28° Taurus, thereby emphasising the significance of the IC-MC axis in the transmission of family fate, karma, genetic inheritance or whatever you wish to term it. I have written about this before (but where, I now forget!) and described my feeling then of having been 'brushed by the wing of a great mystery'.

Recently, whilst thinking about this article, I re-calculated that set of progressions, just in case I had somehow made a mistake all those years ago. The result was the same.

Planets going retrograde, then direct, by progression – and progressed New Moons

When I am preparing for an in-depth astrology reading, I routinely do an SP scan through the ephemeris: planets going retrograde, then direct some years later, usually reveal significant phases in a person's life. Take 'Antonia', for example, aged sixty-one when we met two years ago. She has been living in Scotland for many years. Her Venus went retrograde by progression at age eighteen, when she 'escaped' from a difficult family life in another part of the UK. At age fifty-nine, when Venus went direct, she began to feel the pull back to her home country, as well as feeling greater openness to people – and to the possibility of a significant relationship, after having been single for a number of years.

I also note years where there was a progressed New Moon. Depending on the length of a client's life to date, there may be two or even three of those, if the first one occurred in the early years. May's first progressed New Moon occurred when she was six years old, at which point she moved with her parents to the UK and a new life phase began. Her second progressed New Moon, at thirty-six, coincided with her return to the UK – she had by then been living abroad again for a number of years – and with her marriage and the birth of her child.

By a timeous piece of serendipity, last autumn 2016 as I was beginning to reflect on writing this article, I encountered a client ['Pearl' – overleaf are two biwheel charts showing nativity and SPs at age four and at 35] in her mid-30s who ticked several of the above key SP boxes in one reading. She has very generously allowed me to use parts of her

Pearl birth chart and sp at age 4

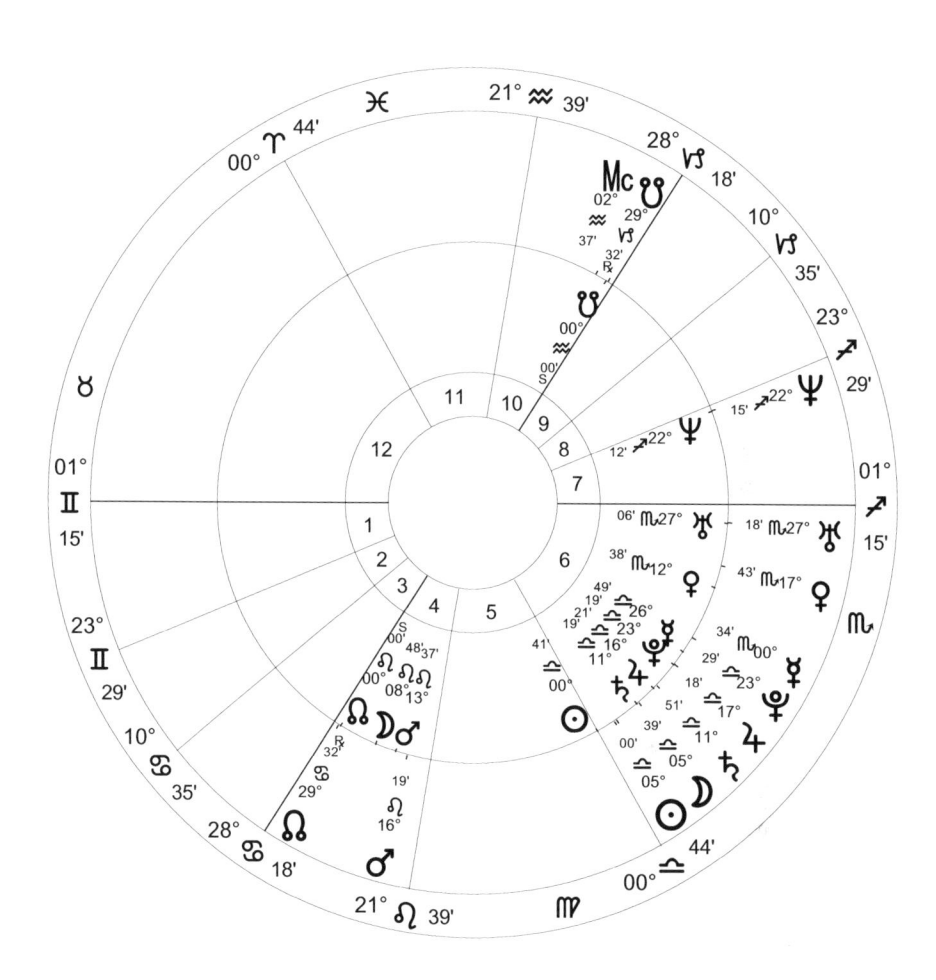

PEARL BIRTH CHART AND SP AT MID 30S

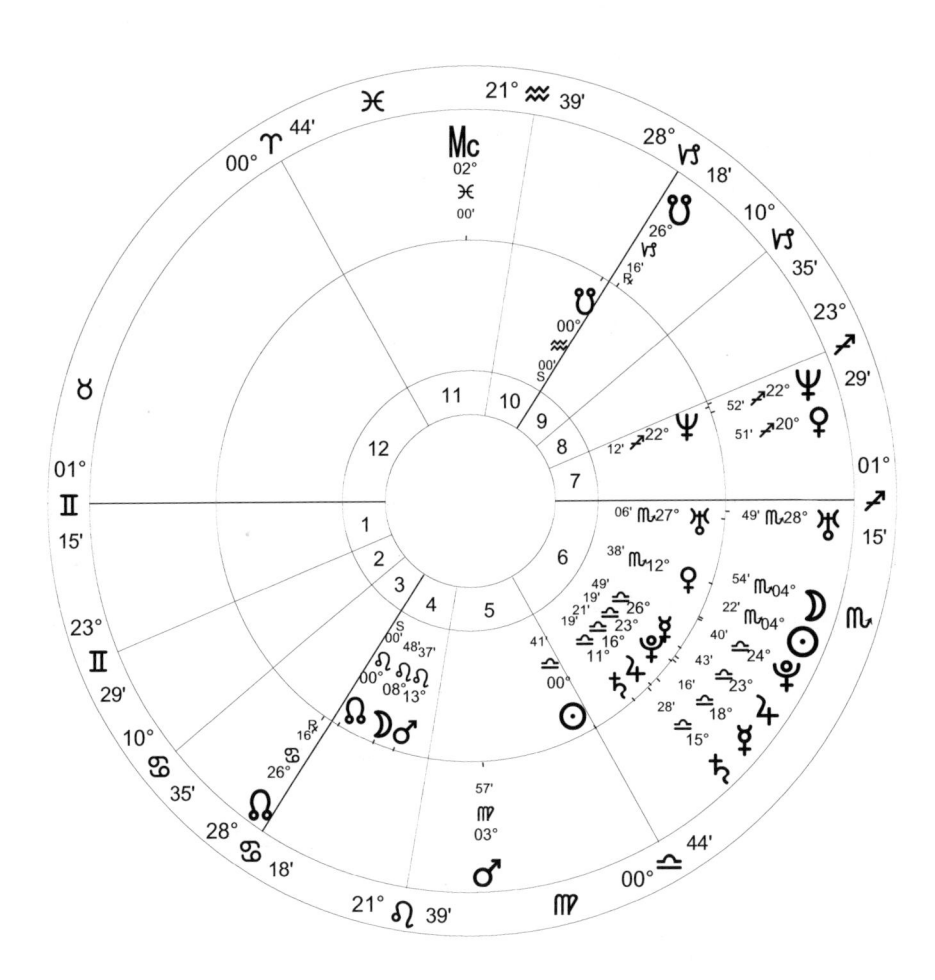

story to illustrate just how much SPs on their own, before one even begins to add the overlay of current transits, can give a vivid picture of an unfolding life. Here is what I wrote in my summing-up notes: 'A most interesting reading with a remarkable young woman who despite a very difficult early life and teenage years has managed to turn her life around.'

The two dominant SP features symbolically structuring Pearl's life's unfolding are the progressed New Moons, and ruling planet Mercury's shifts of sign as well as retrograde then direct motion.

Her first progressed New Moon, at 5° Libra in the 6th house came at age four. At the same age, progressed Mercury moved from Libra to Scorpio, also in the 6th house. She hit puberty at that age and, 'I was overwhelmed by a power I had no idea how to handle.' She was treated with hormone injections. Family, social and school difficulties arose from this, unsurprisingly. Family life was turbulent, they moved around a lot, and her parents separated whilst she was growing up.

Progressed Mercury went retrograde in Scorpio when she was 12, a point at which Pearl became 'a total nightmare' to herself and her family, getting into sex, drugs and all kinds of self-destructive behaviour. She fell in love and had her first serious love affair at fifteen. On the positive side, she was always drawing and painting and into music and the arts. Pearl did various jobs after leaving school, then had her daughter at nineteen. This coincided with the progressed Full Moon, and the start of her grounding herself.

Mercury retrograded back into Libra when Pearl was twenty-two. In her early twenties she had a crisis involving drugs in which 'I nearly died'. From then on, she went from one extreme to the other, turning her life around.

She took up yoga, became vegetarian, and aligned herself with as she put it 'the guidance of the Divine'. She is a yoga teacher, loves teaching, and being a natural performer, is probably very good at it.

She has also been with the same man since her early 20s, but as she has become more independent and self-motivated, the relationship has gradually withered and died. They broke up at the end of 2015, timed with her second progressed New Moon in early Scorpio, and with progressed Mercury's having gone direct in Libra and traversing the powerful natal Jupiter/Pluto conjunction over the next few years.

Pearl feels she is now in a new life phase but is not as yet clear about the way forward. She wants to develop her business and her writing, so I made various suggestions about how she could go about developing them both, pointing out that New Moons, progressed or otherwise, take place in the dark. Just as the familiar Sun-Moon monthly cycle takes a couple of days for the Waxing Crescent to appear, so in the 30-year progressed New Moon cycle, it takes a couple of years for the shape of a new life phase to become clear.

Pearl found knowing about her progressed New Moons' and progressed Mercury's unfolding, as well as the reinforcing information provided by transiting Jupiter's and Saturn's 11/12-year and 29/30-year cycles, extremely helpful and comforting. It gave her a sense of awe, a feeling of being held in something, a meaningful pattern much, much bigger than herself.

I felt the same. Inevitably, you become used over many years to astrological symbolism 'delivering' consistently. Every so often, however, you are privileged to witness the life of another person in which the symbolic tools we work with, in Pearl's case her SPs, speak with such eloquence that it takes your breath away.

Conclusion

I do hope that this guided stroll through some of the highways and byways of SPs and their mysterious significance has some effect in stimulating to consider doing so, especially those of you who have not yet explored that territory. You could start by following the shifts of the progressed MC-IC axis: like the progressed Sun, they are easy to plot since they both move at roughly one degree per year.

Consider this: my SP MC-IC shifted into Cancer-Capricorn, and my Ascendant-Descendant into Libra-Aries when I was thirty-two. SP

1st-house Sun was a mere 2 degrees away from an exact square to natal 10th-house Uranus at the same time. Did anything change? It certainly did! I met both my future husband – Sun and Venus in Aquarius, how literal is that? – and astrology that year. In the three years following, I obtained the Faculty of Astrological Studies Certificate and we moved house so that I could work from home. I also acquired a half share in two small children (still with me, now grown up, both very Uranian) and a very elderly cat.

Who needs transits?

Note: Pseudonyms used to identify all clients in this piece.

The Mountain Astrologer
April/May 2019

Progressions:
astrology's scary delights and a personal progressions story

One scary delight of being an astrologer is the opportunity offered to see one's own transits and progressions shaping up. Opportunities for second guessing the universe's intentions are ever present. This can get tiring.

I clearly recall a day in November 1998, the day I realised, as opposed to having merely noted, that Neptune would enter Aquarius at the end of the month – thereby commencing a long series of oppositions to my five 12th-house Leo planets (or six by Equal House, take your pick) which would not complete until Neptune entered Pisces in 2011/2012.

I reacted by doing what I suspect many enlightened people do when offered useful warning of serious upcoming challenges: I yelled 'Waaah!' to myself, pulled a metaphorical duvet over my head (so far so Neptunian) and carried on regardless.

It took from 2001-2008 to recover from the prolonged family crisis and energy burnout which followed. I did not return to work until 2012. However, all clouds do indeed have their silver lining: I wrote two books whilst lying on the sofa with the laptop, caught up on 30 years' reading and got onto the Internet in 2008 via my first blog 'Writing from the Twelfth House'. I also learned something absolutely essential for persons with an overload of Leo: the world – *somehow* – could manage to cope wonderfully well in my absence.

This year 2018 finds me once again in an especially interesting, possibly scary place: progressed ruling planet Mercury at 21 Scorpio, having stationed on natal 3rd-house Jupiter at 20 Scorpio, turned retrograde at the end of January. For the rest of my life.

I've been trying to approach the whole issue rather more intelligently this time than I did when Neptune was sending a mini tidal wave my way. One of the things which has arisen is an inclination to delve back into that 3rd-house Jupiter in Scorpio territory which has been the core landscape of my whole life since very early childhood.

The mystery of where we came from, where we go to when we leave this world and what the Big Picture may be, has always preoccupied me to a far greater degree than the majority of more sensible people, most of whom prefer to dwell on more concrete and less threatening matters. Grappling with that mystery led me eventually to astrology.

On a recent visit to London, whilst visiting the iconic Watkins bookshop, I chanced upon a deeply thought-provoking book titled *The Super Natural: A New Vision of the Unexplained*, re-appraising that vast territory, by writer Whitley Strieber and professor of religion Jeffrey J. Kripal from which the following quote is taken:

> *'The more deeply we plumb the psyche, the deeper the well appears to go. Somewhere down in there, it would appear that there is a place where the line between the physical and nonphysical blurs, where imagination and reality somehow converge, and events unfold that are not yet understood at all. It is the realm of Jeff's "imaginal" where the electrons of thoughts somehow converge into the molecules of things. But how? The mind knows, but not, perhaps, in ways that it can articulate.'*

It struck me immediately on reading this passage that six-thousand-year-old astrology is *the* language which has always been available to us for both exploring and articulating the imaginal realm as well as the realm of the practical and the everyday.

I am most grateful, however, to the insights which have arisen from what little I understand of quantum physics. As mentioned in my recent progressions article in the *The Astrological Journal*, republished in *TMA* in 2019, modern science has demonstrated that we live, move and have our being as part of a vast energy field which dances between order and chaos in invisible patterns which would appear to hold 4% matter,

23% dark matter and 73% dark energy together in a vast cosmic web.

With Mercury by progression stationed retrograde on 3rd-house Jupiter in Scorpio, I can feel my mind being drawn back into re-reading and re-evaluating my relationship to myth, religion, symbolism, contemporary science, the 'Super Natural' as termed by Streiber and Kripal, Jungian psychology and of course astrology.

I am grateful to astrological writers and thinkers of the calibre of Bernadette Brady, Armand Diaz, Kieron le Grice, Richard Tarnas and Phoebe Weiss, to name a few of my own recent favourites, in the help they have provided me in thinking through what I have long seen as complementary lenses: the astrological worldview and that of the weirdly paradoxical world revealed by quantum physics.

I want to learn more, in more depth, about the 96% of that vast energy field which science has told us is there – but which the procedures of scientific reductionism, centred on the 4% about which we *do* know, seem to be able to tell us very little.

Wish me luck on the journey!

The Astrological Journal
November/December 2017

SCOTLAND:

my own, my native land

This brief analysis of Scotland's horoscope has appeared in several places since I first wrote it in 1999, most recently as part of a long article – for the March 2020 Federation of Australian Astrologers' FAA Journal – on Scotland's increasingly fraught relationship with the UK government headed by Boris Johnson who took the UK out of the European Union when most Scots voted to stay in.

At the time of writing (December 2020), the polls in Scotland have moved further in favour of a second Scottish independence referendum, currently standing at 58% for independence and 42% against: a flip of positions from the defeat of the first referendum in 2014 with 55% of Scots voting to remain as part of the UK. The 2020 COVID-19 pandemic and First Minister Nicola Sturgeon's perceived competence in handling it in Scotland have turned our politics upside down – along with the rest of the world. Despite the UK government refusal to grant a second independence referendum, Boris Johnson's resistance is increasingly looking to be on the wrong side of current UK history.

Watch this space!

[Update on 14 May 2021: a report in The Scotsman *newspaper, shows a changed picture since December 2020:* 'At the end of April 2021, an exclusive poll by Savanta CosRes for The Scotsman *found that support for Yes was as its lowest level since just before the General Election in 2019 … If a second independence referendum was held tomorrow, 42 per cent of voters would go for Yes while 49 per cent would back No, and 8 per cent would be undecided, according to the poll … ']*

Scotland's Horoscope

I wrote this analysis and commentary as Scotland moved towards electing the first Scottish parliament for nearly 300 years on 6 May 1999. Over 20 years later, my closing comments seem eerily accurate.

The most commonly used chart for Scotland is that of the crowning of Malcolm II at Scone on 25 March 1005 at noon (see data at the end of this article). In this chart can be seen quite clearly some of the main themes which the wider world associates with Scotland. In a brief piece like this, one can only cover the most obvious.

The first thing to strike the eye is the powerful emphasis on fire, with Leo rising, Aries MC and both rulers in Aries in the 10th house. Mercury and Venus conjoin the MC from the 9th house. This conjures up a picture of an exuberant, creative and confident nation not wishing to keep its talents to itself but launching them (in the shape of its people) out into the wider world.

Scots are to be found everywhere, and every modern Scot has relatives in Canada, America and Australia in particular. Some of the world's most famous explorers were Scots, two examples being David Livingstone and Alexander MacKenzie, who named the MacKenzie river in Canada.

Uranus, ruler of the Aquarian Descendant, is placed in the 9th house in a watery grand trine with Saturn and Pluto. This conjures up a powerful image of strongly inventive and imaginative abilities which can structure the natural forces of nature in innovative ways: two men who come to mind are James Watt, whose steam condenser led to the steam engine which drove the Industrial Revolution, and John Logie Baird who invented television.

Uranus' conjunction with Mercury, Venus and the MC and trine with Leo Ascendant combine restless travelling with innovative writing and artistic expression: Robert Louis Stevenson and Charles Rennie Mackintosh, neither of whom ended their days in their native land, but both of whom exerted powerful influence as writers and artists, fit this pattern well.

Overall, Scotland is a country which has contributed to the positive dimensions of human endeavour quite out of proportion to its small size.

Inevitably, there is a darker side to this bright picture, as with any nation. Saturn rising in Cancer in the 12th house is the powerful starting place from which to explore the painful side of Scotland's complex sense of national identity. That identity under threat from an oppressive aggressor nation is a strong picture which arises from the square between the 12th house Saturn in Cancer, and Mars in Aries in the 10th.

There are many examples of this oppression by England over the thousand years since Malcolm was crowned at Scone. Memories of the brutal putting down of the 1745 rebellion against English rule, the infamous Massacre of Glencoe and the suppression of the Gaelic language which followed, and the Highland Clearances which forced thousands of Scots to emigrate in the 18th century, still fester in the national psyche.

Mars in Aries in the 10th is exuberant, bold and adventurous; the square to 12th-house Saturn in Cancer shows the undertone of rage and pain at being torn from one's deepest roots which lies behind that bright spirit. Poverty and oppression in many cases were the driving forces behind the Scots' wanderlust.

One of Scotland's many paradoxes is that a great, and justified, sense of national pride seems to co-exist with angry feelings of resentment and a hidden inferiority complex; symbolically, this fits well with the square sitting behind Leo rising.

If you are in any doubt about this, try keeping company with Scots who are the worse for drink, particularly if the location is England! One of the most unattractive facets of contemporary Scotland seems to be the need to put down (with the exception of Sean Connery!) those who have done well, rather than praising them.

Scotland's chart

25 Mar 1005, Sun
12:00 LMT +0:13:52
Perth, United Kingdom
56°N24' 003°W28'
Geocentric
Tropical
Placidus
True Node

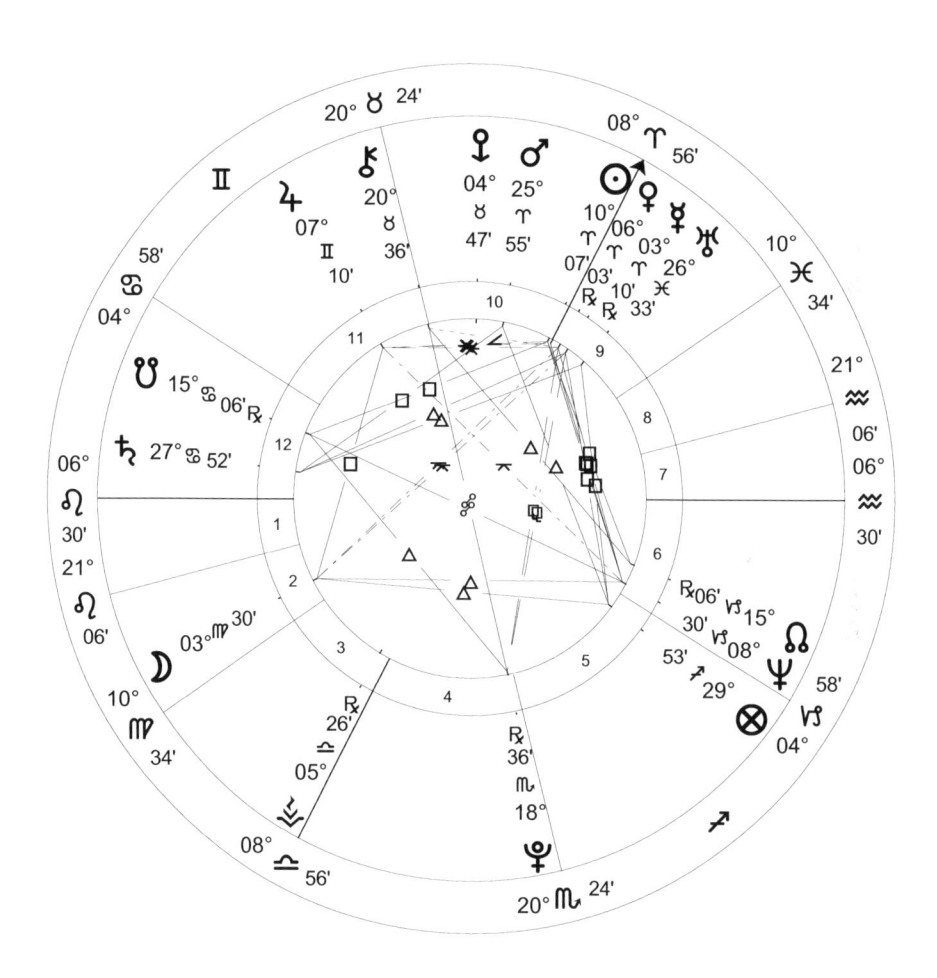

Scotland's passionate and at times tortured relationship with the spirit at its different levels can also be seen from this chart. Look at the dominant grand cross involving the Cancer-Capricorn nodal axis with Neptune, crossing the MC-IC axis t-square involving the prominent Sun and Venus.

This is a highly imaginative, spiritual, musical, passionate, cultured, artistic, adventurous, justice-seeking, visionary pattern in its bright face. It speaks of the many gifts this small nation has given to the wider world, and through which its own national life has been, and is, a rich experience for many of us who live here.

But its dark face is that of the maudlin drunk, abandoned by God, oppressed by England, singing exiles' songs in some parochial bar, longing to return to the unchallenging safety of the womb/home – or failing that, the oblivion of alcohol.

The 1005 chart reflects well the momentous changes which were going on, as we moved towards electing the first Scottish parliament for nearly 300 years on 6 May 1999.

Progressed Uranus at 4° Aries is crossing natal Mercury and Venus (IC ruler) in the 9th house, with progressed Ascendant at 20° Pisces close to natal Uranus, also in the 9th. Progressed Sun (chart ruler) is conjunct progressed MC at 28° Sagittarius, both falling on the natal Part of Fortune – all indications of the radical nature of those changes and the nation's optimism and expansive spirit as it prepared for its first step towards self-government for nearly 300 years.

Transits reinforce this. As the time of the elections approached, Jupiter crossed all the Aries planets at the top of Scotland's horoscope as well as the MC.

During this period (since the sweeping New Labour victory in May 1997) a Scottish parliament was made reality instead of a romantic nationalistic fantasy, with transiting Pluto in Sagittarius opposing Scotland's Jupiter in the 11th in Gemini, square the 2nd-house Virgo Moon. Scotland's Sun-Moon midpoint at 8° Gemini was also opposed by Pluto from Spring 1998 until the end of 1999.

These were very appropriate significators for the debate centred around beliefs and values and the proper allocation of resources which had been going on; also, there is a death/rebirth process going on in Scotland's ties with England and the UK. The outcome of that is by no means clear, many Scots wanting nothing less than the end of the long marriage with the UK.

Scotland data: 25 March 1005, Scone, Scotland, noon (traditional symbolic time for the coronation of the king). Coronation of Malcolm Canmore, aka Malcolm II. This date is given as the start of the year 1005 in the Annals of Ulster, as quoted in *Early Sources of Scottish History* (Volume 1, p. 521), covering 500-1296 AD. This work was collected and translated by Alan Orr Anderson (1879-1958) and first published in 1922 by Oliver & Boyd (Edinburgh). A corrected edition was published by Paul Watkins in Edinburgh in 1990.

(Note: the horoscope in this article is set for Perth, a latitude and longitude so near Scone as to make no difference to the horoscope's planetary positions, Ascendant or Midheaven – the computer hadn't heard of Scone, apparently! And – the date changes to 31 March when calendar adjustments are made from the Julian to the Gregorian calendar.)

The Federation of Australian Astrologers Journal
March/April 2020

Teaching Astrology:
I never knew adult ed. could be such fun!

Pretty often, the reality that we are approaching the ending of something important – e.g., a relationship, a career or career phase, a shift from one country to another – is not apparent until we look back and realise that's just what has indeed been happening.

For me, it's a different story. In 2019 I reached a significant milestone: my 50th year of adult education teaching. Clearly, the inevitable passage of time is pointing to an ending of that career phase, sooner rather than later. Had someone told me at the outset – a very green Assistant Lecturer in English – that I would end up teaching astrology, they would have been dismissed as delusional at least. This thought very much amuses me now.

I have taught a wonderful spectrum of different adults pursuing varying educational aims over all those decades. However, I hardly need tell you that teaching astrology has been by far the most fun, the most stretching, the most challenging, the most heartwarming – and the most rewarding.

Returning to astrology: a lesson in 'never say never'

In the spring of 2003, I packed 18 years-worth of astrology teaching notes into a large cardboard box and sent them to Belgrade. It cost me £96 in postage. I still have no idea whether it ever arrived at a destination whose address I no longer recall. Why did I do this? Because I had decided my career as an astrologer and astrology teacher was over, that there were plenty of astrology teaching notes in English cluttering up the UK and that I'd find someone in Europe who was keen to have some. I did. That was that. Or so I thought.

Fast forward to December 2011. It had taken me from 2001-8 to recover from severe burnout following a long family crisis which stopped my career in its tracks. During the whole of that period, I had resolutely said 'No' to all requests for astrology consultations or teaching, initially because I barely had the energy to get out of bed, latterly because I must have got into the habit of saying 'No'.

However, that December I said 'Maybe' to a young woman who had just embarked on a Faculty of Astrological Studies course and emailed me asking for some back-up tuition. I suggested we meet for a coffee and an informal chat. After an hour Alicia *(not her real name)* who is a senior lawyer by profession, fixed me with a very beady eye and said: 'You cannot possibly keep this knowledge to yourself.'

I went home, somewhat shaken up, to check the ephemeris for the first time in a while. My astrological career had begun following the Jupiter-Uranus conjunction of 1983. In December 2011, the Jupiter-Uranus conjunction of 2010/11 was separating; transiting Uranus – having gone direct at 0° Aries on the day of our meeting – was squaring my natal Mars-Uranus conjunction in the 10th house. Yes, Reader, you've guessed it. I gave in, resuming my astrology practice in May 2012 with Alicia as my first client. Saturn was in late Libra – where it had been in 1983, the first time around.

Alicia moved on to explore other esoterica after a while – very mercurial, that woman! – but we have become friends and every so often, with a chuckle, she reminds me of that kick-ass moment. There was more to follow.

Early in 2014, one of my former students came for an update astrology reading. As she was leaving, she looked at me and said, with a winning smile, 'There are a few of us who would love an astrology refresher course, starting from the beginning again. Why don't you think about it?'

'No, I don't think so,' was my reply. 'I sent all my teaching notes to Belgrade in 2003 – can't be bothered making up beginners' handouts again. I'm getting on a bit, now, you know … .'

'That is no problem', she retorted, ignoring my attempts to pretend I was a bit past it. 'I have all your old notes, filed in order. Why not copy them?'

Our refresher astrology class, an exact Jupiter cycle from the time I posted that cardboard box to Belgrade in March 2003, duly began in August 2014 – the very week my progressed Moon moved into Aquarius in the 6th house, with transiting Jupiter conjunct Mercury (my ruling planet) in Leo in the 12th house.

This October we returned for the 2015-6 session. My students, as usual, were in sparkling form. 'Face it, Anne,' one of them said. 'You are stuck with us. We can always push you along to class on your Zimmer if you get too decrepit.' They tell it like it is, here in Glasgow, Scotland, UK.

It feels great to have been drawn back, albeit in a part-time manner. I am no longer interested in building a career – just want to offer out some knowledge, inspiration and of course entertainment for however long Urania decides is long enough.

I find it humbling to contemplate the striking astrological symbolism describing my departure from and return to the practice and teaching of astrology. Yet again, it would appear, 'To everything there is a season, and a time to every purpose under the heaven' (KJV: Ecclesiastes 3:1). I had no conscious intention of returning to my former career. But that former career had other plans, taking the form of those persuasive women who gave me the right push at the right time.

Through one small individual's experience, then, one can perceive the much bigger reality which those of us versed in astrology's language are privileged to glimpse: Time – in as far as we are able to grasp it – moves in a vast teleology of patterns and cycles of which we are *all* part, whether prepared to acknowledge that reality or not.

'As above, so below'.

The Astrological Journal
January/February 2016

The pleasures of teaching

This post first appeared in my bimonthly column 'The Astro-view from Scotland' in Dell Horoscope's *last ever issue of March/April 2020.*

The students drifted out of class rather quietly for a change. One of them, an older lady, turned round to face me and said with a smile, 'Wow! That was like being in church.' It might not be too hard to figure out what was on the astro-menu that week. Yes – Neptune. After a session of introducing that awe-inspiring planet, then exploring his various symbolic manifestations through the horoscopes of artists, musicians, poets, gurus and clerics, I was feeling pretty stoned myself. Many years later, I still remember my pleasure at that comment.

Nostalgia is a state of being one might justifiably associate with Neptune. Uncharacteristically, it's where I find myself now, as I embark upon yet another decade of being a teacher. This week, early in October 2019, my wonderful tutorial group and I began some sessions called 'Reflecting on Cycles in a Time of Crisis'. My notes on this grew arms and legs and have wound up as an essay under the same title on the Astrodienst website (astro.com) in its Understanding Astrology section. I also repeated the annual injunction I've insisted on uttering in recent years which always makes students fall about laughing, i.e., 'Please, if you think I'm losing it, just tell me to *go!*'.

I have always loved teaching and still do. As well as having a Mercury-ruled horoscope, 3rd-house Jupiter in Scorpio squares six Leo planets in the 11th and 12th houses. There was unlikely to be any escape from declaiming! Having had the good fortune almost always to teach adults who wanted to be there, I have not been up against the types of stresses which I know all too well often burn out good teachers.

However, having blagged my way aged 22 into an adult education college job as Assistant Lecturer in English, there were several early fiery baptisms. My department head was the wonderful but scary Donald MacArthur, a former butcher from my island hometown (an extraordinary coincidence, since our college was nowhere near the Outer Hebrides). Donald had managed to get himself to Edinburgh University as a mature student, emerging with an excellent degree as well as friendships with some of the leading Scottish writers of that era.

During my first week he glared at me, booming: 'How can you have spent four years at university and never have read T.S. Eliot?' I forbore to mention that I had in fact scarcely been to any actual classes, my degree therefore being one of the minor but significant miracles of the Scottish education system. The T.S Eliot omission was duly corrected that first year as well as much else.

Then there was the evening class of mature adults who were allotted the dubious fortune of having me as their teacher. Having popped out on the first evening to collect some forms from our admin office, I overheard a male student in his fifties say in shocked tones: 'Surely that's not the teacher?' Here was a brutal truth: the only way forward was *hard work*. That very student wrote me a thankyou letter on receiving his 'A' pass. It was a long time later, as a result of a chance encounter in a launderette in Bath, England, that I met my horoscope for the first time. The whole edifice hangs upon a very prominent waxing Jupiter-Saturn square. Thank you, Saturn, for pushing me into becoming a competent teacher!

In classic Saturn return style, I changed career at the age of 29, becoming a social worker, latterly working in psychiatry, gradually importing my teaching skills via supervision of students and giving seminars on topics, such as confidentiality and childcare law. Then, on the first Saturn square of the new cycle, at the age of 37, having by then gained my first astrology qualification, came a happy discovery: I had entered this world with 'self-employed' stamped on my forehead. The freedom of organising one's own schedule has never had any downside for me. Could it be Mars-Uranus in the 10th house has some bearing here?

Teaching astrology classes has proved to be the most satisfying and fun part of my long and varied teaching adventure. The sheer variety of folks who attend is just wonderful. I still well remember that first, very small class: two petite ballerinas from the local ballet company and a dreamy young woman who worked with flower essences. As time went on, the classes grew larger, the range of students even more interesting. In one class I recall a consultant psychiatrist sitting companionably opposite a local bus driver, next to a self-declared pagan whose day job was cleaning carpets.

Then there was the class I began one autumn with a stellium of planets in Scorpio including Pluto. To a person, all the students that year were extremely plutonian – as, of course, was their teacher, i.e., moi. It was like teaching a black hole. They said very little, but boy, did they take everything in!

Out of choice, I now only have one small tutorial group of students, some of whom have been with me off and on since the 1990s. Completing the circle which began in that decade with my studies in Psychological Astrology in London with Dr Liz Greene and the late great mundane astrologer Charles Harvey, I now mentor online students studying with John Green and his team for the Mercury Internet School of Psychological Astrology – MISPA.

Being a teacher has been, and continues to be, a wonderful privilege – especially in teaching astrology, which invites students to place themselves symbolically in the context of the Big Picture/the Divine: choose your own term. The student quoted earlier, whose experience of her astrology class felt like being in church was tuning into that level exactly.

I hope I will know, however, when it is time to pack up and go – wouldn't want to create chaos by keeling over in class. If not, hopefully those students of mine will have enough nerve to tell me.

THE BIG PICTURE:
don't focus on the chaos, look for the reason

Being gifted/cursed/both (take your pick!) with no less than five Leo planets in the 12th house – six if you go by Equal House or Whole Sign – I've always been driven to set a Big Picture context to whatever I write. Also, with 3rd-house Jupiter in Scorpio square them all, I've always been addicted to philosophising whenever the opportunity arises. (And even when it doesn't ... ask my friends.)

The tempestuous, disruptive times through which we are currently living provide excellent opportunities for indulging in both – here are some of my philosophical musings on the Big Picture as it appears to me at the moment. I hope you enjoy them.

The Aquarian Age: are we there yet?

*'When the Moon is in the Seventh House
and Jupiter aligns with Mars
Then peace will guide the planets and love will steer the stars
This is the dawning of the Age of Aquarius'*

As predictions go, this one is not impressive. Offered in 1967 via the smash hit rock musical *Hair*, it suffers from its own internal contradictions. For a start, the 'Seventh House' can sometimes be the house of open enemies. Moreover, if you think an alignment of Mars and Jupiter augurs peace in our time, check our former UK Prime Minister Tony Blair's horoscope which has Mars rising conjunct Jupiter.

There is furthermore the annoying problem that contemporary evidence doesn't quite support the theory that the Aquarian Age is ushering in an era of peace and love. As we settle into a new millennium, it is rather noticeable that a maniacal death cult whose avowed aim is to bring down Western civilisation and hasten the Apocalypse has arisen and spread with frightening speed in the last few years.

Also, opinion regarding the fate of planet Earth is divided. For example, in 2013, the thinkprogress.org website produced impressive statistics appearing to demonstrate that life is getting better worldwide, despite the foreground picture of wars and global warming. On the other hand, many scientists think that we are already in the period of the sixth mass extinction, human agency being largely culpable this time.

Moreover, the former Chief Rabbi, the late Dr Jonathan Sacks, stated a few years ago in relation to the self-oriented culture which is rising worldwide as traditional religious belief is declining, that we humans are engaging in the largest experiment in mass selfishness that the world has ever seen.

Respected astrologer and historian Dr Nicholas Campion, in his fascinating book *Astrology, History and Apocalypse* (CPA Press, 2000), describes belief in the Age of Aquarius as 'one of the great clichés of modern astrology.'

He collected a list of almost one hundred dates from around 1260 AD to around 3000 AD 'at which the Age of Aquarius can begin' and this lends weight to Campion's view that the Age of Aquarius is a myth, reflecting our ancient human need to believe that the corrupted old order is collapsing, a wonderful Golden Age being just around the corner. The technical term for this is millenarianism: do read Nicholas Campion's erudite take on that vast and complex subject.

Campion refers to an essay of Carl Jung's titled 'The Sign of the Fish' (from Volume 9, Part 2 of Jung's *Collected Works*) – a must-read for anyone with more than a passing interest in what the Aquarian Age may be, and what it might signify. In essence, Jung concludes that 'the course of our religious history as well as an essential part of our psychic development could have been predicted ... from the precession of the equinoxes through the constellation of Pisces.'

The first point of Aries precesses backwards through a whole constellation during a period of roughly 2,000 years. It is currently somewhere between the first star in the constellation of Pisces and the last star of the constellation of Aquarius.

According to Jung, when the Aries point shifts from one constellation to the next our image of the Divine changes. I was bowled over by this idea, first encountered in a Liz Greene seminar during the 1990s, and have been reflecting on it ever since, watching the wider world to see if there is evidence of this shift taking place.

I think there is. We are going through a vast technological revolution. Science has made fast strides in recent decades: mapping the human genome, beginning to alter the very genetics of life on Earth. The magnificently durable Hubble Space Telescope has hugely expanded our view of the cosmos. And – much of the population of Earth is now linked to the Internet via mobile phone technology.

We even have a new religion: Scientism. This has risen to prominence in recent times complete with our local UK high priests: Aquarius' old ruler Saturn as Richard Dawkins and its new ruler Uranus as Brian Cox. The new paradigm emerging carries with it (as has been the case throughout history) the arrogance of new beliefs: superior – *of course!* – to what went before. Fifty years ago, to be called 'unChristian' was a pretty hefty challenge. Today, being called 'unscientific' has largely taken its place.

Caught on the cusp of crumbling old-world beliefs and the new world order arising, we are a liminal population, projecting the Divine onto enticing promises of a better future offered by scientific progress. This new future needs a name. Why not just call it the Age of Aquarius?

Exciting, revolutionary, disruptive – certainly. Ushering in a new era of love and peace? I don't think so.

The Astrological Journal
March/April 2015

The Fixed Cross: pointer to the new air age?

It's all identity politics' fault. Trying to come up with a Big Picture context for this 21st century phenomenon has led me all the way to contemplating the so-called Aquarian Age, such a cultural cliche by now that I usually prefer to let the ageing braincell focus on fresher topics. However, bear with me. I think I've got to something which might intrigue you.

But first, a definition of identity politics by Nicholas Campion in his book *Astrology, History and Apocalype*: such politics involve 'groups of people having a particular racial, religious, ethnic, social or cultural identity [who] tend to promote their own specific interests or concerns without regard to the interests or concerns of any larger political group.'

Does this suggest the shadow side of the Leo theme to anyone? It certainly does to me. Given that polarity, i.e., the interplay of opposites, is a fundamental generator of the life force (think egg, sperm and first division of fertilised egg here), this by astro-logic brings us to Aquarius, Leo's opposite. Aquarius is fundamentally concerned with the group. As the Aquarian and English philosopher Jeremy Bentham (1748-1832) so famously stated of the utilitarian principle in *A Fragment on Government*: 'It is the greatest happiness of the greatest number that is the measure of right and wrong'.

To be clear: I do not subscribe to the touchy-feely idea that the Aquarian Age, if it exists at all, is bringing or will bring an era of universal brotherly love (or siblinghood of person if you prefer). The evidence from our contemporary world would suggest otherwise. Moreover, Nicholas Campion has collected around 100 dates for the supposed commencement of the Age of Aquarius from around 1260 AD to around 2300 AD. [See previous essay in this collection.]

However, I am intrigued by Carl Jung's notion, set forth in his essay 'The Sign of the Fish' (from *Aion*, Volume 9, Part 2 of Jung's *Collected Works* [1951]) that when world ages change, i.e., when the first point of Aries can be seen against the backdrop of e.g., the constellation of Aquarius, having shifted backwards from its 2000 or so years' traverse of the previous constellation of Pisces – roughly the era of Christianity – we begin to perceive/project the Divine differently.

We have been going through an enormous technological revolution in recent decades as science makes huge strides. Mapping the human genome, expanding our view of the vast universe we inhabit via wonderful Hubble images, and linking much of the human population via the Internet and mobile phone technology are but a few examples. You could even argue that a new religion is arising: Scientism, which holds that only the 5% of the cosmos which we can perceive through our senses or test out through the procedures of reductionism, is worth considering.

It is my view that, as societies become increasingly secular and materialistic throughout the world, we are beginning to project the Divine onto science and technology ... even to the extent in some quarters that the prolonging of human life indefinitely into some kind of techno-immortality is perceived as eventually being possible.

Pushing the boundaries of science forward just because it can be done conjures the spectres of Dr Frankenstein and his monster, immortalised in Mary Shelley's modern myth, *Frankenstein, or the New Prometheus*. It also speaks strongly of the shadow side of the Aquarian theme which doesn't mind how many individual lives it disrupts or destroys in the name of revolutionary change.

Hence its Leo shadow opposite arising, in the shape of identity politics as defined at the start of this column.

Reflecting on the stubbornly fixed positions which have increasingly been taken up in recent times – as expressed in political discourse, religious conflicts and environmental activism – has evoked for me the fixed cross in the horoscope's astrological symbolism (shown): this comprises the four angles upon which every chart hangs: Ascendant (AS), Imum Coeli (IC), Descendant (DS) and Medium Coeli (MC or Midheaven).

Since the Ascendant-Descendant horizontal axis speaks of the here and

Angles fixed cross chart

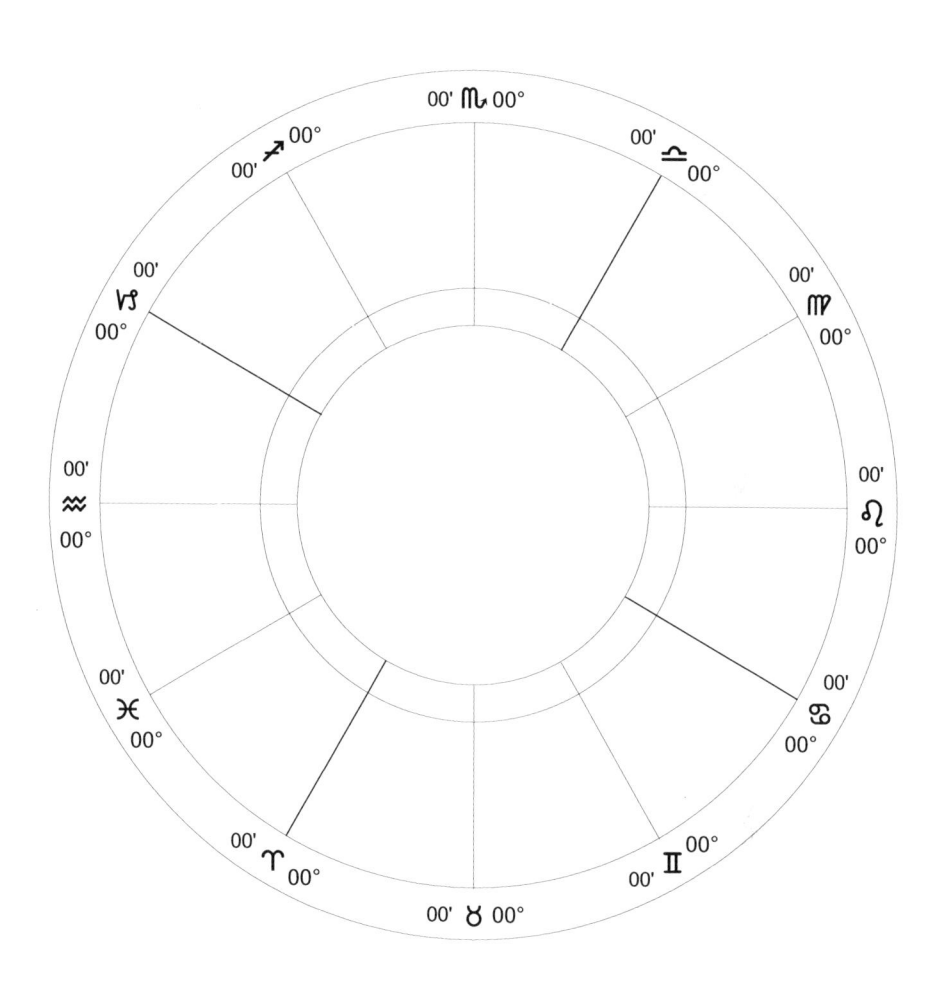

now, of our individual and collective lives, how about placing Aquarius on the AS with Leo opposite on the DS? Thus, we see the march of technological progress for the supposed benefit of us all, not presently getting along too well with individual identities in various forms.

The IC-MC axis speaks of roots (IC) from which our future direction (MC) arises. The Taurus IC is the ground on which we stand, our Mother Earth. Scorpio on the MC opposite speaks of the deep crisis which our home planet is facing. If humanity is to survive into the future, we need to develop radically different ways of living.

The old materialist order is currently dying – the evidence is everywhere. The question is, what will replace it?

I have found contemplating the metaphor of the astrological fixed cross, which condenses the polarised conflicts of our current era into four fundamental themes, powerfully illuminating. We need to find a way forward from our present stubbornly fixed shadow positions to a situation where respect both for the dignity of individual rights and for the greatest good of the greatest number is harnessed and directed towards respect and care for our mother planet.

Perhaps the currently applying harsh pressure on all our institutions and structures via the approaching conjunction of Saturn (old ruler of Aquarius) and Pluto (new ruler of Scorpio) will force us in the direction we need to go.

Dell Horoscope
2019

The air era beckons

What an airy week it's been! I'm writing this column on Sunday, 19 July 2020, in recovery like the rest of our astro-community. I am convinced that our esteemed editor [Victor Olliver of *The Astrological Journal*] is currently lying prone on his chaise-longue in a darkened room, a cold wet flannel cooling his fevered brow, having conducted no less than twelve local radio interviews in less than seven days. Unless you've been hiding out in a tumbledown old shed in the middle of nowhere without a WiFi signal, you would of course have noticed the latest flare-up of Ophiuchus-itis (re: the so-called 13th zodiac sign) which flooded the airwaves and newsprint worldwide this week.

Much has been said, including by yours truly, regarding this recurring, fatuous nonsense. I do not propose to add to that here. However, continuing my musings on the significance of the end-phases of large cycles holding keys to the future arising, this particular Ophiuchus episode has been more fascinating than irritating. Why?

Having now been an astrologer long enough to have lived through a few Ophiuchus astrology-bashing flare-ups – the last major one was I think in the summer of 2013 (always in the silly season: could that be a clue?) – I find something especially interesting about this latest. It has been more febrile, more intensely and widely 'aired' than any before that I can remember. The fact that Victor was on air twelve times in just a few days, explaining why Ophiuchus is not part of the zodiac, is a case in point.

An airborne virus has totally upended our way of life worldwide in a devastatingly short time. This Ophiuchus-fest is a relatively trivial but also widespread collective herald of our impending shift into the new air era, beginning – you could not make the timing of the date up! – on the Winter Solstice 2020 with the dramatic meeting of Jupiter and Saturn at 0 degrees Aquarius.

As I mentioned in a previous column, it was very striking that Saturn's shift into Aquarius in late March 2020 coincided with most of the world – pushed by necessity imposed by lockdown – moving the conduct of both individual and collective life onto the airwaves. 'I am zoomed-out!' is a comment I have heard repeatedly in recent weeks and months. The verb 'to zoom' (from the online web- and video-conferencing company Zoom) is surely set to enter the dictionary as one of 2020's newest additions.

The founder of Zoom has got much more than he bargained for, as this quote (of 17 April 2020 on fortune.com) reveals: 'For Eric Yuan, the 50-year-old founder and CEO of Zoom, adding 90,000 schools – and having to educate them on how to use his product – has become a bit of a nightmare.'

However, this impending shift into a 200-year air era is showing itself in the lives of individuals too: here are just a few examples from my students, friends and colleagues in the last couple of weeks.

One of my students, a well-respected local yoga teacher, has (along with much of the yoga teaching community worldwide) shifted her classes online. This has been a success, but she is now planning ahead for the time when lockdown is further eased, enabling her to add studio-based classes with social-distancing measures in place. Her solution? Moving her current yoga studio to the newly renovated, much roomier upper studio space in the same building. 'It will be very much lighter and airier!' she said to me enthusiastically. There will also be room for her partner and fellow yoga teacher to teach online yoga and have a podcast studio for his planned online freelance coaching work.

A good friend who has been running a successful physically based therapy/hypnosis practice has realised during lockdown that what she really wants is to be an artist. To this end she has been developing a strong online presence exhibiting her art. A consequence of this is that she will shortly have her work exhibited in a reputable London-based gallery. She is also considering developing a support/coaching practice online for fellow women artists, using existing skills developed over the previous twelve years. Thus – a clear move from the physical, earthy dimension to locating her work in air.

As has been the case with many of my astrological colleagues, I have been doing one-to-one work on air for a few years now. However, in April, I successfully began to run my small astrology tutorial group on Zoom, ably assisted by one of my astrology students (who is a veritable Zoom maven) and the delightful 20-year-old Aquarian twins across the landing. They helped me get group-Zoom-literate by allowing me to practise on them and one of their friends.

Since then, I have been talking with a colleague in a different discipline who has an open-minded interest in astrology, considerably amplified by having his chart read several times in recent years. He and I are planning an airy astro-venture at both an individual and group level which we will slowly be evolving for the rest of this penned-in year. Watch this space! I'm sure I am not the only astrologer who thinks that the new 20-year Jupiter-Saturn cycle in Aquarius might be pretty good for launching new airy astro-projects.

Also, after many years of being happy to send out my writing from behind the 12th-house sofa, the impending shift into air has been having the effect of enticing me out. In late June 2020, I was interviewed by my dear friend and colleague Christina Rodenbeck for her popular The Oxford Astrologer website (oxfordastrologer.com). We talked about the impending epochal shift into the air era, the large planetary cycles and much more besides. I am now looking forward to the follow-up.

In conclusion, I'd be most interested to collect some more examples of how impending air is changing your personal and working lives as the 200-year-old 'earth order' winds down. Do email me. If I get enough interesting feedback, maybe *Journal* can publish it.

The Astrological Journal
September/October 2020

Neptune and the 'Gift' of Uncertainty

'The constant dance between form and formlessness, being and non-being, order and chaos, occurs in all epochs and at all levels. Humans have created a range of paradigms and metaphors, from ancient myths to modern cosmology, within which to explore this dialectic. Our ancient Babylonian forebears envisaged the beginning of the world as a battle to the death between the great sea-serpent Ti'amat and her son, the Underworld god Marduk. He vanquished her, creating Heaven and Earth from her divided corpse. Meanwhile, the grapple goes on. Astrology has its own language for this struggle, speaking through the polarity of Saturn and Neptune. Saturn at its core represents the drive to take form; Neptune's teleology is that of dissolution ... ' [28]

Here we are – again. We do not need astrology to tell us that we are in the throes of that epic struggle between Ti'amat and Marduk as the 200 years-long era of the Jupiter and Saturn meeting in earth comes to a messy and turbulent end. The official starting date of the incoming air era is on 2020's Winter Solstice when Jupiter meets Saturn at 0° Aquarius.

The signs are everywhere you care to look: COVID-19 is brutally upending our way of living, which has largely depended on trashing Mother Earth since the outset of the Industrial and Scientific Revolutions. On the one hand, fire ravaged parts of Australia in 2019 and is currently blazing swathes of destruction through California; on the other, the Brazilian rainforests are aflame. Destructive flooding is

---

28 From *The Mountain Astrologer*, 'Contemplating the 12th House: An Optimist's Take on Self-Undoing' by Anne Whitaker, in the Aug/Sept 2014 issue.

on the increase. Species extinction is advancing apace. Social inequality is worse than it has been for a very long time. I could go on and on.

Where astrology *can* be helpful, at least for those of us of a philosophical bent, is via the perspectives which studying the larger planetary cycles can provide. We can thus step back, zoom out as it were (quite the apt expression since much of the world is now zooming) and, with even a sketchy grasp of an historical timeline, reflect upon the scary evidence of an increasingly divided world in turmoil – from a longer-term and possibly more optimistic perspective.

From observing both my own life and that of our wider communities, it seems that the most fear-generating dimension is the profound *uncertainty* which contextualises all our lives at present. None of us can plan with any confidence for anything. Just today, as I write this on Monday, 14 September 2020, the coronavirus 'rule of six' has launched in Scotland – but with different restrictions in other parts of an increasingly fragmenting UK.

Neptune – as 'chaos'– is surely gaining the upper hand. This has been increasingly the case since Neptune's entry into Pisces in 2011/12; Saturn is struggling to maintain order: his shadow, Fascism, with violence as its inevitable companion, is on the rise in various parts of the world.

As is often the case for me (and probably other writers), when I'm reflecting on a possible column topic which has been chewing at me for weeks – in this case the Saturn-Neptune order/chaos dialectic and where uncertainty fits in – I came across an essay on the wonderful aeon.com website last Friday which was really helpful and illuminating: it is about a philosopher whom I only vaguely recollected from university philosophy (aeons ago, in my case!) – Karl Jaspers (1883-1969). The header quote on the essay stopped me in my tracks: 'To Karl Jaspers, uncertainty is not to be overcome but understood'.

Jaspers' work ' ... revolves around the meaning of uncertainty in an increasingly precarious and radicalising world ... he is one of the very few existentialist thinkers ... who did not seek to master, tame or conquer the unknowable and finite condition of human life. Instead, he tried to cultivate a relationship to this essential quality of life and engage it on its own terms.'[29]

Even a sketchy understanding of history reveals that our collective attempts in every culture under the sun ('to master, tame or conquer the unknowable and finite condition of human life') have been held in the vast context of that dialectic between Ti'amat and Marduk, Saturn and Neptune, order and chaos. We have lurched between those extremes, with spells of varying lengths in which we managed to get the two in balance for a time – forever.

The 20-year cycle of the Jupiter-Saturn conjunctions, concluding their journey through the earth element and entering the new air era, can roughly speaking be mapped onto the waning crescent of the 'old order' and the waxing crescent of the new. This gives us a time period from around 2000 to 2040, a time in which, to use Robert Hand's vivid phrase, 'the past has minimum hold upon the present, but the present has a maximum hold on the future.'[30]

We are in a unique time now: not only humanity, but the whole of Mother Earth and all her creatures great and small are suffering the pain and turbulence of increasing chaos as the old order loses its grip. But without Neptune to dissolve the deadening rigidities of Saturn past its sell-by date in any phase of civilisation or culture, life could not go on. Dissolution precedes renewal.

In the meantime, we need to cultivate qualities which do not come spontaneously to most humans, but need to be cultivated these days, probably more than ever before in our long and bloody history: humility, patience and tolerance for one another in the face of our many-faceted differences. Times of uncertainty create great fear, but also greater potential to renew ourselves. Let's not forget that uncertainty

---

29   From aeon.com (11.09.20), an essay by Carmen Lea Dege who is currently writing a book on the theory and practice of uncertainty.

30   From *The Astrology of Crisis*, Llewellyn Publications, 1993, p116.

can be a harsh, but profound gift – which Neptune is offering us right now.

PS: Of course, after writing this I couldn't resist checking out Astrodienst for Karl Jaspers' horoscope and there it was, as I had suspected, right up there in the 10th house in Taurus: Saturn conjunct Neptune, focal point of a grand trine with Moon-Uranus in Virgo and Venus in Capricorn. Maybe we should all be reading him!

The Astrological Journal
November/December 2020

THE TWELFTH HOUSE:
where I live (behind the sofa)

It has intrigued me to note, on re-visiting the next essay and the one following, both of which concern my long quest to make peace with the major determinant of my life's unfolding (i.e., my birth with a heavily tenanted 12th house) that the two essays are separated by 19 years. That, of course, is a complete cycle of the Moon's North Node which is exactly conjunct my Midheaven at 28° Taurus and whose cycles have had a profound impact on shaping my path.

Whom doth the Grail serve?
A personal quest in pursuit of vocation

(My birth chart is on page 14)

INTRODUCTION

We live within, and live out, a profound paradox. On the one hand, there are certain archetypal forces upon whose unfolding patterns through time and space the whole of life is predicated. There is a deeply impersonal dimension to human existence: over the millennia we all live out variations on the same basic set of themes. On the other hand, there is that spark of individual consciousness in each person which says: 'Here I am. I'm special. There's no one quite like me.' Finding a way of reconciling those opposites is one of the fundamental challenges of being human.

I have known this for a long time, and like many other people, have struggled with the paradox. Astrology with its symbolism, which can be used to describe both levels, has been of enormous help. But occasions of deep insight are rare where the dynamic of paradoxical forces can be understood and accepted at the level of both heart and mind.

One such occasion was the first Liz Greene seminar I ever attended in December 1990. The theme explored was that of the interplay of Puer and Senex, the divine child and the wise old man, those archetypal life patterns represented primarily in the horoscope by Jupiter and Saturn. My whole chart is draped round a dominant square of those two planets. I sat rapt, recognising in the weave of the seminar key threads of my family inheritance, my parents' struggles with life in general and each other in particular, and a key part of my own life pattern.

I found the seminar particularly affirming of my sense of teleology. Without needing an image of a personal God, I do need to feel part of an unfolding process which has meaning and purpose. The occasion also offered a corrective to the potential for the individual ego to gorge on its heady sense of uniqueness – 'This path I am walking on, many feet have trodden, driven by the same underlying imperatives. I am special and I am not.'

'I am special, and I am not.' The seminar brought fully home that the paradox which I have long perceived to be at the core of everyone's existence is absolutely fundamental to my own. I was born in the very last hours of the Balsamic phase, preceding the New Moon in Leo: in my horoscope, Sun, Moon, Venus, Saturn and Pluto are all conjunct in Leo in the 12th house, square Jupiter in Scorpio in the 3rd. Ruler Mercury in Leo in the 11th is conjunct Saturn and Pluto, guardians of the 12th-house cusp.

The solar light burns in all of us. Astrology demonstrates that it burns more brightly in some lives than in others. I probably have a greater right than most to address the question of whether an over-allocation of the gift of light is a blessing – or a curse. The Balsamic stage of the Sun-Moon cycle, and the placement of most of the Leo planets in the 12th house, greatly amplifies and polarises the contradiction between the personal and the impersonal which I have been discussing.

How can you be the universally recognised and admired solar hero which all those Leo planets demand when a vast ocean's unending tidal pull is forever drawing you and your powerful ego back into its silent depths?

Looking back over several decades of struggling to bridge the personal and the universal, I think I have at least some idea of what it was like for Parsifal in the Grail myths! The central task of my life has been to find ways of aligning a highly self-absorbed, individualistic, romantic perception of life (and powerful creative drives) with the impersonal requirement to offer self-sacrificing service to the wider community and the higher powers of the universe. For a very long time, not knowing what the task was, I felt like a frighteningly small cork bobbing on the surface of a very big, dark, stormy ocean.

Every aspect of my life has been shaped by this struggle. In keeping with the powerful demands of the 12th house, it is the attempt to respond fully to the vocational call that I have chosen to write about in this essay. As the reader will discover, all attempts to find my way of being a solar hero have been well assisted by a fine collection of solar heroes along the road!

In the beginning

I was born on a small, frequently cold, wet and windswept island off the West Coast of Scotland; an appropriate place for someone with so many 12th-house planets. The sea defined my life: I loved it and feared it, swam in it, sailed on it, walked by it, lived by it – and when I was seven, owing to my father's carelessness, nearly drowned in it.

Childhood was full of larger-than-life male hero figures whose exploits, usually involving water and the sea, inspired my vivid and grandiose imagination. Maternal grandfather Calum's last working years were spent as a Church of Scotland lay missionary sailing round the outer islands, ministering to his flock. He was an eloquent preacher. As a young man he had sailed to South America to work as a rancher, at one point taming wild horses on his own somewhere in the wilds of Argentina. One day he saved a man's life, in the absence of a doctor, by plunging his badly infected arm into a pan of boiling sheep dip.

Paternal grandfather Fred was of genteel English upbringing. He had been a Royal Navy gunner in the First World War. Locked into his gun turret with his men, he was told to come out victorious or dead. He died at 81 years of age; I was given the medal he won for that episode.

My uncle Norrie was a wireless operator on a ship in World War 2. He drowned when his ship was torpedoed in the last two weeks of the war. His was the only body found. Having swum a long way to the French coast, he died of exposure on the shore. My uncle Red Murdo, the salmon poacher, was featured in a leading article in *The Sunday Times* in the 1970s. He was offered a great deal of money after that for his autobiography but declined, saying, 'What do I want money for? I'd only piss it against a wall.'

My father George combined the official occupation of senior local government officer with the unofficial one of the most notorious poacher in the Hebrides for over 30 years. He used to go out in his boat to check his nets in working hours in full public view. 'Why not?' he'd say. 'I've done my public duty for the day!' He was tried for poaching in the 1950s in a case that made national headlines: the QC he and his friends had hired secured them a Not Proven verdict. George had taken the precaution of dropping the bolts of the guns they had used over the side of his boat and into the sea as the police were arriving to arrest him. This produced the immortal line in court: 'My Lord, how could Mr. Whitaker have shot twelve deer with guns without a bolt?'

These characters, both present and in family memory, were the norm throughout my childhood. It never occurred to me that most other people's lives did not have quite the same bright thread of derring-do running through them as mine.

The feminine principle was most powerfully represented by Granny Whitaker – clan matriarch, with a Leo Moon rising and strong Pluto aspects. The first female town councillor in the Outer Hebrides in the 1920s, she brought up three children of her own and her sister's two when she died young. Running a shop, and latterly a boarding house, she had great style but never any money. Like maternal grandfather Calum, she tended to give what she had to others in need. She was also a great environmentalist, fighting the local town council for years over the fate of a tree which was getting in the way of a new housing development. She won. To this day a wall can be seen which was diverted to go round the tree! Granny was a strongly masculine, strongly feminine woman – a kind of female solar hero – regarded by her community as a woman ahead of her time. I wanted to be like her when I grew up.

My first encounter with the archetypal feminine in literature came through the vivid writings of H. Rider Haggard, an English Victorian author whose myth-steeped adventures set in colonial Africa fascinated me. Ayesha,[31] the beautiful, sexually alluring, anciently wise and

---

31   Ayesha appeared in *She* by H. Rider Haggard, Penguin Popular Classics 1994: first published in 1887.

terrorisingly destructive queen who had found the secret of eternal life which eventually destroyed her, fuelled my dreams and my nightmares. I was very afraid of the dark in childhood, fascinated by death, what might lie beyond, and why we were here at all, spinning at unimaginable speeds through space on our tiny planet. I had a secret inner life driven by avid reading, with Grandpa Calum my only confidant.

I never felt safe during childhood. Pluto's transit through the 12th house, crossing Venus, Moon and Sun, then squaring the MC-IC and crossing the Sun-Ascendant midpoint, all took place in the first 10 years of my life. Pluto first crossed my Ascendant when I was 14. From 10 to 17, Uranus crossed the Leo stellium, gradually catching up with Pluto. I grew up with unhappy parents in a stormy, unpredictable and sometimes violent marriage made worse by my father's womanising and alcohol abuse.

I left school early at 16, having the previous winter submitted my application to go to university to study English, Psychology and History. The triggering event, as transiting Uranus crossed my Ascendant, was an assault by my father. As the progressed Sun crossed the Ascendant to join Uranus and Pluto, I emerged from 'prison' with my father as the governor, little realising that I was entering a different form of prison, this time with myself in charge. Escape into the intoxication of running my own life had motivated my departure from home – not any kind of reasoned vocational choices. I was the first member of my family to go to university and was already regarded as strange.

INTO THE WORLD – BUT OUT OF IT

What did I want to do when I grew up? I had decided at eight years of age that I wanted my independence as soon as possible, would never marry and never have children. This was in response to the frightening emotional mess in which I grew to adulthood. At 12, I had passionately wanted to be an archaeologist. But this had been dismissed as a stupid idea.

Having been fired up and inspired by all those solar heroes, the bright side of my family inheritance and the central figures of my voracious childhood reading, I certainly didn't want a traditional island woman's life. I would be a free spirit! The conviction also burned deep inside me that I was different, special and would be famous one day. There was no one around then to tell me that this was archetypal Leo grandiosity, vastly amplified in my case!

The university years were a mess. Without the container, however unsatisfactory, provided by family and community, I nearly fell apart. Neptune in Scorpio in the 3rd house squared the Leo stellium for the entire period and beyond. Uranus conjunct Pluto ran with the progressed Sun in the 1st house. I didn't know who or where I was. I had eating, drinking and relationship problems, and seventeen addresses in four years. The only stable male in my life was killed when I was 19. The following year, my first love fell over a third-floor tenement staircase in questionable circumstances and died. Another man nearly killed me twice. There were regular periods of deep depression, culminating in a long dark night of the soul experience at 20. At the end of it, I decided not to kill myself (despite the depth of my misery) but to choose life.

Why? There were human reasons. My love for my little brother, only a toddler when I left home, whom I did not want to saddle with such a legacy. Although desperately angry with my parents, I did not doubt their love for me, flawed though it was, and understood that destroying my life would also destroy theirs. But there was something at work in me during that long dark night for which I still cannot find adequate words. The feeling is of having been touched by the grace of God in the very depths of despair. Which deity, I shall never know.

A solar hero played a major part in shaping my future – Ken, my adviser of studies and an Aries Sun like my father. He was a diabetic who swam in the North Sea every day of the year including Xmas. His response to losing a leg because of his illness was to get an artificial one and take up long-distance cycling. We knew each other for twenty years until Ken became too ill to keep in touch. He bailed me out of all sorts of scrapes, including being thrown out of university twice, and wrote the references for my first two careers. He was my good, safe father. There has been a mentor of that nature at every important developmental stage in my life.

It took four years to complete a minimum subject ordinary Master of Arts degree. To this day I regard its acquisition as one of the minor miracles of the Scottish education system. One vignette sums this up. I submitted a third-year essay on the origins of the American War of Independence to my now eminent tutor, Owen Dudley Edwards. It was as late as it could possibly be, and had been dropped in a puddle in my rush to his office to hand it in. He returned it to me with a mark of 55%, and the comment: 'This essay bears all the hallmarks of the triumph of innate intelligence over little or no material. Your bibliography [I had cited Winston Churchill's *A History of the English-Speaking Peoples*, having once had a cursory glance through it] I assume is a joke.'

POSTGRADUATE

Following graduation, it was my intention to live on a Greek island for a year and work at any old job, letting the future decide itself. Still only 20, I had to be 21 before applying for my own passport. Throughout university years, my father had resolutely refused to sign my passport form, thereby exercising the one bit of external power he still had over me. 'Don't try forging my signature,' he had said. 'I know you're capable of it. I'll get Interpol onto you!' Knowing he would, I didn't. The Greek island was out. This decided the next stage in the vocational quest.

Glimmerings of a dawning realisation of where my energies could be going determined the next choice. I had emerged relatively sane and moderately able to function from the nightmare of my university years because of the virtually unbreakable creative spirit which had mysteriously kept me going even when I seemed, on the surface, hell bent on self-destruction. Not being aware of this at the time, for many years I could not quite understand why I hadn't died.

The other major saving grace was the healing power of love – this I did recognise at the time. My adviser's consistent behaviour towards me had been of patient loving kindness. A small coterie of determined friends got me through my exams, re-sits and more exams. At one point they had a rota to get me out of bed, make sure I got to the library, and wouldn't let me away until enough work had been done for me to scrape by. I owed my degree and future to the alliance of my inner spirit and their love.

I was now beginning to realise that surviving harsh, formative experiences might just be a qualification for helping other people in their struggles. I had been a nihilist for years, feeling the world was going to hell and nothing I could do was of any value. But having chosen to live, I knew how important the love given to me, one small person, had been. The desire to return this love to the wider community began to grow. I was groping towards being a child of the 12th in an affirmative rather than a destructive manner. But there was a long road still ahead.

I embarked on a one-year postgraduate course in Personnel Management, thinking vaguely that this was something to do with caring for people. Having discovered it was about being as minimally reasonable to the workforce as management could get away with, in order to get as much work out of them as possible, I became very Marxist and started to rebel. This, combined with the all-consuming nature of another tempestuous love affair, led to my being asked not to turn up for graduation. 'We don't want people like you as personnel managers,' I was told. How right they were!

Enter another solar hero. One lecturer had inspired me throughout the course. A sociologist, he was a specialist on the relevance of Further Education to industry and supervised my thesis which was on that very topic. The college did not like me – but they kept my thesis for their library. This lecturer reminded me of the best aspects of my own father: incorruptible, he gave not a damn for bureaucracy or any authority he didn't respect. He was very much on the side of the students. I admired him, and he turned me onto the idea of becoming a lecturer in Further Education. The very next year, I did.

Honest but very good references from him and my university adviser added to my own ability to sell snow to the Eskimos when required and all this got me my first Adult Education job.

First career

My teaching began with Saturn squaring the Leo stellium from the 9th house, on the waning quarter of the progressed New Moon cycle which began shortly after my birth. I was 22 and very scared of the responsibility.

My remit was to teach university entrance English to mature students as well as Liberal Studies to a wide range of obstreperous apprentices in various trades, most of whom were male and all of whom were bigger than I was. It was in this first job that I began to develop the only tool which exerted any leverage on those lads: humour. 'Miss, fancy coming out with me tonight – we could go over my homework.' Loud sniggers. 'Young man, when I take up baby-snatching, you will be the last to hear about it.' Silence.

I coped with the Liberal Studies, loved the English teaching, and have never worked so hard in all my life as in that first year, making the joyous discovery that I was capable of shouldering professional responsibility and inspiring trust and confidence in my students. However, restlessness still drove me. In seven years, I taught in five different parts of Scotland and England, picking up a postgraduate Diploma in Education along the way. In the mid-1970s, with my progressed Sun crossing 1st-house Urania, a strange little Irishman I met in a launderette in Bath told me I would become an astrologer in my 30s. I thought this was tosh. [See my earlier essay in the Fate section, 'Prediction and a Personal Story'.]

I enjoyed teaching adults, and was popular with my students, always putting them first. But I hated the bureaucracy of the system, and the small-minded people who ran it. My bosses knew that my priorities didn't fit theirs and were deeply suspicious of me.

Second career

At age 27 (as Saturn moved into the 12th house, progressed Moon began to cross all my Leo planets in its return to its own position and Mercury progressed into Libra to square Mars) I returned to my native island to become a full-time writer, having written on and off all my life, with phases of having poetry and articles published. I also wanted to support my father. Scottish local government was being reorganised and he was having to apply for his own job in the new Western Isles local authority. Old scores were settled for his defiance, incorruptibility and poaching exploits. He was given the Deputy's job but couldn't bear not to be the boss; so, he started early retirement proceedings as well as a major escalation of his drinking habits.

Despite a daily writing routine in a cosy little office in the air traffic controllers' building in the local airport, I could only stand living at home for four months and moved back to mainland Scotland. At one point I had three part-time Adult Education jobs, teaching university entrance English in one college, Drama in another and Business Studies English in the central institution down the road. There followed two years during which, as one of my oldest friends succinctly put it, 'You locked yourself up in that daft wee flat in Dundee and nearly drove yourself crazy!'

Pluto, ruler of the IC, was transiting Neptune throughout this time. It was a long and desperate, poverty-stricken period of confronting my illusions about who I was and what my life meant. It was another, less intense but more protracted dark night of the soul. On realising that I had writing talent but lacked the ruthless drive which keeps people at it full-time, the adventure ended. I couldn't make a career out of writing and also discovered my terror of failure: it was now staring me in the face. Now nearly 30, I couldn't be a wanderer all my life. Whatever came next, I resolved to stick to it.

The most important thing to emerge, at last, from many years of restlessness and suffering, was a belief that something meaningful was going on which slowly, relentlessly, was forcing me to grow. A fragile sense of personal connection with forces much greater than myself was starting to form.

I was beginning to be able to swim in the deep dark waters of the 12th house. For many years I had had a recurring dream of being swept away and drowned by a tidal wave. At the end of this period the dream came again. In the dream, knowing I had been drowned before, this time I knew what to do. Turning to face the shore, letting the wave carry me, I knew I would be all right.

After that dream, life began gradually to curve upwards. My last serious depression occurred at 38, the year after my father died. There have been no more since then, despite many hard times. Faith that my bright thread is woven into a meaningful pattern continues to provide an increasingly strong foundation for focusing and directing my creative energies.

THIRD CAREER

As the progressed Moon emerged from the 12th house, crossing my Virgo Ascendant on the way to meet the progressed Sun, and transiting Uranus in the 3rd crossed Chiron, I got out of bed one morning and on impulse phoned the local social work department. 'I want to be a social worker, what do I do?' Six unqualified social work jobs were just being advertised and I got one of them, despite having an argument about poor wages with a scruffy little man who turned out to be the director of social work for the region. What they saw was who they got!

Right from the start I felt I had found my path. Loving the variety, unpredictability and challenge which social work brought, the high degree of mobility and autonomy which could be found within a structure of accountability, I also relished the opportunity to be an advocate for the rights of the vulnerable. I enjoyed the eccentricity and humour of my closest colleagues and admired the courage of my clients. Quickly feeling committed to a social work career, I applied for training as my second progressed New Moon took place in the 1st house in Virgo. Saturn was still transiting the Leo stellium in the 12th house, and Uranus had started squaring it from the 3rd house. Yet again, a major life change was about to be dictated, apparently, by accident.

My degree lacked a social science component. Not thinking I was eligible to do a one-year postgraduate course, I had resigned myself to doing two years of training. However, to my great surprise I was offered a selection interview for Glasgow University for a one-year course. Discovering later that I had mixed up the course numbers on my university clearance form – and that finance would not have been available for two-year courses – it really felt as though Fate was intent on my going to Glasgow.

At the end of the interview, the interviewer, a rather aristocratic English lady, said: 'Miss Whitaker, you seem very keen. What would you do if we turned you down?' I looked her straight in the eye and replied: 'Miss Ford, I would undoubtedly go home and shoot myself.' For a wavering moment, she thought I was serious. Then we both laughed. I got a place and obtained my Diploma and Certification in Social Work the following year. I have lived in Glasgow ever since.

A social worker for nine years, I worked in only two different settings in the six and a half years following qualification. I was slowing down and sticking in at last and finding exactly the same priorities that had caused me to abandon an official teaching career: organisation first, clients second, workers last. But I stayed with my awkward priorities: clients first, workers second, organisation last. I loved the work, and with Saturn in the 1st house in Virgo approaching the progressed Sun, had begun to develop specialist expertise in childcare: very appropriate for a 12th-house Leo with many childhood wounds still to heal in herself.

My experience of adult education was utilised through rapid involvement in staff training and the supervision of student social workers. I also carried on writing, formally this time. My social enquiry reports and Children's Hearing reports were often singled out for praise. Those diverse creative abilities were beginning at last to come together in one context.

My boss was another solar hero, last heard of flying in rickety planes to and from the Urals whilst establishing orphanages for abandoned East European children. In 1996 we met on the London shuttle, not having seen each other for 15 years. Within 10 minutes he had offered me a job as a social worker in a Romanian orphanage. I said no on the grounds that I was now an astrologer and had a husband and stepchildren to consider. 'What sort of an excuse is that?!' he said, mischievously. He was wonderful. Sharing my maverick attitudes, he supported me to express my commitment in my own way. I was a highflier in the world of childcare, expected to move up the promotional ladder quickly.

I ended my own career in social work over the fate of an abused and vulnerable three-year-old boy, having been told to place him in a third-rate children's home too far away from Glasgow for me to visit regularly. There were no foster parents available. I defied every manager I had, saying that this constituted such bad practice that doing it meant I had no professional ethics and might as well leave. Eventually, my boss found some 'lost' foster parents with whom the little boy thrived. But my card had been well and truly marked.

I applied for a post in a newly created childcare team where there were six jobs. Saturn was transiting the progressed Sun. I was turned down. Knowing my career was over, I obtained a transfer to psychiatric hospital work where I went shortly after my beloved boss left, remaining in retreat there for four years until the next Saturn square.

Fourth career

Teaching, writing and social work gave me ways of offering my energy creatively to the wider community. That was satisfying. I found that I could have the variety and challenge which I realised my restless spirit would always need, without the destructive discarding of jobs and relationships and roots which had characterised my late teens and the whole of my twenties. But connection with the bigger picture was what my soul still craved.

At age 33,[32] just before my retreat into the 12th-house of psychiatric work, progressed Sun with transiting Saturn was squaring 10th-house Uranus; transiting Uranus was on the IC-South Node, Neptune trine and Pluto sextile the Sun. The Jupiter-Saturn conjunction at the end of the year was due to fall exactly on radix Neptune sextile Mercury. Any astrologer could have told me the Big Picture was about to require my presence! A male Aries friend, to whom I had said very little about an increasing interest in astrology, gave me a copy of Alan Oken's *Complete Astrology* for Xmas. I opened it and could not close it – the connection was instantaneous, like a lightning bolt.

I met both astrology and my Aquarian husband Ian in the same year and have remained closely involved with both of them ever since, Ian providing the human love and stability which has supported me as I have slowly worked to develop a deep connection with the impersonal symbolic world represented by astrology.

SYNTHESIS

I became self-employed as Saturn made its first square to my Leo stellium after the Saturn return, feeling strong and mature enough by then to attempt to bring all the diverse parts of myself together in my own project. I was a frightened but determined solar hero, taking on my biggest self-challenge! In his usual role of providing the big obstacle to spur my growth, my father dropped dead the month after I set up in private practice, just as Saturn squared the Sun, with progressed Sun moving into Libra semisextile the Sun/Ascendant midpoint.

Since then, I have been successful in bringing my talents, abilities and experience together in a way which honours my creative diversity without being superficial. I work as an astrologer, astrology teacher, counsellor, counselling supervisor, occasional broadcaster, public speaker and writer. Since Pluto went into Sagittarius, Uranus into

---

32 For more on why the 33rd solar return is so special, I refer the reader to 'Exploring Preliterate Sources of Astrology' by Robin Heath, pp. 17-20, *The Mountain Astrologer*, Volume 10, No 3, April/May 1997.

Aquarius and Saturn into Aries, all triggering the Leo stellium again, I have completed a demanding astrological study course and sent more of my written work out than ever before. Having come more to terms with the 12th house, I feel less afraid of the outside world.

My aim is to aid others in their efforts to be all they can be whilst doing the same thing for myself. The great delight of astrology is being able, through its symbols, to function as a bridge from the personal to the universal for other people, thereby creatively living out the paradox which has so dominated my entire life, for a long time almost destroying it.

My current verdict on the over-allocation of the gift of light? It is both a curse and a blessing.

Apollon, the Journal of Psychological Astrology, 1995
The Mountain Astrologer magazine, 2000

Contemplating the 12th house: an optimist's take on self-undoing

(My birth chart is on page 14)

A tiny frog, barely half an inch long, lay flopped and dead on the tip of a teaspoon as I gently lowered it toward the plughole of my kitchen sink. Soon, I'd turn on the tap. Its fragile little body, already liquefying, would be washed down the drain.

Yesterday, it had been leaping around, full of life, inside the plastic refrigerator box in which I had created a little aquarium with water, moss and stones. The tadpoles which I had brought home a few weeks previously had all survived. My satisfaction and pleasure at having achieved this, however, was tempered by the growing knowledge that my delightful new pets would soon have to be returned to their original habitat.

But this little fellow would never go home.

That small incident, which occurred more than 40 years ago, offered such a poignant illustration of the fleeting fragility of life that it has never left my memory. There are times when something tiny and transient can illustrate much larger truths. The constant dance between form and formlessness, being and non-being, order and chaos, occurs in all epochs and at all levels.

Humans have created a range of paradigms and metaphors, from ancient myths to modern cosmology, within which to explore this dialectic. Our ancient Babylonian forebears envisaged the beginning of the world as a battle to the death between the great sea-serpent Ti'amat and her son, the Underworld god Marduk. He vanquished her, creating Heaven and Earth from her divided corpse. Meanwhile, the grapple goes on.

Astrology has its own language for this struggle, speaking through the polarity of Saturn and Neptune. Saturn at its core represents the drive to take form; Neptune's teleology is that of dissolution. For example, the unglamorous wrestle, which we all go through from time to time to act effectively in the face of a bout of profound inertia, is a tiny manifestation of that polarity. There are times when it just seems easier to give up, lie on the sofa with a good book and have a long snooze.

But where do we go when we sleep? Where do we go when we give up the fight? Where do we go when we drift, allowing fantasy to take over? Where do we go when we die? Where *do* we go when we give up struggling within Saturn's realm and allow Neptune's flow to take us over? Astrology has a name for this inchoate territory where everything dissolves into the primal waters.

It is called the 12th house.

Meltdown

I have six planets in Leo – five of them in the 12th house – with Virgo rising. My entire life has been spent wrestling with the profound contradictions contained within that astrological description. Starting in 2001, a long series of transiting Neptune oppositions to the Leo planets, and a shorter but more disruptive period of transiting Uranus oppositions also through my 6th house, were backed up by the progressed Moon crossing a natal 12th-house Saturn-Pluto conjunction in August 2001, at the same time as the Saturn-Pluto opposition of 2001/02 was in trine and sextile to it. All of this symbolised an energy meltdown and a need for almost total withdrawal from the world for a very long time.

At the end of 2001, after dealing with a severe, prolonged family crisis in tandem with a busy career, I collapsed, barely able to get out of bed for the first six months of 2002. During 2002-08, I spent much of my life – out of necessity, my energy being perilously low – on activities that required little physical output or contact with the wider world. I look back on that period now as a very productive time of writing, reading, contemplation ... and rest.

There are so many ways in which I could write about that profound and at times terrifying 'night sea journey'.[33] The whole seven years are recorded in detail in diaries, notebooks and an imagery journal, none of which may ever see the light of day. Keeping a record, along with the loving support I was fortunate to have, was a significant part of what kept me sane. Of necessity, this account takes only one thread from the weave.

The main route through my life's difficulties of whatever kind has always been to set a goal which would hopefully bring me to a place of greater balance with greater understanding of where I stood in relation to the Big Picture. This understanding, however, has always been retrospective, sometimes with *decades* of hindsight involved!

True to form, as soon as I realised that I was cast adrift with no landmarks in sight, I had to find a project to get me through the loss of much of life as I knew it; I had to try to make some sense of what had happened – and why. The rest of this article describes briefly what that project was and where it took me, a process of profound relevance to my astrological self. A very lengthy time of immersion in the secret sea that is the 12th house provided me with an opportunity to understand more deeply what the 12th house is, what being a 12th-house person means, and how to live in a more creatively balanced way with this house's challenges and extreme contradictions.

I hope that, by sharing an account of one dimension of my 'night sea journey', I can help other 12th-house people to see their relationship with that complex, mysterious place in space in a clearer and more constructive light.

Understanding of the 12th-house deepens

During the 2002-06 period in particular, I felt strongly motivated to use the enforced gift of unrestricted time to give free rein to my long-term interest in the overlaps between religion, mysticism, myth, symbolism,

---

33   C.G. Jung, *Analytical Psychology*, Routledge & Kegan Paul, (London), 1976, p. 41.

science and the paranormal. In essence, I have long felt that all those lenses are focused on phenomena arising from the same underlying ground.

I also set myself a writing project to accompany this inner journey. From the summer of 1970 until the autumn of 1999, I had had a series of sporadic paranormal episodes, ranging from prophetic dreams to seeing ghosts to premonitions and included mediumship, poltergeist phenomena, telepathy, etc. All of these had appeared unbidden whilst on the surface I was leading a fairly reasonable, responsible, grounded life. They were unwelcome and unwanted. Mostly, I told no one. As an open-minded sceptic and rationalist, I was also rather offended that they should have appeared to me at all!

So, in 2002, I decided to pull together all these experiences, since many had been recorded in notebooks or diaries at the time, and others could be confirmed in location and date from my husband's diaries from 1980 onwards. I also decided to set them as best I could in a context of rational analysis, drawing on the insights of open-minded contemporary scientists. The objective was to make peace with my 'other' side, an inheritance from my maternal great-grandmother's dubious gift: the 'second sight'. [34] In the process of doing so, I was also unexpectedly led to a deeper level of understanding of the 12th house.

To contextualise this writing project, I looked back at core texts and commentaries arising from the great religions – re-reading more than once psychologist William James' brilliant *Varieties of Religious Experience*. James' considered view of experiences occurring outside 'normal' parameters is as follows, quoting from his book:

> *'The whole drift of my education goes to persuade me that the world of our present consciousness is only one out of many*

---

34   Second sight is a form of extrasensory perception, the supposed power to perceive things that are not present to the senses, whereby a person perceives information in the form of a vision about future events before they happen (precognition) or about things or events at remote locations (remote viewing). See Wikipedia for further understanding and reading material.

worlds of consciousness that exist, and that those other worlds must contain experiences which have a meaning for our life also; and that although in the main their experiences and those of this world keep discrete, yet the two become continuous at certain points, and higher energies filter in ... the total expression of human experience, as I view it objectively, invincibly urges me beyond the narrow 'scientific' bounds.'

This perspective was profoundly supportive of my own conventionally inexplicable experiences.

I also returned to what the scientists had to say, finding some wonderful works such as David Abrams' *The Spell of the Sensuous*, Russell Targ and Jane Katra's *Miracles of Mind*, and Brian Swimme's *The Secret Heart of the Cosmos* whose poetic vision of a unified cosmos I found wonderfully inspiring, educative and supportive of many of my own conclusions regarding the kind of world we live in.

With Swimme's help in particular, I have grasped not only in my head but in my heart the notion of the vast sea of energy which constitutes the whole of existence, the quantum vacuum of physics, from which particles that we cannot see flash constantly in and out of existence. In my imagination, these take the form of diamond sparks – appearing, disappearing, reappearing like fireflies in and out of the 'dazzling darkness'.[35] As Swimme puts it in *The Secret Heart of the Cosmos*:

> 'The ground of the universe then is an empty fullness, a fecund nothingness ... The base of the universe seethes with creativity, so much so that physicists refer to the ground state as "space-time foam"'.

---

35   From the poem 'The Night' by Henry Vaughan (1621-95), v. 9.

The pull of dissolution

Through a very long period of varied reading and reflection, I have gradually come to understand more clearly how matter arises out of the universal energy sea and returns from form to energy again. This process is enacted always, within and beyond time, at every level, from the invisible depths of all life on Earth to the birth and death of galaxies, universes and multiverses.[36] We are part of the universal process: our whole being participates whether we know it or not.

It has also taken me some time to comprehend that the apparently solid material world we perceive through our five senses is not the world which quantum physics has revealed. Our limited perceptual apparatus creates material 'reality' from energy and a sprinkling of stardust.

Reflecting on the insights offered by quantum physics has also provided me with a form of proof that the boundaries between 'real' and 'imaginary' are arbitrary and artificial – something that my own intermittent, uncomfortable and unsought paranormal experiences over a very long period of time had led me to believe was the case anyway.

I also find it very powerful to contemplate the apparent ratio of matter to energy in the universe – 4% matter, 23% dark matter, 73% dark energy – and to consider that the pull on matter to break down and become energy again is constant at every level, from the minute (us) to the vast (supernovas).

All in all, I have come to the conclusion that the place of dissolution ...

where all forms disperse, and flash back into life again
where boundaries are impossible to draw
where our experiences dissolve into our collective, tribal,

---

[36] The multiverse (or meta-universe) is the hypothetical set of multiple possible universes, including ours, which together comprise all of reality. The different universes within the multiverse are sometimes called parallel universes. Multiverses have been hypothesised in cosmology, physics, astronomy, philosophy, transpersonal psychology and fiction, particularly in science fiction and fantasy. The specific term 'multiverse' was coined by psychologist William James (Wikipedia).

familial, and personal past
where the seeds of the future lie
where 'reality' and 'imagination' overlap
where paranormal experience takes place
where religion and myth's 'sacred time' resides
which myth describes
which the collective unconscious evokes
which can be perceived as God, Goddess, the Void, Brahman, the Zero Point Field ...

... is that which astrologers call the 12th house.

12TH-HOUSE PEOPLE IN ESSENCE
From my journal notes (20 June 2007):

> *'Feeling of my returning fire co-existing with clear awareness of ever-present underlying vulnerability ... particle poised to flip back to the wave ... we are all vulnerable as creatures of this Earth. Mostly we do our best to shield ourselves from this awareness. Personally, I find it liberating. I feel closer to knowing my true nature than I have ever been. My true nature as a 12th-house person is also a tiny pointer to humanity's true nature ... we are all particles poised to flip back to the wave ... .'*

Deep in our cell memory may be the knowledge that quantum physics has uncovered in the 20th century what has been divined and expressed intuitively in our cosmologies, religions and myths from our very early days as humans trying to understand why we are here. We blip endlessly in and out of the Quantum Vacuum, the Void, God, Goddess, Brahman, the Cosmic Egg, the Collective Unconscious.

Matter has a strong pull at all levels towards dissolution, then reforming somewhere else as something else ... as multiverse, cosmos, star, solar system, planet, individual life forms. We humans are part of the universal process. Thus, our destiny, periodically within an average lifetime, is to be dissolved – undone. The ultimate dissolution for any one lifetime, of course, is death. In this way, I have come to think of that ancient (and none too popular!) description of the 12th house, 'the house of one's own undoing', as an accurate piece of description and *not in itself negative.*

At a deep cellular level, then, I consider that 12th-house people are more aware than others of the essential fragility of form and structure – and of that Vastness to which form returns. This awareness is initially unconscious, developing only gradually (if at all) as their lives unfold: over decades rather than just years. Likely there is always, underlying even the most apparently successful public life, this 12th-house undertow; this pull towards the Void. The more planets located there, the greater the pull.

With this awareness probably co-exists a greater level of fear for 12th-house people than for the rest of the population. If form is so *fragile,* it can easily dissolve. Therefore, ties of love and friendship, community, material possessions, worldly status, sanity (as defined by common consensus) – all the certainties of life that more grounded people take for granted – can be much more tenuous and fragile for the 12th-house tribe.

Until they make peace with this fear, they are likely to deal with it by holding on too compulsively to some or all the above. Or, going to the opposite extreme, they may do their best to avoid becoming involved with any, some or all of the above, depending on which kinds of attachment carry the most powerful positive or negative charge.

The 12th-house challenge

Being able to see our tiny lives as diamond sparks in relation to and part of the 'dazzling darkness' of eternity, finding our own way to frame and live out this relationship – whether it be through conventional religious affiliations or whatever framework fits our era, culture and psychological makeup – this is a big task for anyone. But it seems to me to be the particular one that we 12th-house folk are asked to undertake to a greater extent than other people are.

This challenge, which at times is very painful and disruptive to ordinary dimensions of life, appears to demand periodic sacrifice, renunciation and withdrawal from the so-called real world into that world whose compass is oriented to eternity. These are rites of passage, which 12th-house people must go through to enter into deeper and deeper levels of connection and a more creative, positive relationship with what belonging to the 12th house means.

The horoscope's great gift is to show each of us our unique take on the human drama. We are all connected to a Bigger Picture. Archetypal patterns shape and structure our whole life from birth to death. The great gift of a mature perspective, perhaps deepened by the midlife crisis transition, is an eventual realisation that these particular challenges *must* come our way. At best, they can be met over time with grace and acceptance rather than resistance and fear, bringing the reward of inner peace. To paraphrase Jung's wise dictum: freewill is the ability to do gladly that which we must do anyway.

Consent, faith – and respect

For 12th-house people, though, arriving at a state of balance and acceptance of such a profound paradox as that of the relationship of (to put it in one of many ways) *being and nothingness* is no easy process. Jung's concept of the 'night sea journey' is powerfully descriptive here. There are times when being a 12th-house person means being lost in the darkness, tossed by mysterious storms whose origins are unknown and perhaps unknowable, unable to stand upright long enough to take a compass bearing, not knowing where the journey is leading, when it will end, or whether one will survive at all. As André Gide so eloquently wrote: 'One does not discover new lands without consenting to lose sight of the shore for a very long time.' [37]

During such trials, one's greatest strengths are *consent* to the

---

37   From his novel *Les faux-monnayeurs* ('The Counterfeiters'), 1925.

experience, however harsh it may be, and *faith* that, whatever the outcome, one's own tiny speck of matter is in meaningful relationship to eternity.

Although life was generally tough and a lot shorter in times preceding the Scientific Revolution, it may well have been easier for 12th-house people to find their balance then. In that era, living was tied to the pace of the diurnal cycle of night and day and the cycles of the seasons. People generally did not travel far. The pace was much slower. Most people's lives unfolded within the context of religion and ritual. The twin practices of contemplation and retreat were thus much more accepted as a normal part of life.

Nowadays, within a ubiquitous cultural context whose thrust is towards increasingly frenetic participation in material preoccupations on a 24/7 basis, *doing* is very much emphasised over *being*. People who wish and/or need to withdraw from the quotidian world on a regular basis tend to be seen as odd or lacking in some way.

I've never forgotten a Centre for Psychological Astrology seminar in the 1990s in which Liz Greene, talking about the demands that planetary transits place on us, said something to this effect: 'You have to give the god what the god wants. And if it's Mars, don't offer a bunch of flowers!'

Whether the world considers us odd or not, I think that a major key to entering the 12th house as a willing visitor, rather than a fearful and reluctant guest, is eventual recognition by 12th-house people that they need to offer conscious respect and honour to the 12th house, prioritising time there on a regular basis throughout their lives.

Twelfth-house time is radically different from ordinary time. For example, contemplating and making art; making, playing and listening to music; walking in solitude, communing with nature; sharing communal rites in church, mosque, temple or the church of the open air: all these activities take one into sacred time where the moment and eternity are one and where the numinous hovers. I feel that 12th-house people need those experiences of being in sacred time more than do other people.

They also need to give themselves permission to retreat, to dream, to be out of the everyday world. This can take whatever form fits the life pattern, life demands, and temperament of the person concerned – from regular formal retreats to allotting a chunk of time each day to withdraw into a room alone with a book, music, meditation or yoga practice. Drifting and doing 'nothing', wandering in space/time, seems to me an essential quality of being for 12th-house people, if they are to maintain balance together with good mental and physical health.

Twelfth-house people need to learn a way of being in the world, but not of it which enables the intangible dimensions of their makeup to have the room they require.

A personal testimony

Until my energy collapse forced me to have huge amounts of rest, I considered an hour without activity (apart from holidays or the necessity of sleep) to be an hour wasted. However, I slowly came to realise that sitting in the park in the sunshine staring at a bee for an hour was equally as valuable as, say, spending an hour catching up on paperwork. I also realised – and it is a humbling realisation, especially for someone with as many Leo planets as I have! – that the world was managing to carry on perfectly well without me.

If we die or disappear, life goes on. We are special, and we are not. Because of this realisation, one of the many gifts of my timeout has been a failure to recover the same sense of urgency I used to feel about getting everything done. This may at times infuriate my nearest and dearest, but I enjoy being a lot more relaxed and laid back than before. After years of a very restful life – reading, writing, thinking, lying around drinking tea and doing 'nothing' for many a peaceful hour, strolling in the park nearby watching the seasons change – I realise just how developmental all this has been. I feel full of spiritual and imaginative energy and am happy to be back at work, albeit part-time.

I do not wish, however, to minimise how terrifying it was to lose my personal power. Going from being strong and self-reliant to having to depend heavily on family and friends for all sorts of help has been an exercise in humility, to say the least. Not knowing if I would ever recover generated a great deal of anxiety for a long time. To keep my head above the deep waters of fear, I needed to use every tool acquired in decades of both working on my own process and supporting other people's as a teacher, therapist and astrologer. Mindfulness practice was the biggest aid, and I owe a huge debt to Buddhist wisdom. Pema Chödrön, Jack Kornfield, Jon Kabat-Zinn: thank you so much!

Ultimately, the love of those closest to me, along with my own consent and faith, pulled me through. Having learned the hard way that *being* is every bit as important as *doing*, I now honour and act upon my need to enter 12th-house time on a regular basis. I feel much at peace, at last, with both the gifts and the limitations that the 12th house brings.

The Mountain Astrologer
2014

PS: WINDOWS TO THE FUTURE
Mary Shelley – with Greta Thunberg – has the last word

21 December 2020 was a truly momentous day. With the Jupiter-Saturn conjunction at 0° Aquarius, we were witnessing two major celestial events. The beginning of a whole new 20-year cycle of the Great Chronocrator – as that conjunction is called – began right on the day of the Winter Solstice: both the conjunction aspect and the Winter Solstice representing important cyclical turning points in the cosmos. Thus, the symbolism of death and rebirth, ending and new beginning, was doubly highlighted on that date.

Moreover, the conjunction's Aquarian entry point signified the ending of just over 200 years of Jupiter-Saturn conjunctions travelling through earth signs. They will now be travelling through air signs for roughly the next 200 years. This represents an even more significant point of deaths and entrances. As a human community we are at a time of major epochal shift. A deadly airborne virus upended our way of life in 2020. Major cultural, political and environmental turbulence is set to continue, radically altering the way we live on planet Earth.

Mary Shelley – as we have seen in an earlier part of this book – issued a prescient warning at the outset of the earth era through her 1818 masterpiece Frankenstein *of what the consequences might be for humanity if we allowed science to run unchecked by either ethics or compassion. Greta Thunberg, another very young woman appearing at the very end of the earth era, has run with the consequences of that warning in speaking environmental truth to materialist political power.*

The resonance between their horoscopes is truly fascinating. It bowled me over. I cannot get away from Mary Shelley, it would appear. And this seems a very fitting piece with which to conclude Postcards to the Future.

Waning and waxing crescents: windows to the future

'Teach me your mood, oh patient stars!
Who climb each night the ancient sky'

– 'Fragments on Nature and Life' by Ralph Waldo Emerson

THE LUNAR CYCLE: A TEMPLATE FOR LIFE'S UNFOLDING
I grew up on a small, windswept island off the West Coast of Scotland, where environmental pollution was negligible. The night skies were wonderfully, deeply dark. Dazzlingly dark – especially on cold, clear winter nights. Becoming utterly fascinated by the heavens above me, I was gradually able to discern some of the patterns made by the stars, learning to spot even Saturn at certain times of the year.

However, what I especially loved was the comfortingly predictable rhythm of the Moon's monthly traverse across the night sky. I waited eagerly to see – intermittently because of our frequently stormy and cloudy weather! – the fragile silvery sliver of the waning crescent. Then darkness. And a couple of days later – again, if I was lucky and the skies were clear – the welcome appearance of the fresh, new waxing crescent Moon.

That was outdoors. Indoors, things were uncomfortably unpredictable to say the least as I slowly emerged from childhood, gradually gaining agency culminating in an early departure from home in my late teens. The one steady source of comfort as I moved towards that goal was a picture: a stylised Art Deco image of a tall, elegant, ethereal lady clad only in a wispy translucent garment, reaching up for the fragile Waxing Crescent Moon. Its dreamy blue/green colours entranced me. I knew nothing whatever about that picture apart from its title: 'Reaching for the Moon'. No one in the house seemed to know where it had come from. Only many years later, thanks to Google, did I find out who created it – an American painter called Edward Mason Eggleston 'who specialised in calendar portraits of women, fashionable and fantastic', according to Wikipedia.

This image inspired me in my teens to reach towards the waxing crescent of my slowly forming future life. Only many years later, on receiving a hand-drawn horoscope from the Faculty of Astrological Studies' cartographer as part of their Certificate course in the early 1980s, did I discover that my birth had occurred on a Sun-Moon conjunction in Leo in the 12th house – just a few hours before the New Moon. No wonder the soli/lunar cycle had fascinated me in my childhood; cycles have increasingly continued to do so ever since.

Whether the cycle is huge, like the 500-year Neptune-Pluto one, or small, like that of the monthly Sun-Moon, the same basic stages apply: seeding, germinating, sprouting, flowering, ripening, harvesting, dying back in preparation for the new. These stages describe developmental processes from gnats to galaxies: we can thus apply the basic template of what we see enacted above us in the heavens every month to the ebb and flow of everything, including cultural phases and the rise and fall of whole civilisations.

In midlife, during one single decade, I had to negotiate a passage through the endings of not one or two or three but four major cycles, amplified by a long Uranus then Neptune transit opposing my 12th-house planets. This necessitated a lengthy period of contemplative retreat and slow re-emergence which was both personally purging *and* a wonderfully close-up qualitative research opportunity (you have to look on the bright side!). Although aspects of this 10-year period were devastating, I emerged with both deepened insight into – and fascination with – the waning and waxing crescent phases of cycles great and small, personal and collective.

The times we are currently living through are devastatingly disruptive and at the moment we have no real idea how – *or who* – we are going to be when we eventually emerge. It struck me recently that the very last 20-year Jupiter-Saturn cycle in earth could roughly be mapped onto the waning crescent of that 200-year period; and the cycle's first 20-year journey through the subsequent air era could be thought of as the waxing crescent of a very different time unfolding.

Three major cycles' endings

At times symbolism seems to step down a level, manifesting in a very literal way in the world we ordinary mortals inhabit. I experienced such a moment of symbol becoming strikingly 'real' in the week following Saturn's first entry into airy Aquarius on Sunday, 22 March 2020: Mother's Day in the UK. This was also the day that the UK government declared that we were in lockdown owing to the threat posed by the COVID-19 airborne pandemic, thereby joining much of the rest of Europe and parts of North America. Much of Asia had got there weeks before us.

A few days later, it seemed as though the human community had literally taken to air en masse – via Zoom, Skype, WhatsApp, FaceTime, Facebook etc., – a powerful, immediate, adaptive response to the locked-down world.

Along with many of my astrological colleagues, especially those of us who have been tuning in to the larger planetary cycles which span aeons of time, I have been observing the turmoil and difficulty of the very ending of the 1982-2020 Saturn-Pluto cycle and its manifestations in the reality of life on Earth with grim fascination.

I have also been very aware that the long sojourn of the 20-year Jupiter-Saturn cycle through the earth element, which began in 1802, will terminate on 21 December 2020 with a dramatic symbolic flourish following its full entry into air, with the two planets meeting at 0° degrees Aquarius on the Winter Solstice, no less.

We are not only at the end of the Jupiter-Saturn cycle begun in Taurus in the year 2000, but the end of a whole era of that cycle's moving through earth. This shift is 'the transition of the conjunction from one element to another – the "Mutation Conjunction" – [and] has always been considered to be of particular importance marking a major shift in emphasis and orientation in the world'.[38]

This triple whammy of Moondark in 2019 and 2020, involving the very ending of no less than three major cycles of 200, 33-38 and 20 years respectively, points to those years as being especially, symbolically significant.

We have increasingly been handing over the conduct of our 'civilisation', for good and ill (the usual inextricable twins), to the airy Internet in recent times, gaining pace from the Jupiter-Saturn conjunction's first, brief, 20-year appearance in air (Libra) in 1980/81: creating an increasingly interconnected cyber-world. However, the last week of March 2020 powerfully brought home to me the literal reality of the symbolism I'd been observing. At the end of the waning crescent phase of the Jupiter-Saturn cycles travelling through earth, the air era truly is almost upon us.

We are seeing the seeds of the next 200 years beginning to push through the darkness of the future. As the earth era loses power and agency in its waning crescent, a new world order is gradually emerging.

Deaths – and entrances

It feels as though we humans – tiny chips of the huge prevailing energies of turbulence and change – are living …

> *'On almost the incendiary eve*
> *Of deaths and entrances'*

---

[38] From *Mundane Astrology* by Baigent, Campion and Harvey who also describe the conjunction as 'the ground base of human development which marks the interaction between perception of ideas, potentialities (Jupiter) and their manifestation in the concrete world (Saturn).'

... as Dylan Thomas so powerfully put it his poetry collection *Deaths and Entrances* (1946). It is a very ancient human tendency, when knowing that a stage of life has come to an inexorable end, to look back to wherever the beginning might have been in trying to come to terms – and in starting to contemplate the largely unknown future.

That has very much been my recent experience. My husband Ian was felled by a stroke on 12 January 2020, three hours after the opening crescent phase of the new Saturn-Pluto cycle in Capricorn: a brutal opening for me to a new way of life. One of my ways of dealing with his loss has been to go back, back to just before the opening 1982 Saturn-Pluto cycle in Libra, when we were married nearly forty years ago, to reflect on what that precious time may have meant both in my life and his – and where I go from here.

However, having been born with many Leo planets in the 12th house, I have made it always my way to seek creative perspective on whatever happens to me and in the wider world by setting personal dramas. if possible, in the context of a bigger picture.

Thus, as we all sit in 2020 – penned in and fearful as a deadly airborne virus takes down not only individuals, over half a million as I write in July 2020, but also much of the economic and social structures upon which the earth era rests – I have been very strongly drawn to reflecting on another ending and beginning on the very large scale: the closing crescent phase of the Jupiter-Saturn cycles through the element of fire in 1603 which ended with the conjunction's first meeting in earth in 1802.

What a turbulent ending and beginning that was! The waning crescent of the fire era hosted not one but two major Western revolutions: the American Revolution between 1775 and 1783, and the French Revolution from 1789 to 1799. These occurred against the backdrop of the combined forces of the accelerating Industrial Revolution and the Scientific Revolution, which really got underway from the Jupiter-Saturn cycle's shift into earth in 1802 and the rise of the materialist era thereafter – rooted firmly in exploitation of the resources of planet Earth.

It needs only a sketchy knowledge of the historical timeline, looking back, to realise that those revolutionary upheavals at the waning crescent of the old fire era were largely responsible for the rise and pan-global impact of Western civilisation as the new earth era took shape.

One of the fascinating seeds of the coming air era emerging in the waning crescent phase of our current earth era has been the undoubted rise and expanding influence of the East, spearheaded by the expansionist, exponential rise in worldly power and influence of China: its dominance and global influence via sophisticated technologies has given us at least some idea of what shape the air era will take. A manifestation of the negative dimensions of this airy shift has been the rise of cyber-warfare in recent years.

Powerful new Earth-based technologies, e.g., Big Oil (the powerful supermajor top six or seven oil and gas companies), arising in the materialist era have provided lifestyles and opportunities undreamed of by our ancestors, in the wealthier parts of the world. But, uncoupled from any agreed collective sense of responsibility towards our mother planet, they have placed her very survival under threat as the earth era draws to a close. Clearly, as the opening crescent of the new air era takes form, we will need urgently to develop technologies which no longer depend upon sawing off the branch on which we are all sitting.

From the collective to the personal: Mary Shelley, prophet; Greta Thunberg, climate activist

Some individuals have a more powerful impact than others on the way history and culture take shape, as Greta Thunberg herself neatly put it in her first book's title: *No One is Too Small to Make a Difference*. As my reflections on the waning crescent phases of both the 1603-1802 fire era and the 1802-2020 earth era continued, the impact of two very young women – Mary Shelley and Greta Thunberg – struck me forcefully as individuals whose lives and work bracket the beginning and ending of

Mary Shelley's Chart

30 Aug 1797 NS, Wed
23:20 LMT +0:00:40
London, United Kingdom
51°N30' 000°W10'
Geocentric
Tropical
Placidus
True Node

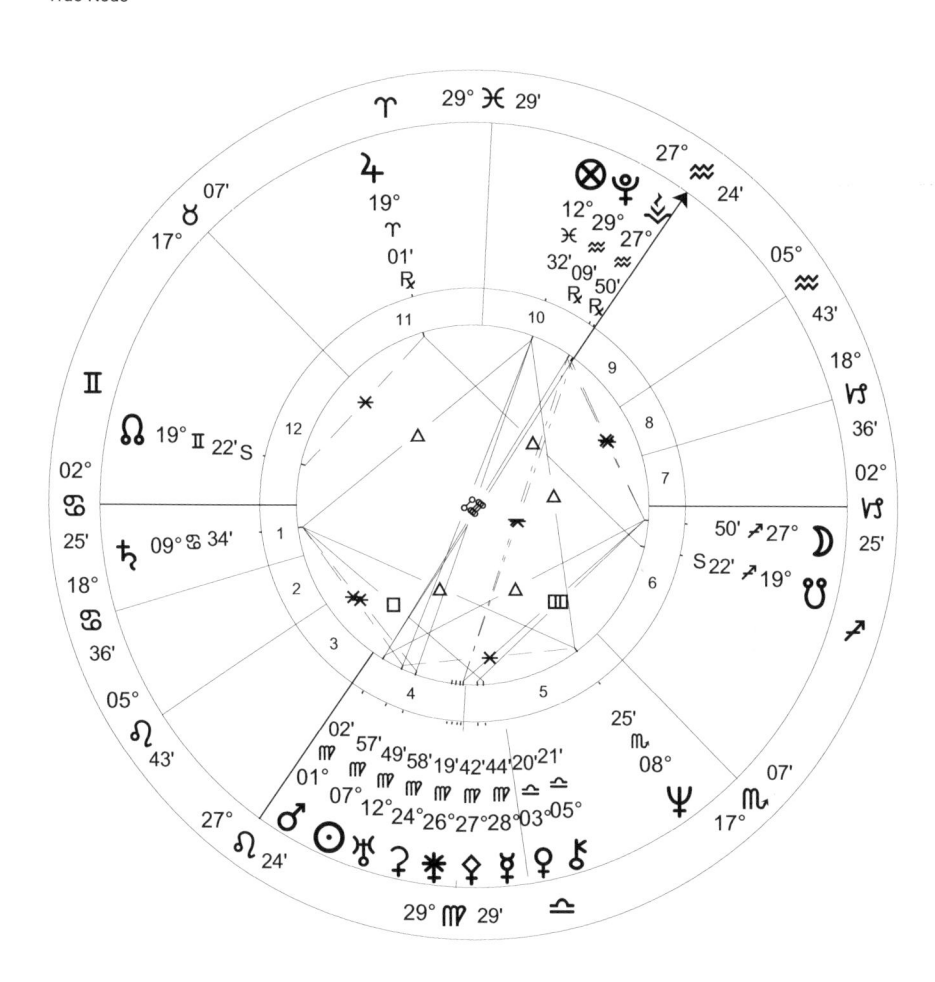

Greta Thunberg's chart

3 Jan 2003, Fri
12:00 CET −1:00
Stockholm, Sweden
59°N20' 018°E03'
Geocentric
Tropical
0° Aries
True Node

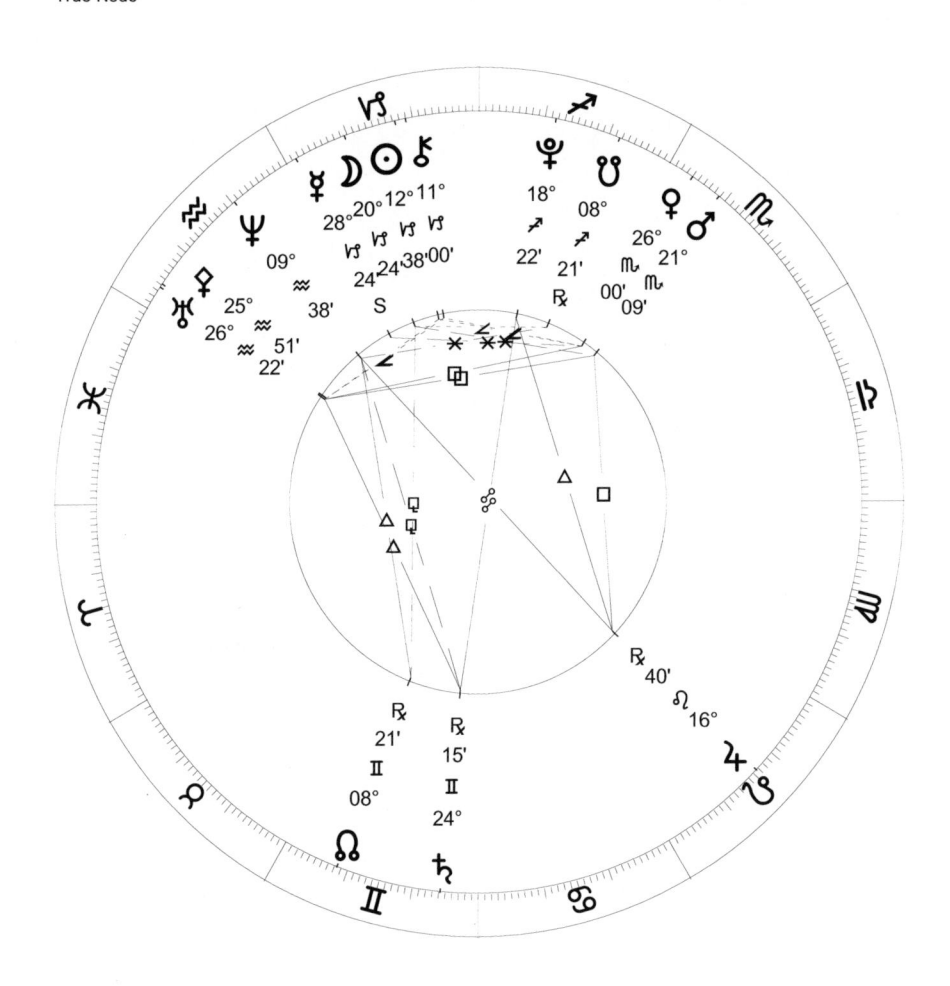

the earth era, as well as setting the tone for our entry into air.

Mary Godwin Shelley was born on 30 August 1797 (full birth data in the chart caption). Daughter of the famous philosopher and writer William Godwin and the early feminist writer Mary Wollstonecraft, who died 10 days after her birth, she made her entrance in the turbulent final years of the dying fire era, its waning crescent.

Little did her parents know that their child (at the time of her first nodal return whilst only 19 years old, in the waxing crescent phase and the first 20-year Jupiter-Saturn cycle of the new materialist earth era) would write an enduringly famous book which has created a modern myth. *Frankenstein; or, The Modern Prometheus* (published on 1 January 1818) issued a prescient warning of the grim results which might well follow from scientific endeavour being pursued without compassion or due regard for ethics or morality. As Emily Sunstein puts it in her wonderful biography, *Mary Shelley: Romance and Reality*:

> 'Mary Shelley ... will be best remembered for her perception in Frankenstein ... that the Promethean drive is at the heart of human progress and yet a bringer of new ills if not focused on ethical means and ends.'

At the end of the waning crescent of the earth era, and the outset of the final Jupiter-Saturn cycle in earth, Greta Thunberg, another globally significant young woman, entered the world; her birth taking place at an earlier stage of an era's end than Mary Shelley's: her preoccupation being the dangerously damaged state of Earth, our mother.

I find it fascinating, if chilling, that the warning issued by Mary Shelley via *Frankenstein* can be seen clearly now to have been so prophetic: that the materialist era's wanton disregard for the health and wellbeing of our world and all its creatures, largely in the name of profit, is reaping its consequences in terms of planetary and climate upheaval which now threatens our very survival.

None of us had heard of young Swedish girl Thunberg, born on 3 January 2003, until she began her solo protest against climate change in August 2018 at the age of 15. By the end of 2019, she had been declared *Time* magazine's 'Person of the Year'. Here are the bare bones of her story, in the words of the publication's 23/30 December 2019 issue:

> *'Thunberg began a global movement by skipping school: starting in August 2018, she spent her days camped out in front of the Swedish Parliament, holding a sign painted in black letters on a white background that read "Skolstrejk för klimatet" (School Strike for Climate). In the 16 months since, she has addressed heads of state at the U.N., met with the Pope, sparred with the President of the United States and inspired 4 million people to join the global climate strike on September 20, 2019, in what was the largest climate demonstration in human history. Her image has been celebrated in murals and Halloween costumes, and her name has been attached to everything from bike shares to beetles. Margaret Atwood compared her to Joan of Arc.'*

We do not know as yet what Thunberg will do as we all step over a powerful threshold into the opening crescent of the new air era on 21 December 2020. She has already published two books: one of her speeches, the other a memoir featuring her family. What we do know is that her challenges, issued at the closing crescent of the 1802-2020 earth era, have birthed the Extinction Rebellion movement, thereby setting the agenda for one of the defining themes of the opening air era – and of the Jupiter-Saturn cycle at 0 degrees Aquarius with which it begins – i.e., we can no longer ignore the grim reality that our planet is under threat to its very survival.

It would seem likely, therefore, that the waxing crescent of the air era will involve the development of new, community-based politics which are a radical departure from the old, broken, top-down model. It will also need to evolve technologies which facilitate the conserving of our planet and its abundant but limited natural resources and find a way of doing this relatively quickly. Youthful leaders are already arising from the Millennial generation. I imagine that Greta Thunberg will be one of them.

Mary's and Greta's horoscopes

Surely, I thought, there must be significant connections between their birth charts? Indeed, there are. There is much upon which to reflect with those horoscopes, both individually and in conjunction. But I'm confining myself to commenting on the three sets of links which struck me as most significant. I am sure readers will find more … we do not have a birth time for Greta. But the 0° Aries chart [shown] I have used is still very descriptive.

Mary's painful Saturn rising in Cancer (signifying her maternal loss and the alienated monster in *Frankenstein*, abandoned by his creator, friendless and alone) opposes Greta's powerful Sun-Chiron conjunction. This signifies her very extreme, wounded response to the pain of our planet which set her off on her protest and may also point to her autism and other personal wounds: the classic 'wounded healer' significator. One can see in this linking the powerful sensitivity to woundedness in them both which fuelled Mary's writing and fuels Greta's campaigning.

Greta has an exact conjunction at 26° Aquarius between rebellious, political, potentially fanatical Uranus and Pallas, the asteroid signifying warfare, wisdom, skill, strategy and commitment to fairness and justice. This falls closely conjunct Mary's 27° Aquarius MC, conjunct Pluto. I was stunned to find that Mary's progressed Moon is crossing this combination, at 26°.5 Aquarius at the Winter Solstice 2020. This link between Mary and Greta as rebels, innovators and visionaries hardly needs explanation.

I have saved the most significant connections till last. Mary Shelley's North Node at 19° Gemini in the mediumistic 12th house, opposite the South Node at 19° Sagittarius in the 6th, squares her Sun-Venus, Sun-Mercury and Uranus-Mercury midpoints in Virgo, making a powerful t-square. This potent combination speaks of a visionary writer whose task,

Mary Shelley & Greta Thunberg's charts with tr Neptune station direct

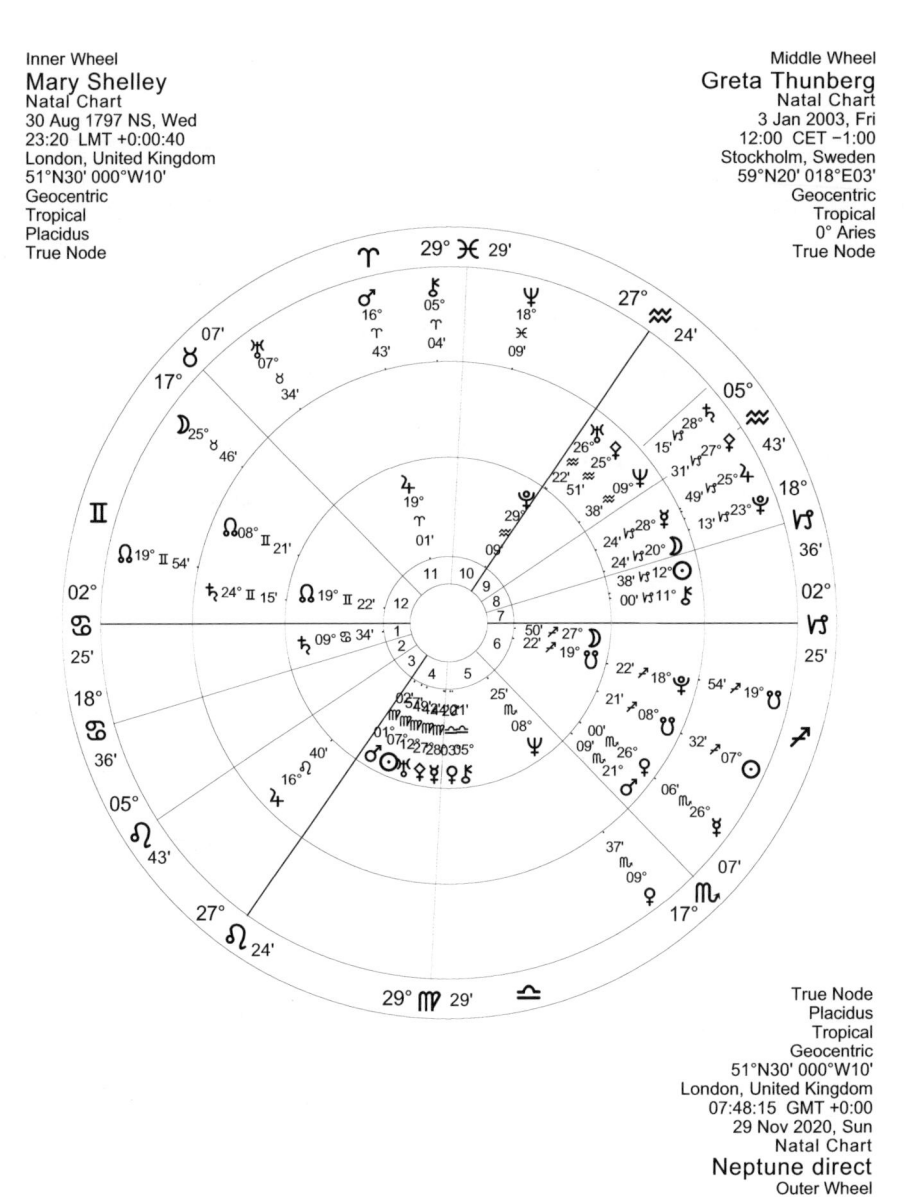

Inner Wheel
Mary Shelley
Natal Chart
30 Aug 1797 NS, Wed
23:20 LMT +0:00:40
London, United Kingdom
51°N30' 000°W10'
Geocentric
Tropical
Placidus
True Node

Middle Wheel
Greta Thunberg
Natal Chart
3 Jan 2003, Fri
12:00 CET −1:00
Stockholm, Sweden
59°N20' 018°E03'
Geocentric
Tropical
0° Aries
True Node

True Node
Placidus
Tropical
Geocentric
51°N30' 000°W10'
London, United Kingdom
07:48:15 GMT +0:00
29 Nov 2020, Sun
Natal Chart
Neptune direct
Outer Wheel

set by the North Node's position, was to send out a futuristic, ground-breaking challenge and warning which was to echo down the ages.

Her first nodal return with its attendant eclipses triggering off this pattern coincided with the birthing and publication of *Frankenstein*.

Greta's nodes are in the same pair of signs, at 8° Gemini-Sagittarius. Her Pluto at 18° Sagittarius sits on Mary's South Node. What a fated connection! And here's the knock-out nodal link which took my breath away when I saw it. The North Node is in airy Gemini, midwifing the shift from the earth to the air era on the Winter Solstice 2020: at that point, the nodal axis is at 19° Gemini-Sagittarius: exactly conjunct Mary Shelley's nodal t-square – and Greta Thunberg's Pluto. Coincidence – or Fate?

At the Winter Solstice of 2020, as we make our dramatic transition into the new air era, transiting Neptune having turned direct at the end of November 2020 will be at 18° Pisces, squaring the transiting nodes at Gemini-Sagittarius, Mary Shelley's nodes and Greta Thunberg's Pluto.

From all those stunning overlaps, it certainly looks as though Greta Thunberg, one way or another, is set to continue where Mary Shelley left off as we step into our airy future.

Voices of the Great Mother

There was a stand-out moment for me last spring 2019 when the South Node met Saturn-Pluto in Capricorn: at that time the very Capricorn Greta Thunberg strode onto the world stage, forcefully confronting us all – and our political leaders in particular – with the dangerous state of our mother planet and challenging us to do something about it.

Listening to this slight 16-year-old girl speaking so passionately, articulately and forcefully, I had one of those moments where one gets a shiver down the back and becomes tearful – accompanied by an eerie sense of listening to the voice of the Great Mother calling to us through the voice of a woman barely out of childhood.

Thinking about this, and Greta's evocation for me of the voice of the Great Mother, brought to mind an article I had written featuring Mary Shelley published in *TMA* June/July issue way back in 2001 at the opening crescent of the final Jupiter-Saturn cycle through earth, called 'Mary, Dolly, and Andi: O Brave New World?' [See 'My Mary Shelley Obsession' section in this book.]

In this article, I wrote about the exact links between Mary Shelley's Placidus 9th-house cusp at 5°43⏴ Aquarius: the February 1997 Jupiter-Uranus conjunction at 5-6° Aquarius and the public announcement of Dolly the Sheep at that time; followed in January 2001 by the birth of rhesus macaque monkey Andi, the world's first genetically modified primate, just when Neptune at 5-6° Aquarius went over Mary's 9th-house cusp. I wrote the following:

> *'This is a stunning piece of synchronicity. How do we interpret it? The long traverse of Neptune through Mary's Aquarian 9th house, which has now begun, could be seen as a metaphor for the slow, inexorable consequences of what she foresaw seeping into every facet of human life, radically altering it forever. An image arises of Mary Shelley, standing alone on the shoreline of her imagination and her dreams, calling out a message to the far future like the Oracle in ancient times.'*

As the human community prepares to step into the challenge, terror and exhilaration of a largely unknown future, we have already been provided with significant clues regarding the shape of what lies ahead for its waxing air crescent – and what we must do if we are to survive for the next two hundred years.

Has the Great Mother indeed spoken to us? And are we listening?

The Mountain Astrologer
December 2020/January 2021

Acknowledgements

Most of the articles, essays and columns in this book have appeared over the years in the following publications:

> *The Mountain Astrologer, The Astrological Journal, Dell Horoscope, Astrodienst, Apollon, The Mountain Astrologer* blog, *Infinity Astrological Magazine, The Federation of Australian Astrologers Journal*

I am truly grateful to the editors past and present of those fine publications for their support of my work. It has been such a pleasure to work with you all!

The pieces not appearing in the above have featured on my two blogs *Astrology: Questions and Answers* and *Writing from the Twelfth House*.

My colleague and longtime astrology practice supervisor, Juliet Sharman-Burke of the Centre for Psychological Astrology, has steadfastly supported me professionally and personally for many years. Thank you so much, Juliet! Special thanks to dear friend and colleague Christina Rodenbeck of The Oxford Astrologer website for her encouragement all along regarding this project. Also, for her frank comments on my initial subtitle and Contents list, leading to considerable improvements. I would also like to thank Victor Olliver who edited this book, Frank C. Clifford whose foreword to this book is most generous and Cat Keane who designed the covers. And my gratitude also to Rosamund Saunders for designing and producing this book.

About the Author

An internationally recognised essayist and columnist, Anne Whitaker has contributed to many publications, including the UK Astrological Association's *The Astrological Journal*, USA's *The Mountain Astrologer*, *Apollon* (the Journal of Psychological Astrology 1998-2001), the *FAA Journal* in Australia and the Switzerland-based *Astrodienst* website at astro.com. She wrote a bimonthly column 'The Astro-view from Scotland' for USA *Dell Horoscope* magazine in its last three years. Her articles and essays have also been translated and published in Czech, Finnish and Mandarin. Anne has an M.A. degree, postgraduate Diplomas in Education and Social Work, and holds the Diploma from the Centre for Psychological Astrology in London, UK. She is a member of the Association of Professional Astrologers International.

Anne was born and raised in Scotland's Outer Hebrides and for many years now has been based in Glasgow, Scotland. She has a long background in adult education as well as generic and psychiatric social work. Anne has also written in one context or another all her life, having had her first newspaper column at the age of 22 in that renowned local Hebridean paper *The Stornoway Gazette*. There were also interesting vocational detours in her younger years, such as when she acquired her honourable discharge papers from the British merchant navy after an educational spell as a stewardess for Caledonian MacBrayne ferries. She was also thrown off a Personnel Management Diploma course following her degree – for being too Marxist. However, in the early 1980s Anne and her 10th-house Mars-Uranus conjunction settled down happily to the career she has pursued ever since as a professional astrologer and astrology teacher. She no longer does astrology readings, but mentors international students studying with reputable courses, most notably MISPA – the Mercury Internet School of Psychological Astrology.

Anne can be contacted in the following ways:
Website: anne-whitaker.com: 'Writing from the Twelfth House'
Facebook Astrology Page: Astrology: Questions and Answers
Email: info@anne-whitaker.com
Instagram: stargazerh12   Twitter: @annewhitaker

Printed in Great Britain
by Amazon